A Decade of Economic Reforms in India

A Decade of Economic Reforms in India

Prof. C. Narasimha Rao
M.A., Ph.D. (KIEV)

Centre for Scientific Socialism
Nagarjuna University
Nagarjuna Nagar-522 510
Guntur (Andhra Pradesh)

SERIALS PUBLICATIONS
New Delhi

First Published–2004

ISBN: 81-86771-41-7

Published by

Head Office : **SERIALS PUBLICATIONS**
4, B.S.S. Hall, Khyber Pass Market,
Civil Lines, Delhi–110054 (India)
Phone: 23245225
Fax: 91-11-23272135
e-mail: serials@satyam.net.in

Branch Office : 4830/24, Prahlad Street, Ansari Road,
Darya Ganj, New Delhi-110002 (India)

Printed at : R.K. Offset Process, Naveen Shahdara, Delhi-110032

Foreword

The need for economic reforms in our country is well recognised. However, divergent opinions have been expressed as regards the content of reforms, their sequencing and method of implementation. It is necessary now, after a decade of implementation of these reforms to objectively assess and evaluate their impact on the macro-economic situation, different sectors of the economy and different sections of population, in the light of the large body of information now available on various aspects.

The reforms have undoubtedly made a positive impact in stabilising the economy of the country. Inflation rate declined considerably. Balance of payments position has improved and there is a sizeable accumulation of forex reserves. The growth of GDP per capita has accelerated. On the negative side, the rate of growth of agricultural output has declined, basically on account of the decline in public investment in rural infrastructure. This is attributable to the lop-sided priorities, slow growth of revenues and rise in inessential expenditure. There has also been a big decline in the industrial growth rate. Inequalities in income-inter-state, rural-urban and intra-urban-have increased. The impact on employment and social development, in general, has not been encouraging.

An attempt has been made by the Nagarjuna University, Guntur, to undertake an evaluation of economic reforms implemented in the country by organising a National Seminar on "A Decade of Economic Reforms in India - Retrospect and Prospect". Papers on the major economic and social dimensions of economic reforms were presented at the seminar representing different points of view in an atmosphere of free and frank discussion. The present volume is the result of this seminar.

The present volume would be useful not only for teachers and students, but also for policy makers. The efforts of Prof. Narasimha Rao and his colleagues in facilitating the publication of this useful book are commendable.

18th September, 2003
Centre for Economic and Social Study, Hyderabad

Ch. Hanumantha Rao

Preface

The last decade of 20th century has been a decade of economic reforms in India. The structural adjustment programme has completed a decade and the second-generation reforms have been started. It was stated that these new reforms would bring great changes in economy and would help to improve the living standards of people. The people of this country, especially the urban middle classes, enthused very much and welcomed these reforms. The electronic and print media has successfully campaigned about these reforms. The multinationals and the India's big capital, on the name of the economic crisis successfully utilized the reforms for their advantage.

After a decade of economic reforms the people of our country experienced the bad taste of the reforms in several fronts. This is not only the experience of our country but also of other Asian, African and Latin American Countries where the economic reforms have been implemented. Liberalization, Privatization and Globalization under the pressure of Neo-Liberalism has met with resistance not only in our country but every where on the globe. Indeed, the resistance is very acute in the major capitalist countries.

After a decade of economic reforms, the much promised industrial growth rates have not been realised. The agriculture sector is in great crisis. Absolute majority of our population is dependent on agriculture and allied sectors.

The forming community especially the small and medium farmers and agricultural laborers have suffered a lot. The rate of unemployment and under employment has gone up. The economic reforms have not reduced the problem of poverty. Disinvestment policy paved the way to sell away P.S.U's for cheaper prices to the capitalist monopoly. The living standards of the people of India have gone down. Most of these reforms have direct and indirect bearing on the lives of the people and unrest amongst them has been wide spread in the country.

There are several issues that need immediate attention of the government. The government and the policy makers have to examine the adverse impact of these reforms on the various facets of our economy.

In this context, a national seminar is organised at Nagarjuna University, Guntur in which various scholars and academics have addressed several of these issues. I hope this will greatly help to understand about a decade of economic reforms and their implications as well as finding relevant solutions to these problems.

Prof. C. Narasimha Rao

Acknowledgements

The center for Scientific Socialism of Nagarjuna University, A.P. has organized a U G C sponsored National Seminar on "A Decade of Economic Reforms in India: - Retrospect and prospects" In the month of January 2003 and the proceedings of the seminar are published in this volume. It contains twenty one papers contributed by eminent Social Scientists from the States of Kerala, Tamil Nadu, Karnataka and Andhra Pradesh. I express my thanks to all the paper contributors.

I wish to express my sincere thanks to our beloved Vice-Chancellor Prof. L.Venu Gopal Reddy, M.Com. Phd,, Who extended his all-sided help in organizing this National Seminar successfully. I am also thankful to UGC for its financial assistance to organize this National Seminar. The Chairperson and rapporteurs deserve special thanks for conducting the proceedings of the seminar and presenting the report in the plenary session.

I place on record my sincere thanks to Prof. K.R. Chowdary, who helped me practically in all aspects of organizing this National Seminar and also to bring-out this publication. I am very much thankful to Prof. Ch. Hanumantha Rao, for his affection towards this center and also for writing his valuable foreword to this volume. I am very much thankful to my colleagues N.Anjaiah, Dr. K. Somasekhar and Dr. V. Divya Thejo Murthy who made tireless efforts and rendered their services in organizing this National Seminar and also in bringing out this publication.

We express our thanks to all those who directly or indirectly helped in making this National seminar a real success and brining out this volume. I thank Serial Publications (Pvt) Ltd., New Delhi for their co-operation to publish this Book in record time.

C.Narasimha Rao

Contributors

1. **Prof. K.R. Chowdary (Rtd),** N.G. Ranga Agricultural University, Hyderabad, A.P.

2. **Prof. K. Aravanidakshan**, G.149, Panampily Nagar, Kochi-682 036.

3. **Prof. C. Narasimha Rao & N. Anjaiah,** Centre for Scientific Socialism, Nagarjuna University, Nagarjuna Nagar-522 510.

4. **Dr. K. Somasekhar & Dr. V. Divyathejo Murthy,** Department of Rural Development, Nagarjuna University, Nagarjuna Nagar-522 510.

5. **Prof. K. Nageswara Rao,** Professor of Economics, Sri Krishna Devaraya University, Anantapur, AP.

6. **Dr. P. Purushotham,** Professor & Head, Centre for Rural Industry & Employment, NIRD Rajendra Nagar, Hyderabad.

7. **Dr. Y. Gangi Reddy,** Assistant Professor, Centre for Rural Industries & Employment, NIRD Rajendra Nagar, Hyderabad,

8. **Dr. M.V.S. Koteswara Rao,** Associate Professor, Department of Political Science & Public Administration, Nagarjuna University, Nagarjuna Nagar-522 510.

9. **Dr. N.V. Madhuri,** Assistant Professor, NIRD, Rajendra Nagar, Hyderabad.

10. **Prof. K. Aravindakshan,** G.149, Panampily Nagar, Kochi-682 036.
11. **Dr. D. Dakshina Murthy & Dr. BKS Prakasa Rao,** Department of Management Science, RVR & JC College of Engineering, Guntur.
12. **Prof. Noor Basha Abdul,** Professor of Commerce, Special Officer, NUPG Centre, Ongole-523 001.
13. **Prof. M. Sundara Rao,** Professor of Economics, Special Officer, AUPG Centre, Etcherla, Srikakulam.
14. **Prof. S. Jankarajan,** MIDS, Gandhi Nagar, Adayar, Chennai-20.
15. **Dr. K. Hanumantha Rao,** Associate Professor, NIRD, Rajendra Nagar, Hyderabad.
16. **Prof. S. Subramanyam,** CESS, Hyderabad.
17. **Prof. K.S. Chalam & Dr. D. Francies,** Academic Staff College, Andhra University, Visakhaptnam-530 003.
18. **P.A. Vasudevan,** Aksharam, Vidyut Nagar, Palghat, Kerala-678 001.
19. **G. Sri Devi,** ISEC, Banglore.
20. **Prof. K.C. Heremath (Rtd),** University of Agricultural Sciences, Dharwad, Karnataka.

Overview

The process of deregulation and liberalisation of the Indian economy had been initiated in 1980's and dramatic changes have taken place in 1991. The Indian industries were given almost full freedom without any restrictions and regulations on production and trade. Private sector was permitted where it was not allowed in the past. Import tariffs were drastically reduced and the rupee was devalued significantly. This made the ruling classes to be further strongly committed for further liberalisation and economic reforms.

Sweeping changes have taken place in financial sector. Subsidies for various products such as fertilizers, food etc are drastically cut down. Disinvestment and privatisation of public sector enterprises which started in 1992 has gained movementum with second generation economic reforms. During the period of economic reforms the rate of growth of agricultural production has gone down drastically and for the first time the rate of agriculture's growth has turned negative. The removal of quantitative restrictions on agricultural imports had a tremendous impact on Indian farmer due to lack of proper prices for their agricultural products. The dumping of various goods from other countries put the small scale industry in great difficulties. Industrial growth had deteriorated sharply since the middle of the 1990's and the performance of Industrial sector collapsed in 2001-02. The impact of the economic reforms on employment and poverty is obvious. Employment in the organised sector has been virtually stagnant for some time. The rural employment expansion has begun to stagnate in the recent period. The stagnation of employment in organised sector and also in the agricultural sector will have its impact on poverty. The head count ratio of rural poverty which has declined noticeably during the 1980's has ceased to decline over the nineties but it has been marginally increased.

Prof. K.R. Chowdary, who delivered the inaugural note address expressed that the structural adjustment programme can rightly be called L P G policies. The policy prescriptions or conditionalities are imposed by the two international financial Institutions i.e., I M F and I B R D. The economic reforms, particularly the stabilization measures, have been undoubtedly successful in the initial period in stabilizing the economy of our country. However, these achievements were short lived. He briefly presented the negative impact of economic reforms on different sectors of the economy and different classes of the people of the society of our country. The deceleration of the sectoral growth during the decade of reforms is quite conspicuous. The average annual sectoral growth rates in primary, Secondary and Tertiary sectors decelerated. The level of food grain production has been widely fluctuating. The growth rate of production of all crops declined, the substantial decline in the percapita day net availability of cereal and pulses and the share of public investment and gross capital formation in agriculture declined. This decline has led to the crises in agriculture sector. Subsides to irrigation, Power, Research and Extension, Inputs, Credit and Prices have been reduced which has undoubtedly affected the agricultural sector adversely.

Research on Poor Peoples' crops, such as Jowar, Bajra, Small millets and Ragi is neglected Research is concentrated on crops which are normally cultivated by rich formers shows the class bias against the poor peasants in research and extension. Extension services for transferring technology to the farmers has virtually collapsed. The deceleration in industrial growth was wide spread encompassing all the three major sectors. As a part of economic reforms, the disinvestments of P S U 's is being done with all vehemence and rapidity. He also sited the example of power sector reforms. He further says the impact of the reforms on various classes. The prices of all agricultural inputs have gone up and the prices of agricultural commodities have not increased in proportion. The farmers are in distress conditions. It is reported that the wages plus salaries dropped drastically in the period of reforms. The rate of unemployment has increased and the total percentage of G D P spent on social sector was reduced drastically in education and health. The economic reforms have adversely effected the lives of women, dalits, Rural Artisans, Fishermen, Adivasies etc and threatened their lively hood security.

The middle classes and poorer sections disillusioned with these economic reforms. Prof. Chowdary concludes that in the alternative policy-frame, self reliance should occupy the center stage. Livelihood security and food security should be accorded top priority.

Prof. K. Aravindakshan in his paper on "Wither Financial Sector Reforms" discussed the salient features of these reforms i.e. banking sector and financial markets. He made a quick survey of the trends in the banking sector in India in the Pre and Post Nationalisations periods. The definition of priority sector lending was extended in the period of reforms to extend loans to MNC's. He felt that banks have shifted an increasing share of their funds in favour of financial investments than credit. Priority sector lending, subsidised interest rates, differential interest rates so on, has virtually come to an end. The agricultural credit advanced by commercial banks has come down. Regional disparities and imbalances in credit disbursement have also deepened. Big chunk of the bank credit is swallowed by corporate sector, upper middle class and urban elite. He expressed that at the cost of national interests to the benefit of the defaulters, crores of rupees were written off on the name of 'one time settlement' etc. The RBI, as a part of second generation reforms, has generously liberalised erstwhile policy on investments abroad by Indian business houses, individuals and firms so that they could expand globally. On the other side servicing costs of external capital for India are very much higher than the higher out put and employment generated through FDI and further explained various dangers to the developing countries in general and for India, in particular. In the era of liberalisation and globalisation of Indian economy, the people have come across lots of frauds and crimes in the financial markets. The irony of the situation in the Indian financial sector is that the successive governments in India have been promoting the financial casino as part of the economic reforms imposed upon by the IMF, World Bank, WTO-Trinity. Some regulatory methods have been suggested to prevent volatility in the stock markets.

Prof. K.C. Hiremath in his valedictory address on "Reforms for Making Indian Agriculture Strong, Sustainable and Globally Competitive" expressed his views that good or bad, a new chapter has been opened in our economic policies and development strategies. Although these economic reforms have not worked wonders, a good beginning has been made. While comparing the P.V. Narasimha Rao, Man Mohan Singh model with Nehru - Mahalnobis model he felt the farmer broke a new path in economic policies. He explained the agricultural scenario and felt that the government had been more particular about food security rather than about livelihood security. In the new economic policy reforms, the agricultural sector remained unprotected, while many developed countries of the world continued to protect their agriculture. He sees the innate strength and competitiveness of Indian agriculture and says the Indian agriculture is by and large, competitive and capable. Fruits, vegetables, flowers and cotton are the potential exports since they are even now export competitive. We should also create a congenial environment for attracting more private sector investment and involvement in storage, transport, post-harvest management and processing. Further agriculture being a state subject, needs large scale participation of state government in reforming agriculture. The serious tariff and non-tariff barriers imposed by the developed countries have added to the problems of promoting our agricultural exports. The ceiling on land holdings has been a major stumbling block for high capital investment in agriculture. He supported the contract farms and says that input subsidies system has been unbearable fiscal burden. In his concluding remarks he pointed out that there should be a strong and solid partnership between agriculture and industry, centre and the states, the internal and external agriculture trade, and the Macro economic policies at the national and state levels.

Prof. K. Aravindakshan who was a Chief Guest to this National Seminar spoke on "New Dimensions of Globalisation and the Relevance of Communist Manifesto", writes that now there is so much talk about globalisation and was prompted to find out whether there is any reference to globalisation in the Manifesto. He quoted Marx on globalisation. He also mentioned about the two famous books "The End of the Nation State" and "Border less World' which dealt with the imperialist propensity of global capital, which is capable of making a clean sweep of the economies of the developing countries. In his view Kenichi Ohmae felt that investment, industry, information technology and individual consumer, these factor move across the globe quite freely and it is through these four factors that imperialism has been able to establish it self over the entire world. James Peetras and Veltmeyar stated that globalisation has been able to refashion itself as the imperialism of the 21st century. He quoted Marx how "the bourgeoisie has, through its exploitation of the world market has given a cosmopolitan character to production and consumption in every country. He also quoted Henry Kissinger "Globalisation is just another term for US domination" and expressed that capitalism has been re-fashioned as neo-liberalism, which is hardly different from neo-colonialism and Imperialism. Joseph Stightz described the policy of 'Privatisation' which forms an integral part of globalisation policy package, asbbriberasation. Global capital is a hot pursuit of new avenues of exploitation of the masses of people in developing countries and thereby add to their profits and mentioned the experiences of his own state Kerala, and also the experiences of Latin America. Of late, even law courts and the legal system too have come under the influence of globalisation. He concludes, in short, the sweep of globalisation is virtually full and total, embracing all productive sectors, import-export sectors, banking and financial sectors, social service sectors as well as intellectual property.

Prof. G. Sai Baba, presented a paper on "Globalisation, Economic Reforms and Social Sector Development: Some emerging areas in India," made an attempt to analyse the several aspects of social development in the pre and post reform period. He felt globalisation is creating new threats to human security both in rich and poor countries. Around the world, there is wide spread unease about the growth of social and economic insecurity and inequality. The recent decades show all too clearly that there is no automatic link between growth and social development. He expressed that poverty alleviation and raising the standard of living have been the central aim of economic planning in India but it has failed to trickle down in order to fulfill the objectives of social protection. He narrated the reform process and analysed during the period of reforms the non-plan expenditure has increased and expenditure both in plan and non-plan on social sectors has fallen. However, economic reforms have their transition costs which were to be borne more by poorer sections need a special correction mechanism to the loopholes of the new economic policy. The development strategy of ninth plan and its implementation with regard to the social sectors have been analysed Drinking water, housing and health issues were discussed. In the 3rd section he dealt with some emerging trends and area's like. old age, child labour, employment, women and development issues. He concludes by stating that the ongoing economic reforms process should be reappraised and revitalised to give the entire national development effort a more human face. Finally, the goal of social protection is not mere survival but social inclusion and preservation of human dignity.

Dr. S.Janaka Rajan presented a paper on "Economic Liberalization: Prosperity or More Poverty" opined that the I M F and World Bank were instruments through which conditionalities were enforced. When these rules and regulations and conditionalities were framed, there was not iota of concern whether developing and poor countries have the capacity to absorb them. He looked into India's performance with some key indicators during the period of a decade of Economic reforms. Agriculture production has slowed down, paradoxically, despite declaring growth rate in food grain production, the buffer stock has swollen due to increase in P D S prices. The economy is flooded with a variety of luxury and consumer goods which as indeed let down our domestic industries very badly and overall industrial performance was dismal. The rate of poverty has increased due to lack of purchasing power among agricultural workers and other weaker sections, which is due to steady increase in P D S prices of food grains and declining employment opportunities. He felt that some of the key services, which could drastically effect the poor are legal, medical, veterinary, education at all levels and Transport of all kinds. In addition, services such as electricity generation and distribution, drinking and irrigation water, insurance, Tele-communications and banking where the poor population will be very badly affected.

Prof. P.A. Vasudevan in his paper "The Post-Reform Thoughts on Trade Union Movements" expressed that the state, which had a pro-labour attitude, took to pro-employer attitude, which led to serious problems to TU movement. American managerial capitalism aimed at capturing world market, with lower unit cost and higher competitiveness and adopted a strategy to incorporate trade unions in a drive to lower cost of production through a package deal. The Japanese variant, the collective capitalism aims at still higher profit, through further lowering of labour cost. The new technology is more labour serving rather than energy and input serving which is an ideological distortion on the part of the capital owners in the new era. He expressed his concern about the absence of awareness among workers about the new economic and technological changes and sweeping shift in ideological field and advocated for union schools to train the workers. The sharp reduction in the permanent work force, aggressive attitude of employers due to pro-employer legislations, the fast disintegration of organised sector has created more problems than prospects. He calls for a new operating strategy to strengthen the trade union movement. He suggested that trade union should be a part of a right social process and is essential to establish global solidarity with global workers unions.

Prof. D. Dakshina Murthy and Dr. B.K.S. Prakasa Rao in their paper on "Banking Sector Reforms, The Challenges Ahead" felt that over the years the Indian banking and the financial system have made impressive progress in terms of both geographical spread and functional reach. They acknowledged the fact that in Post-

Nationalization era, banks have ceased to be the institution of the privileged. The last three decades after Bank Nationalization bank deposits had increased by 178 times and the same trend bank credit also increased 120 times. While discussing the banking performance they explained that the gross N P A's of the 27 P S B's shot upto Rs. 54,773 cores which have not only reduced the yield on advances but also has an adverse impact on the profitability of banks. They concluded that the reform process cannot be entirely pain less. There are achievements and pitfalls as well. There has been an increase in the rate of growth of both bank deposits and bank investments but a decrease in the rate of growth of bank credit. The banks have invested in government securities a much larger portion of their deposits than is warranted by the prescribed S L R. The deregulated environment has not resulted in any marked improvements in the efficiency of P S B's with the exception of a few.

Prof. S. Subramanyam in his paper on "Impact of Economic Reforms On Growth And Poverty" discussed the India's post independence development strategy briefly and later reviewed the economic reforms. The evidence from growth of real wages and growth of food grain prices relative to the growth of overall price index do not support the hypothesis of poverty reduction in the nineties. The growth rate of whole sale price index as well as that of food grain prices are higher in 1990's as compared to 1980's. He concludes that full scale liberalization has not helped the country either in poverty reduction or in reducing regional inequalities though over all growth could be maintained. The sector wise growth trends indicate that this growth is not sustainable.

Prof. B. Purushotham presented a paper on "Impact of Liberalisation on Rural Non-farm sector and Rural Livelihoods". He felt that Indian agriculture, due to various reasons is less than competitive as compared to the farm out put in developed countries. The Indian dairy industry is predominantly small farmer- oriented and providing subsistence income to millions of rural households. He explained that due to lack of subsidy from the government, the imports from the west, and the high subsidies given by the west to its farmers created serious problems to the Indian dairy industry. The state is not providing infrastructure to the small dairy farmer and lot of negative campagin has been carried out by the west against the Indian dairy products. Thus Indian small dairy farmers are not able to benefit much from the globalisation by way of exports. Handloom industry is the most important economic activity in rural areas as it provides employment to over 12 millions of people. Following the economic reforms the government has withdrawn its assistance and the cheap textile imports from other countries have become a threat to local textile products. Hence the handloom weaving industry in the country facing difficulties. The poultry industry which provides employment to 1.6 million people with the current exposure to globalisation is threatening the industry. The khadi and village industry which has been providing full and part time employment to over 1.5 million rural people is affected by the economic reform process. Salt manufacturing industry which provides self employment to over five hundred thousand households at once become helpless to compete with the large, modern and aggressive brand pushers. Liberalisation has led to the commercialisation of rural economy and put premium on several rural resources which were at one time owned by the community and were called common property resource. He also suggested some policy interventions.

Prof. K.Nageswara Rao in his paper on " Reforms in Industrial Sector-prospects of Indian Industry" expressed the view that India was compelled to accept some conditionalities which were reflected in the structural adjustment programme. As a result, Indian industrial growth experienced a series of mixed trends during the period of liberalization compared to earlier decades. Industrial sector launched into a high growth phase during 1980-90 and during 1990-94 the index of industrial production declined every year. During 1994-98 the general index of industrial production staggered. He is of the opinion that the period of economic reforms began with stagnation of industrial production. The annual average level of employment in public sector units is increased prior to the reform period and decreased during the period of economic reforms i.e., 1990-1999. He has concluded, that the industrial growth rates in some sectors, during 1991-95, slowed down indicating an industrial recession. The average annual industrial growth rate achieved after liberalization is lower than that achieved in the decades before liberalization.

Prof. K S Chalan in his paper on "New Economic Policy in India: The Caste Dimension" analyzed caste needs to be understood as property in India. He feels that the dvija castes are given the right and opportunity to education, assets, weapons etc., which naturally accumulate capital over a period of time and improve their value of human capital which was denied to the sudras and untouchables. With regard to the distribution of resources in India he felt Brahmins remained arbiters and enjoyed the patronage of both the winners and also the runners. He analyzed the post independent economic reforms as an absolute co-operation and understanding among the three groups of dvija's and explained how they shared the fruits of the economy. The Brahmins who have swelled their private exchequer with public money thought that it would not be beneficial any more if they continued in the public sector. They felt that it becomes risky if public sector continues further as the dalits are emerging as a formidable force. Therefore, they thought that it would be beneficial for them to survive both economically and politically if the economy is made private and linked it to the international market.

The Brahmin experts in the World Bank and Brahmin bureaucracy in Delhi conspired and mortgaged the economy when the bahujan were emerging as a force to manage the economy and enjoy the benefits of it. The prescriptions that were implemented in new economic policy have really helped the dvijas project to intensity its operations. The V R S as an exit policy targeted the dalits and O B C's to drive them off the public sector. The fifth pay commission abolished around five lakh jobs mostly belonging to the backlog vacancies. With regard to the changes in macro economic indicators it has to be examined in detail with reference to the socially disadvantaged groups. Out of the super 100 firms reported in business in India, none appears to be owned by a dalit. He concludes that the impact of new economic policies appears to be adverse and serious in the case of dalits. After liberalization the living conditions of groups like fishermen, service castes and dalits have deteriorated.

Prof. M. Sundara Rao and Mrs. A. Sailaja Devi in their paper on " One Decade of Economic Reforms and Indias' External Sector" says that, there have been intense discussions in the academic as well as policy circles regarding the second generation economic reforms. Loans that we took at that time to salvage India's credibility in the world financial market, the second generation economic reforms have been guided by our compulsions, to confirm to the norms set by the W T O in matters of trade policy. Many of the changes that are now contemplated in the functioning of the Indian economy are basically the off shoots of the standards and norms prescribed by the W T O. They are of the opinion that the external sector reform has not bestowed its much favourable influence on the Indian economy. The full benefits of external sector reforms are yet to be achieved. Trade growth and F D I inflows to India have yet to come in a big way and reforms are yet to influence the exchange rate regime and external debt front on more favourable lines. However India's external sector has emerged with considerable inner strength to meet the challenges of foreign as well as domestic shocks, following the economic reforms in 1990's.

Prof. Noor Basha Abdul in his paper on " Indian Banking Sector Reforms: An Appraisal" expressed that one of the widely published purposes of the banking sector reforms was to introduce a healthy competition among the banks but the experiences are proved totally different. Competition has been infused in the Indian Banking Industry by allowing new private sector banks and more liberal entry of foreign banks. The public sector banks are slowly but surely losing out to the more aggressive new private sector banks which have increased their market share. He explained various difficulties caused by the V R S with banking industry. The impact of manpower reduction has been strictly heavy during the post V R S scenario due to the fact that most of the banks functions had not been computerized. During the period of reforms agricultural credit has steadily declined and similar is the case with tertiary sector. By contrast the share of the industrial sector in the total bank credit has registered a sharp increase in post reform period. He concludes that lending to agriculture in general and to the small and marginal farmers in particular needs to be enhanced beyond the prescribed target levels, since the definition of agriculture is unreasonably widened.

K. Hanumantha Rao in his paper "An Enquiry into the Poverty Decline in Rural India during 90's" discussed trends in poverty indices, agricultural growth and rural poverty. He has also explained the changes in labour market and says that the inflationary trends confirm the view that poverty in rural India had declined in the first phase of the new economic reforms and also the in inequalities among the poor have also shrinked during the period. Effects of economic growth was uneven, rates of poverty reduction differed across Socio-Economic groups and the share of SC's and ST's in poverty had gone up in the reforms era. The growth rates of unemployment and under employment were higher in the second phase and female workers were at a disadvantage. The rising unemployment levels for both males and females warn that the initial era of the new economic reforms were unfavorable to rural workers.

Dr. Y. Gangi Reddy in his paper on "Impact of Economic Reforms On Power Looms Industry in Andhra Pradesh" explained the spread and status of Power Looms industry. The major factors i.e., Power sector reforms, technological changes and liberal import policy, the three major factors are the result of new economic reforms led to the power loom industry into a sudden crises. He explains that the power sector reforms have invited the large scale hike in tariff, but failed in providing the quality power to the power loom industry. The power supply interruptions have also increased and further effected not only the running of power looms but also livelihood of worker weavers. Since the wages are linked to the production of cloth, Power cut means cut in wages of worker weavers which led to the crisis in the livelihood of worker weaver. The textile policy based on the recommendations of Satyam committee report adversely affected the employment. The technology upgradation fund could not attract any of these power loom industry owners as it invites large scale investment. Due to liberal import policy the crisis was precipitated by a sharp increase in yarn prices and dumping by countries such as china and Thailand, which led to a fall in the market for the textile products. Several suggestions were made to improve the power loom industry. He concludes that suicide deaths of the weaver workers were caused by distress attributable to liberalization policies and the government has to foresee and assess the likely impact of reform process on employment and incomes of the working poor.

Dr. N.V.Madhuri Presented a paper on " Power Sector Reforms - A Case Study of Andhra Pradesh" and explains that since independence the central thrust of the India's energy policy has been on augmenting the country's energy system. As a result of this, there has been a substantial expansion of, and shift in, the country's energy sector and yet India still suffers from energy shortages. Eighth Plan could not reach the plan targets due to various reasons and the prospects of power sufficiency in the Ninth Plan do not appear to be very encouraging. Huge system losses unchecked over a period of time have led to deep crisis. This was compounded by the government failure to provide subsides to meet the deficits. As a net result of years of criminal neglect, rampant corruption and rank incompetence of electricity boards are now facing severe financial crisis. Every single percentage of Power loss in the system means a loss of revenue to the tune of nearly Rs.100 cores. At least 20 percent power, supplied to the system is being stolen or lost because of incompetent management, corruption and poor infrastructure. Even now, no rational policy for farm sector power has been evolved. She advocates the removal of corruption and inefficiencies, improvement in capacity utilization, co-generation and captive generation of electricity.

Dr. M.V.S. Koteswara Rao presented a paper on "Power Sector Reforms in Andhra Pradesh" and stated the spectacular growth of power sector and its characteristics in Andhra Pradesh. The power supply to agricultural consumers has become a perpetual source of losses for not only APSEB but also to all Power Boards of South India and the decision of the state government to give up the metering system made the situation much worse and proved to be a short sighted one. The state government never bothered to give subsidy to the APSEB. It is in this background that the state government decided to privatise the power sector. The government of Andhra Pradesh has stated three reasons for power sector reforms namely to bridge the gap between demand and supply, improve the financial performance and control the commercial losses. Government of Andhra Pradesh, based on the recommendations of Hiten Bhaya Committee, projected 53,000 crores as minimum requirement to make power available to every one. The recommendations of the Hiten Bhaya and salient features of the reforms were presented in the paper. He says the practical side of the reforms was a rude shock including to those who believed privatisation as a penacea. The Indian public money ultimately financed the Independent power projects and to this extent several details were given. He concluded by stating the negligence by the state government was the primary reason for the crisis in power sector and felt the figures were cooked up, manipulated, the people were given wrong information and what was provided was much worse, much inefficient and anti-people.

G. Sri Devi in her paper on "Food Security and working of P D S in Andhra Pradesh" felt that Indian economy has been exposed to economic liberalization and globalization. Reducing food subsidies is seen as an important means of reducing public expenditure. She has discussed at length about the changes made in P D S in Andhra Pradesh by both congress and Telugu Desam governments. The micro level studies reveal that a large number of poor households do not have ration cards. With regard to the trends in procurement and distribution, the quantity procured is increasing with the increase in production but the quantity distributed is declining. During the last five years, the quantity distributed through P D S has not changed much, while the population of the state has been steadily increasing and there fore, the percapita quantity distributed has declined. She explained the subsidy on rice scheme and says that nearly 15 percent of rice supplies in Andhra Pradesh do not reach P D S consumers and blames the government for its inefficiency, relative to private trade, in delivering food grains through the P D S. She feels that the extent of food security provided by P D S appears to be better in rural areas, but many of the beneficiaries are non-poor. Urban poor are prone to be more food insecure when compared to the rural poor. Disparities in access to P D S among the districts and three regions were also discussed. She concluded that a large number of poor house holds do not have ration cards, while may non-poor households have white cards. About a quarter of the households in rural area could not buy rice because either they had no entitlement or no ration card. The P D S price paid by the higher income groups is not substantially higher than the price paid by the poor groups. The present P D S favours better off districts and developed villages and hence it is unlikely to reduce the regional in balances. She advocated for non-corrupt and efficient and decentralized delivery system.

Prof. C. Narasimha Rao

Contents

1

Reforming the Economic Reforms (Inaugural Address)

*Prof. K.R. Chowdry**

I am honoured to have been called upon to deliver the inaugural address at this National Seminar. I am grateful to Dr. Venugopala Reddy, the Vice-Chancellor of the Nagarjuna University and Prof. Narasimha Rao for giving me this opportunity to say a few words at this gathering of the scholars, economists, political scientists, academicians, and other distinguished personalities.

The theme of this Seminar is "A decade of Economic Reforms in India—Retrospect and Prospect". I must congratulate the organisers for choosing this subject. I think this is a right subject chosen at the right moment and by the right people. This is a right subject because there is an absolute need for a thorough review of the performance of economic reforms today when these reforms have completed ten years by existence. Even P.V. Narasimha Rao, the former Prime Minister, who initiated and implemented economic reforms in the country, pleaded some time back in this very city of Guntur for a national debate on economic reforms.

Economic reforms, as you are all very well aware, consists of two parts, namely stabilisation measures and

* Former Member Secretary, APCOST, Government of Andhra Pradesh, Hyderbad.

Structural Adjustment Programme(SAP). Stabilisation measures include three aspects and these are:

1. Management of balance of payments.
2. Control of inflation and
3. Adjustments in fiscal sector

The structural adjustment programme (SAP) consists of the following:

1. Adjusting the foreign exchange rate
2. Foreign investments
3. Liberalisation of imports
4. Encouragement to exports
5. Rationalisation of tariffs and taxes
6. Reforms in financial sector
7. Abolition of permit-licensing system
8. Disinvestment of public sector undertakings(PSUs)

All these aspects, I think, can rightly be called LPG policies, that i.e., liberalisation, privatisation and globalisation policies. I would like to draw your attention, in this context, to the policy prescriptions or conditionalities imposed by the two international financial institutions, namely the International Monetary Fund and the International Bank for Reconstruction and Development World Bank). These Institutions urged the Government of India as measures of stabilisation to cut drastically the fiscal deficit. The conditionalities included are as follows:

1. Reduction in the Government expenditure
2. Cut in the expenditure of social sector
3. Cut in the subsidies
4. Increase the issue prices of the commodities by the Government of India

5. Enhance the irrigation and power tariff
6. Inviting the foreign Investments and
7. Devaluation of Currency.
8. Taking loans from IMF.

I may add those SAP aims at removal of licenses, restrictions, regulations in all sectors; privatisation in all sectors and priority to exports rather than self-reliance.

I think, a thorough review and assessment of economic reforms has to be made in this background, of course in an objective, dispassionate and impartial manner. Although different versions are available about the performance of economic reforms in India during the last decade, no one claims any achievement or celebrates ten years of reforms.

I would like to draw your attention to the macro-economics crisis, which the country was facing before the introduction of reforms. The crisis manifested in the form of accelerating inflation and unsustainable fiscal and current account deficit. There was a steep fall in foreign exchange resources to about 1 billion dollars and a sharp downgrading of India's current rating and a cut-off of foreign private lending. The rate of inflation was as high as 13 percent and it was rising. The public and current account deficits were large.

In this scenario, we have to assess the impact of reforms in India, I am sure, the economic reforms, particularly the stabilisation measures, have been undoubtedly successful in the initial period in stabilizing the economy of the country. The rate of inflation was brought under control slowly but steadily to about 5 percent from 13 percent. The balance of payments position improved. The foreign exchange reserves increased to $21 billion by the end of March, 1995. The current account position was comfortable. The dollar value of exports grew at around 20 percent per annum. However, we should note that these achievements were short-lived and could not be sustained. From this positive impact, now let us move to the negative impact of the economic reforms.

The economic reforms encompass or engulf all the sectors of the economy and all the classes of the people of the society in the country. I would like to present a few aspects briefly.

Macro-economic Situation

To begin with, let us like the case of macro-economic situation. The deceleration of the sectoral growth during the decade is quite conspicuous. The average annual sectoral growth rates in primary sector decelerated to 1.91 percent in 1996-2000 from 5.72 percent in 1986-90. Similarly, in the secondary sector, the same decelerated to 4.99 percent in 1996-2000 from 8.66 percent in 1996-2000, while the same was 7.20 percent in 1996-2000 from 8.83 percent in 1986-1990 tertiary sector.

In the guise of controlling fiscal deficit, both plan and non-plan outlays were brought down. This affected the crucial infrastructure field.

Agriculture

Now, I would like to discuss the agriculture sector. The level of foodgrain production has been widely fluctuating during the past years. The country has failed to achieve the target of 234 million tones of foodgrain production fixed by the Ninth Five Year Plan. The downward trend was also observed in many commercial crops.

Further, as per the Economic Survey Report 2001-2002, the growth rate of production of all crops declined from 3.19 percent in the decade of the 80s to 1.73 percent in the 90s. Productivity has declined from 2.56 percent to 1.02 percent. Another disturbing feature is the substantial decline in the per capita day net availability of cereals and pulses compared to the position in 1991. The per capita net availability of cereals and pulses together was 510.1 grams per day in 1991 and the same has declined to 417 grams per day in 2001. These averages may be misleading, as the poorer sections do not get even 417 grams per day. The average annual growth in foodgrains production has also declined to 1.67 percent in the 90s - a rate lower than the population growth rate of 1.9 percent. The above discussion clearly shows that agriculture has declined during the period of 1990's, the decade of reforms.

The economic reforms policy prescribes the reduction of state's role in agriculture. When there is input, it is well known that there would be output. The state's input, in other words, the investment in agriculture has declined from 1.6 percent of GDP in1993-94 to 1.3 percent of GDP in 2000-2001. This declined is mainly due to decline in public investment. Electricity, irrigation, research and extension, markets, storage etc., are crucial for the overall development of agricultural sector. But the capital formation in the public sector came down from 15.3 percent in 1980-81 to 4.9 percent in 1996-97. The share of public investment in agriculture declined from 33 percent in 1993-94 to 24 percent in 2000-2001. The share of gross capital formation in agriculture in the total gross domestic capital formation was 19.1 percent in 1979-80, which declined to 9.4 percent in 1996-97 and 5.5 percent in 1998-99. This decline in investment in agriculture has led to crisis in the sector.

Subsidies are extended generally to irrigation, power, research and extension, inputs, credit, prices, etc. However, subsidies on all these items are reduced and hence they became costly. This has undoubtedly affected the agricultural sector adversely.

Financing institutions are catering to the needs of agro-industries, agro-processing, etc. Credit is also provided to high tech agriculture that includes prawn culture, fish culture, horticulture, floriculture, biotechnology etc. Heavy machinery is also given importance and hence credit to purchase the same is provided. As a result of all these, crop loans have declined. Credit for minor irrigation and land development has also declined. The share of small and marginal farmers in the total credit disbursed is only marginal. Lack of credit for agricultural purposes and to small and marginal farmers has been a major obstacle for the development of agriculture.

Despite the fact that a large number of institutions of Indian Council of Agricultural Research (ICAR) and State Agricultural Universities are functioning in the country, no useful technology suitable to landless, poor, small and marginal farmers is generated and no dependable technology for rainfed areas is available. Research on poor people's crops, such as jowar, bajra, small millets and ragi is neglected. Most of the research is concentrated on paddy, sugarcane, horticulture and other commercial crops, which are normally cultivated by rich farmers. The class bias against the poor peasants in research and extension is quite visible.

It may be noted that extension services for transferring technology to the farmers has virtually collapsed. This is mainly due to the policy of downsizing the department of agriculture.

The government has announced a policy of dismantling of procurement of agricultural commodities, abolition of essential commodities (ACT) and introduction of hedging and futures trading in agriculture. All these will undoubtedly affect the prices adversely and the farmers would simply be ruined.

The above discussion clearly establishes the fact that reforms had a negative impact on agriculture in our country. Hence, 70 percent of the people of the country depending on agriculture have been suffering from misery and poverty.

Industry

The Indian industry continues to function as a drag on the overall growth of the economy, with necessary conditions continuing to operate in the sector. Industrial growth decelerated to 2.3 percent in 2001-2002. The growth in the second five-year period, (1997-98 to 2001-02) as well below the average growth rate of 8.2 percent assigned to industry in the Ninth Plan. The deceleration in industrial growth has widespread encompassing all the three major sectors, namely, mining, manufacturing and power. The main factors for constraining growth in the sector have been the slowdown in domestic and global demand. Further, infrastructural bottlenecks especially in the power and transport and communications sectors; high interest rates, lower speculative demand in automobile and real estate sectors, low level of productivity due to low volumes, obsolete technology and slow response to increased competition have been some of the crucial factors responsible for slow down recession in the sector. Further, the flow of manufactured goods into the country from abroad caused the collapse of domestic industry, particularly in small scale sector. India's small-scale sector is quite large with 3.3 lakhs units in 2000-01. About 1.8 percent people are employed and it had an output of Rs.66,250 crore. The collapse of small scale sector ruins millions of people engaged in production, distribution and trade.

According to the Statesman, April 22, 2000, in a briefing to the BJP Members of Parliament, the then Finance Minister, Yeshwant Sinha stated, "the country's small-scale sector is likely to be wiped-out". Because of the W.T.O. commitments, he said, "The Government might not be able to provide any protection to the country's small-scale sector and they would have to face competition. It would not be possible for the Government to raise import duty or extend the time period for the small-scale sector to gear up for the competition. Either they prepare for the competition or phased out by 2001".

The fall of small scale sector is not only due to flood of cheap imports but also due to de-reservation of key production lines in the sector and opening out of this sector to big business in general, and foreign capital in particular.

Disinvestment of Public Sector Undertakings and Privatisation

Over the years, the Government laid a sound foundation for industrial growth through public sector. As part of economic reforms, the disinvestment of PUSs is being done with all vehemence and rapidity. The enterprises worth hundreds of crores of rupees or the huge assets created are being sold for a song. I need not give a list of these companies and enterprises. As per the Budget for the year 2000-2001, the Government decided to bring down its equity in all non-strategic PSUs to 2.6 percent or lower, if necessary. The disinvestment of PUSs is certainly not considered to be in the interest of the country. Privatisation means profits and hence, the people will loose an account of privatisation in different sectors. I would like to give one example to consider power sector reforms. Generation and distribution are being privatised. The Government entered into agreement with private companies for purchase of power. The Government agreed to purchase the power at the rate of Rs.4 to Rs.5 per unit from these private companies against the price of Rs.2/- per unit from NTPC. The state governments are giving guarantees to the companies agreeing to give 16 percent of profit even before the generation is started and a counter guarantee is given by the Government of India. Orissa is the first state which implemented the power sector reforms quite early and now we can see that the whole system has been collapsed. I must say that privatisation is not a panacea for all ills of the country.

Trade

The share of India in the International Trade continues to be negligible despite the liberalisation. Our exports have not picked up as expected. But imports increased substantially. The trade gap has increased from a mere Rs.6,860 crore in 1991-92 to a whopping Rs.73,530 crore. The liberalisation policy is said to help the multinational companies to loot the people of the country.

Impact on Various Classes

Peasants

It is because of the policies of the Government that the prices of all agricultural inputs have gone up. At the same time, the prices of agricultural commodities have not increased in proportion. Hence the incomes of the farmers decelerated. Further, the import of agricultural products caused not only the decline in demand for the products produced by our farmers but also a crash in the agricultural prices. Hence, it has resulted in a crisis in agricultural sector. The farmers are in distress conditions and it is manifested in a number of forms such as, farmers' suicides and farmers' selling of kidneys etc.

Workers

It is reported that the wages plus salaries dropped drastically by over 12 percent in the decade of economic reforms and hence the working class suffers a lot.

Employment

The rate of unemployment has increased from 1.91 in 1983 to 2.23 in 1999-2000. The reforms have failed to make economy to absorb more workforce. Further, the closure of several industries has thrown the people out of employment. The workdays for the labour in the agricultural sector have also come down because of a crisis in the sector and a shift in the cropping pattern, mechanisation.

Social Sector

The total percentage of GDP spent on social sector was reduced drastically.

(a) *Education:* The percentage of GDP spent by state and central governments on education was about 3.8 against the commitment of 6.0 of GDP. The resource constraint is evident for primary education all over. Neither the higher education is in a better position.

(b) *Health:* The health delivery system is weak. The PHCs are inadequately provided with equipment and manpower, the poorer sections suffer due to poor health care system, which is totally neglected as a result of reforms.

(c) *Poverty:* It is reported that neither growth under SAP through trickle-down, nor the growth under PAP (Poverty Alleviation Programmes) through pull-up have been of much help to the poor. Further, the economic reforms have adversely adverted the lives of women, dalits, rural artisans, fishermen, advasies, etc., and threatened their livelihood security.

Ladies and Gentlemen

The issues I discussed here not exhaustive. There are many more issues and many more angles for this subject. I am sure the scholars present here have done some academic work and they would discuss the same in depth in this seminar.

Friends

The economic reforms, as some scholars point out, have created both favourable impact on certain aspects but failed miserably in several others.

Mr. P.V. Narasimha Rao himself admitted, while speaking at Hyderabad a few months ago, that reforms did not help the majority of the people, but served the interests of only upto 10 percent of the people of the society. Now the disillusionment of the middle classes and poorer sections regarding the benefits of economic reforms is amply clear. The optimists plead for economic reforms with a human face, while the critics reject the same outright. I leave it to this august body to discuss and deliberate on these aspects of the subject and also suggest the alternatives and amendments to the reforms.

In the alternative policy frame, "self-reliance" should occupy the center stage. Livelihood security, and food security should be accorded top priority. Enhancing the states role in economic activities becomes all the more important. Agriculture should be given priority. Infrastructure, namely, irrigation, power, credit etc. and also institutional reforms particularly land reforms are absolutely needed for agriculture development. In the field of industry, public sector should continue to play a crucial role. The rural industries also should be encouraged. The Government should create the necessary infrastructure and also marketing facilities. The people of the country should be saved from the onslaught of the domestic and multinational marketing forces. Equity and justice should be the goal of the alternative policy.

With these words, I would like to thank the organisers again for giving me this opportunity to deliver the inaugural address and I wish this seminar a grand success.

Thank you.

2

New Dimensions of Globalisation and the Relevance of 'Communist Manifesto' (Message of the Chief Guest)

*Prof. K. Aravindakshan**

At the very outset, let me express my thanks to the organizers of this Seminar for having invited me to be the Chief Guest at the inaugural functions. I do consider it as the honour bestowed on my State, the State of Kerala as well as on me personally. On this Occasion I deem it fitting and proper to speak on the 'Communist Manifesto', in the era of globalisation especially since the Seminar is being organized under the auspices of the Centre of Scientific Socialism, Nagarjuna University.

Now that there is so much talk about globalisation, I was prompted to findout whether there is any reference to globalisation in the 'Manifesto'. Yes there is. Not just one reference, but quite a few references. Referring to the globalisation propensities of capitalism, the 'Manifesto' published in 1848, that is, more than one and a half decades ago, states:

"The need of a constantly changing market for its products chases the bourgeoisie over the whole surface of the globe. It must nestle everywhere, settle everywhere,

* Prof. K. Aravanidakshan, G.149, Panampily Nagar, Kochi-682036.

establish connections everywhere......... In place of the old local and national seclusion and self-sufficiency, we have intercourse in every direction, universal interdependence of nations........"

This aspect or dimension of the global spread of capitalism has found expression due to the emergence of the phenomenon of a borderless world. Two books written by Kenichi Ohmae are relevant in this context. These are "End of the Nation State" and "Borderless World" which deal with the new imperialist propensity of global capital, which is capable of making a clean sweep of the economies of developing countries. Kenichi Ohmae is of the view that four is dominate the present day world with the disappearance of bi-polarism and the establishment of a unipolar world, with US as the sole arbiter of the world. These four is are Investment, industry, Information Technology and Individual Consumer. These factors move across the entire globe quite freely, without any let or hindrance. It is through these four factors that imperialism has been able to establish itself over the entire world. And, according to James Petras, Prof.Emeritus of Sociology, State University of New York and Henry Veltmeyer, Professor of Sociology and International Development Studies, University of Mexico, Globalisation has been able to re-fashion itself as the imperialism of the 21st century. In fact, the very title and the sub-title of the book authored by these two scholars – "Gloabalisation Unmasked – Imperialism of the 21st century" – make interesting and relevant reading.

The process of economic exploitation by global, imperialist capital initiated by the British East India Company in India for over two centuries about which Dr. Dadahbai Naoroji evolved his famous "Drain Theory", is now being carried out by US global finance capital in tandem with MNCs, IMF, World Bank and WTO. Incidentally, it must be remembered that Lenin, while enunciating his theory of imperialism, refers to Naoroji as the great Indian economist (for his contribution to the revelation of the exploitation character of imperialism). Now, in the modern world the process of imperialist exploitation continues with greater intensity and spread. Let us see what 'manifesto' has to say about this.

"The bourgeoisie has, through its exploitation of the world market has given a cosmopolitan character to production and consumption in every country.........All old-established industries destroyed. They are dislodged by new industries, whose introduction becomes a life and death-question for all civilized nations, by industries that no longer work up indigenous raw materials but raw materials drawn from the remotest zones, industries, whose products are consumed, not only at home, but in every quarter of the globe..........".

It is worth recollecting in this context, the candid remarks made in the course of a speech in 1999 by Henry Kissinger, US Secretary of a state under both Richard Nixon and Ford, former US Presidents. According to Kissinger: "Globalisation is just another term for US domination". In fact, from our experience with regard to globalisation we may describe it as "US imperialism of the 21st Century". Global Capitalism, we know very well, cannot tolerate equality, social justice and security of workers' interests. These are barriers to the sustenance and survival of capitalism as a global social system. We also know that now capitalism has been re-fashioned as neo-liberalism, which is hardly different from neo-colonialism and imperialism.

One of the new dimensions of global capitalism is corruption. Prof. Joseph E. Stiglitz, Nobel Laureate in Economies in 2001 who had served as the Chairman of the Council of Economic Advisers under US President Bill Clinton and also as Chief Economic Adviser of the IMF, in his book, part of globalisation policy package, as "briberisation". In his opinion at least 10 percent of the benefits accruing from privatisation go to the Swiss bank accounts of politicians and bureaucrats who are privy to the disinvestment of public sector undertakings in developing countries.

Global capital is hot pursuit of new avenues of exploitation of the masses of people in developing countries and thereby add to their profits. In the small Latin American State of Bolivia, the entire people of 'Kochabamba' region are on a war path against an MNC which has taken on a long-term contract basis for a water-bottling plant a vast length of the river which used to serve as the only source of drinking water. The people of the entire region are denied access to drinking water by this MNC. In the Chattisgarh State in India, about 100Km length of Sheonath river has been sold outright to an MNC for the bottling of water for commercial use. In Kerala, a popular agitation by people, cutting across all political parties and persuasions against the proposed move of the UDF Government to sell the Periyar river water in Ernakulam district and water in the Malampuzha Dam in Palghat district to a private company for similar purpose,under the guise of bottling of water for industrial use. The people of Plachimada in the Chittur region of Palghat district have been on an agitational path for quite some time against Coca-Cola bottling plant which has drained away water from almost every tank and well in the area, creating acute scarcity of drinking water.

Of late, even law courts and the legal system too have come under the influence of globalisation. The latest concrete instance of this is the Legal Services Authorities (Amendment) Act of June 11, 2002 in terms of which it has been stipulated that in case of any dispute relating to public utility services involving an amount of up to Rs. 10 lakhs it will have to be settled outside the authority of the law courts. These public utility services include transport,

P + T, telephones, water supply, electricity, sanitation, hospitals and insurance. All such disputes shall be settled by a 'Lok Adalat' having three members. Its Chairman will be a retired judicial officer not below the rank of an Executive District of Additional District Judge and the two members will be those with 'adequate' (?) experience in the field of public utility services, nominated by the Central/ State Government as the case may be. As for the right to appeal against any decision of the Lok Adalat there is still some uncertainty and confusion.

Apart from this Act, the Government of India has also enacted the Indian Patent Act(1970) Amendment Act, June 2002 which, in effort, would mean the surrender of all patent rights to MNCs even in the case of products of Indian origin in the Pharmaceutical industry.

In short, the sweep of globalisation is virtually full and total, embracing all productive sectors, import-export sectors, banking and financial sectors, social services sectors as well as intellectual property.

3

The Impact of Economic Reforms on Agriculture: A Study of Groundnut

*Prof. C. Narasimha Rao**
*N. Anjaiah***

While the official media claims that India has become self-sufficient in agriculture, tenth largest industrial power in the world, sixth technologically advanced nation to have conquered the outer space, the UNDP's 1999 Human Development Report has ranked India a lowly 134th in the comity of 174 nations in the human development index and the 144th in the per capita GNP index. It is now widely admitted that in the fifty years of plans and programmes to promote development and eradicate poverty, despite some progress in agriculture and industry and income poverty reduction, India's track record is mixed, and the country remains a land of stark contrasts and disparities.

Structural Adjustment Programme (SAP) was expected to benefit agriculture in an indirect way. With the dismantling of the urban industrial interests, agriculture was expected to take off, and its exports were supposed to be the main earner of foreign exchange, along with light industries, such as textiles, for meeting the costs of imports

* Prof. C. Narasimha Rao, Head, Centre for Scientific Socialism, Nagarjuna University, Andhra Pradesh.

** N. Anjaiah, Assistant Professor, Centre for Scientific Socialism, Nagarjuna University, Andhra Pradesh.

of other goods. These expectations have not materialised. In a general way, agriculture has done badly under SAP. Lowering or withdrawal of subsidies for fertilisers has caused higher input prices. The larger, surplus producing farmers have gained from agricultural prices, while small farmers and rural producers have suffered on account of curtailment of public expenditure on irrigation, power, roads, education and health. As the Approach Paper to the Ninth Five Year Plan (1997-2002) clearly points out, investments in the agricultural sector, particularly towards the creation of irrigation potential, have fallen short of targets. Production of foodgrains in 1995-96 declined, and wheat production was also below target. Capital formation in agriculture-has been declining in real terms, and the quantum of bank credit directed to agriculture has declined. The most serious defect in the reforms has been ignoring the most basic structural issue in agriculture, namely, land reforms.

In the Economic Survey of the Government of India for 1997-1998, it has been pointed out that while the Eighth Plan (1992-97) had stipulated that the level of investment in agriculture should be raised to at least 18.7 percent of the total investment, it could at best reach only 11 percent. Investments in the agricultural sector, particularly for the creation of irrigation potential, fell short of targets despite efforts to reverse the trend by introducing Accelerated Irrigation Benefit Programme (AIBP).

Relative share of agriculture in the Gross Domestic Product (GDP) of India has been on the decline. From 45 percent in 1970-71 this share declined to 38 percent in 1980-81 and further to 31 percent in 1990-91. The rate of decline slowed down somewhat during the decade of 1990s.The contribution of agriculture to the GDP of India stood at 27.9 percent in 1998-2000. The need for stability and acceleration in the growth of agricultural sector can hardly be overstated.

A decline in the rate of growth of agricultural production from 3.4 to 2.2 percent in the 'post-reform' period (Period II) makes it clear that there is a strong indication of a slowdown in the agricultural production.

The reforms so far introduced in the agricultural sector include: (a) reduction of fertilizer subsidy, (b) selective removal of domestic restrictions on the movement of agricultural commodities, (c) decanalisation and rationalization of export of some agricultural commodities and (d) bringing agriculture under GATT agreement.

Above all the desirability of exporting agricultural produce in large quantities to earn foreign exchange is itself questionable – given the widespread poverty and hunger prevailing in India. India needs 230-240 million tonnes of foodgrains to feed its population. Export of foodgrains adversely affects 43 percent of the population living below the poverty line. Even today we are self-sufficient only to the extent that those who can afford food can have it. More than 200 million Indians go hungry to bed every night.

During the period 1990-91 to 1996-97, when reforms were implemented, the growth rate of total agricultural production as well as foodgrain production declined sharply. The growth rate of foodgrains declined from three percent during the period 1980-81 to 1990-91, to 1.73 during the reforms period. A deceleration in foodgrains production during the 1990s has occurred in all regions of the country except the western region. In the eastern region the growth rate has fallen from 4.22 per annum during the 1980s to 1.2 per annum during the 1990s.

Indian agriculture is perhaps going through the worst phase since the food crisis of the mid-sixties. The depression in the prices of various agriculture commodities has started hitting the farmer hard. What is more worrisome is the fact that no state or commodity has remained insulated from the depression in prices. Moreover, this depression in prices has not been on account of any breakthrough on the production front. In fact, in the last decade we have witnessed a negative growth rate in agriculture for the first time since the green revolution. Even in the current year (2001-2002), according to quick estimates, the growth rate in agriculture is expected to be negative. The situation of glut has been witnessed not only in foodgrains and horticultural commodities like potato, onion, but also in plantation crops like coconut, arecanut and cash crops like cotton. The decline in prices has also been witnessed in milk, poultry, fish and meat industry. A decline in output growth coexisted with crumbling prices in agricultural commodities. The paradox is easily understood in terms of collapse in demand for these commodities on account of lack of purchasing power.

The decade of reforms has also witnessed decline in investment in agriculture, which has had adverse effect on Gross Capital Formation. GCF in agriculture as a percentage of the total gross capital formation in the country has declined to just around 5 percent in 1999-00 from 18 percent in 1980-81. The share of public investment in agriculture has declined to 23.6 percent. While the public sector investment in agriculture has fallen, the private investment has grown by 25.18 percent during the same period.

Coupled with the fact that gross cropped area in the country in 1996-97 was around 190 million hectares or 19 crore hectares while the total institutional credit available in that year was Rs. 26,411 crore, the average credit available per hectare does not exceed Rs. 1,400. In the year 1996-97 the short-term credit was around Rs. 900 per hectare. The inadequacy of credit for making improvements in agriculture is highlighted by these averages.

As per the quick estimates, from 1995-1996 to 2000-2001, the share of primary sector in the GDSP of Andhra Pradesh was reduced from 33.32 percent to 30.32, in the secondary sector it was reduced from 23.54 percent to 23.75 percent and in the service sector it has increased to 43.14 to 45.93 percent. The share of agriculture, got reduced whereas the share of service sector has increased and the secondary sector has stagnated is not a healthy trend, where 70 percent of the people are living in rural areas. The capital investment of the state government in agriculture has gone down from 33.9 percent to 23.6 percent. The non-plan allocation to agriculture in Andhra Pradesh during 1998-99 had been Rs. 9317.20 lakh, lagging behind Maharashtra with an allocation of Rs.15586.74 lakh and Tamil Nadu with an amount of Rs.13691 lakh.

Since 1996-97 to 2000-01 the amounts that were allocated to agriculture, under various heads, have not been fully spent in any financial year. The net result is the share of agriculture in GDSP when compared to 1980 has got reduced in 1990s. The state investments in agriculture have gradually fallen. During the period 2000-01 and 2001-02 the fall in agriculture prices due to lack of minimum support price, the stocks of foodgrains in FCI and the failure of mansoon put together created several problems to the agriculture sector.

The foodgrain production was 25 lakh tonnes in 1970s has increased by another 14 lakh tonnes in 1980s and during the 1990s, that is in the period of economic reforms the production of foodgrain has not crossed the additional production of 14 lakh tonnes. In 1996-97 the state has produced 136.8 lakh tonnes of foodgrain and has not moved an inch in the year 1999-2000 and it was only in 1998-99 that the production has reached to 149 lakh tonnes. The crop of rice has stagnated at 106 lakh tonnes. The produce of jowar and few other crops were also reduced. The foodgrain production in 2000-01 was quite good in Andhra Pradesh and the cropped area has increased to five lakh hectares is perhaps the reason for this growth.

Study of Groundnut

Groundnut is a major oilseed crop in India, occupying over 8.0 million hectares, of which 85 percent is rainfed and 15 percent irrigated. The crop is cultivated in 46 percent of India's total oilseed growing area and accounts for 59 percent of the oilseeds produced in the country. Although India ranks first in area and production (7.2 million metric tonnes) in the world, average yields are low (I tonne/ha) in the rainy season and 2 tonnes/ha in the post-rainy season.

About 91 percent of the total groundnut area and production occur in the states of Andhra Pradesh (2.39 mha, 2.21 mt), Gujarat (1.91 mha, 1.24 mt), Karnataka (1.24 mha, 1.03 mt), Tamil Nadu (1.09 mha, 1.49 mt), Maharashtra (0.76 mha, 0.81mt), and Orissa (0.32mha, 0.43 mt). The remaining area is scattered through other states.

The proportion of the groundnut area that is irrigated is around 20 percent or less. It is thus apparent that a sizeable proportion of the groundnut area is without irrigation support. This is a factor which cannot be ignored while analysing the growth and stability of the groundnut economy in India

Groundnut is grown on over eight million hectares in India. This accounts for around 40 percent of the world's total area under groundnut. In terms of production, India's share in the total world output is 32 percent.

Groundnut oil is also used in the preparation of cosmetics, soap making, used for preparing common lubricants, as an energy source, the groundnut oil makes an excellent substitute for diesel fuel. For pharmaceutical purposes, the groundnut oil finds varied usage. It is used as a substitute for olive oil in making, ointments, liniments and plasters; it also acts as vehicle for vitamins A and D, and hormones. The major portion of groundnut cake or meal produced after the extraction of oil is either exported or finds its way either direct as cattlefeed or farm manure.

The average groundnut yields in India are 700 to 800 kg per hectare. Even under irrigated conditions the average yields have ranged from 1.3 to 1.8 tonnes per hectare. On the other hand, in several European countries and in the U.S.A. they range from 2 to 3 tonnes per hectare. The country has to import about 4 million tonnes of edible oil every year which has inflicted a major drain in the otherwise meagre foreign exchange resources. Groundnut ranks first among the oilseed crops of India constituting about 59 percent of the total oilseed production. Groundnut being the most important oilseed, the prices of various oilseeds and oils generally move in line with its prices. So in order to keep the prices of oilseeds under control, the yield of groundnut has to be increased.

This was particularly true of the non-foodgrain crops, notably oilseeds, whose producers not only suffered a large loss in output but also received sharply lower prices for their produce. It should be remembered that the material distress of farmers is higher whenever lower production is accompanied by terms of trade loss. More generally, it should be noted that the current year is the third since 1995-96 when agriculture's terms of trade have moved adversely, and in each of these years (1995-96, 1997-98, and 1999-2000) agricultural output has either declined or remained stagnant in comparison with the previous year.

World market prices in these commodities had fallen over a period. The international prices of palm oil and soyabean oil which had averaged $670 and $630 per tonne respectively during 1998, averaged only $440 and $ 430 during 1999, and fell further to $360 and $ 330 per tonne in February 2000. The corresponding figures for wheat (HRW, Gulf ports) were $126, $112 and $ 105 per tonne, respectively. Even for pulses, for which international markets are thin and price data not readily available, there are indications of a decline in international prices by 10 to 15 percent. For all these commodities there was sustained fall in international prices throughout 1999 and by the beginning of the marketing season these were lower than the corresponding domestic production. In the case of edible oils, earlier expectations that the government would increase import duties had led to an unusually large build up of imported stock even as world prices continued to fall, so that when duties did not rise by harvest time there was both an overhang of stocks and disappointed expectations.

While the subsidies now being given to farmers and for food are being questioned, the outgo on non-merit subsidies and revenues foregone in the form of concessions, duty exemption and leakages are many times more. While the subsidies by States and Centre taken together for farm and food sector are around Rs.40,000 crore (though whole of these are not subsidies to the farmers), direct and indirect subsidies to other sectors are around five times more than this level. The subsidies enjoyed by non-poor be phased out first to release more resources for agricultural and social development.

Andhra Pradesh is occupying first place in the production of groundnut. An average of 5 years in three regions of Andhra Pradesh reveals that the area of cultivation of groundnut in the coastal region in 72,142 ha. while in Rayalaseema 1,45,129 ha. and in Telangana 1,55,220 ha.

Though there was a growth in production the agriculturists could not sell their crop at remunerative prices. The millers have reduced the prices and the peasants lost heavily. During the period of economic reforms from 1990-91 to 2000-01, the cultivated area and yield of groundnut in Andhra Pradesh decreased. In the year 1990-91 the production of groundnut was 3.96 lakh tonnes, which declined to 2.33 lakh tonnes in 1999-2000. The yield per hectare was 1409 kilograms in 1990-91 and it declined to 936 kilograms in 1999-2000. Due to lack of monsoon and a variety of diseases to groundnut crop, yield levels decelerated. Good number of oil mills were closed down and the remaining mill owners have purchased the groundnut from other states and this has put the agriculturists in great difficulties and some of them have committed suicides in various parts of Andhra Pradesh.

Empirical Study

A study is conducted to assess the impact of economic reforms on groundnut crop in the drought-prone Anantapur district. Three revenue divisions of the district namely Anantapur, Dharmavaram and Penukonda were chosen for the study. One mandal in each division based on the criteria of highest, moderate and lowest extent of cultivation of groundnut crop was selected. The sample consisted of 120 households by covering 40 respondents from each of the divisions. Out of 120 households/respondents, 69 are small, 26 medium and 25 big. It is found that the total number of working persons among the three categories are 240 members. Out of 240 members, 128 belong to small, 57 to medium and 55 to big households. With regard to the land particulars, it is found that selected farmers possess 685 acres of dryland and 79 acres of wetland, totally 784 acres. It shows that the groundnut cultivation in Anantapur district is mostly in dryland and a limited extent of groundnut cultivation is under wetland.

(a) Costs and Returns of Groundnut

The details of cost of cultivation of groundnut per acre are given in Table 1.

Table 1: Cost of cultivation of Groundnut per acre

Sl. No.	*Particulars*	*Total in Rs.*
1	Material Cost	1,300-00
2	Human labour cost	780-00
3	Bullock power cost	750-00
4	Machinery	-
	Total	2,830-00

As per the Table 1, the cost of cultivation per acre in the form of material cost i.e. seeds, fertilisers, pesticides, manure's worked out to Rs.1300/-. Human labour which includes both family and hired labourers is estimated to be Rs.780/-. The bullock labour cost is around Rs.750/-. The use of machinery is almost nil. As per the collected data, it is estimated that Rs.2,830 is the cost of cultivation per acre. It has to be noted that Anantapur district is a drought-prone area where the wages of agriculture labourers are comparatively low. The human labour cost is about half of the cost on materials.

The average groundnut production in the sample area is 4 quintals per acre and the price of each quintal was Rs.1,050/-. Per acre average cost of cultivation has been calculated based on the group discussions with the farmers in three revenue divisions. The difference between the cost of cultivation and per acre average gross returns is not much. The groundnut farmers are spending Rs.2,830/- as cost of cultivation per acre and getting income of per acre Rs.4,200/-. This meagre income is fluctuated quite often. This is due to a number of factors such as the conditions of mansoon, market price and availability of inputs.

(b) Marketing

Marketing plays an important role in the price determination of groundnut. The agricultural markets are not very nearer to the villages. In such a situation the farmers are bound to sell their product through middleman in the villages. As per the details given in Table 2, out of the total 120 groundnut farm households, 88 percent of households sold their groundnut product through the middleman and 98 percent farm households sold in regulated market. The remaining 3 percent of households sold their groundnut product in unregulated market. The above information reveals that middlemen's role in marketing is substantial and they exploited the farmers.

Table 2: Marketing Practices

Sl. No.	Place	No. of farmers
1	Village itself	106 (88.00)
2	Regulated Marketing	10 (9.00)
3	Un-regulated Marketing	04 (3.00)
4	Directly to mill owner	– –
	Total	120 (100.00)

Note: Figures in the brackets are percentages to the total.

Besides this, several other important factors played a crucial role in the lives of groundnut farmers.

(c) Droughts

Anantapur district is commonly known for its drought-prone conditions with an average rainfall of 544 mm, next to the Jai Salmeer of Rajasthan state. A natural calamity is booming large over this area since decades. In this context, it is not out of place to mention that in the name of economic reforms, Government of Andhra Pradesh has not undertaken any major irrigation projects in the state. So the neglect of irrigation projects has caused serious damage to the farmers of the district. The only source of irrigation to the entire Rayalaseema particularly to Anantapur is Handri Neeva Project. The foundation stone was laid years back and so far the project has not been completed.

(d) Neglect of Research and Plant Protection

In the recent past the groundnut crop in Anantapur district is facing an acute crisis due to bud Necrosis. It is because of the new economic reforms the research and extension in agriculture has gone down steeply and private sector which has entered into this area has naturally no interest in finding out solutions to this problem. On the other side, the farmers are totally ruined due to this peculiar disease to the groundnut crop and they have repeatedly brought this matter to the notice of the concerned authorities but failed.

(e) Credit

In the name of financial sector reforms, the bank credit to the priority sector has gone down. Advances to agriculture constituted only 15.5 percent of the net bank credit at the end of March 1999, which is less than the credit available in 1991. Long-term trend in priority sector advances showed that their share in total bank credit was 38.9 percent on an average during the period 1981-91 which diminished to 32.5 percent during the period 1992-98. Coupled with the fact that the gross cropped area in the country in 1996-97 was around 119 million hectares while the total institutional credit available in that year was Rs.26,411 crore. The average credit available per hectare does not exceed Rs.1400/-. In the year 1996-97 the short-term credit per hectare was around Rs.900/-. As a part of economic reforms, the financial sector reforms made the life of the farmers vulnerable and they were left to the mercy of moneylenders.

(f) Increased cost of Inputs

The economic reforms have made a significant impact on the cost of agricultural inputs. The subsidy that was reduced on pesticides and fertilisers increased the cost of cultivation which led to further ruin in farming community.

(g) Imports

WTO has played a havoc in the life of the farmers. There was a deep international crisis of palm oil and soyabean oil. The prices were ruling at $670 and $630 per tonne respectively, during the 1998. These prices decelerated to $440 and $430 during 1999. Further, they decelerated to $360 and $330 per tonne in February 2000.

The crisis has been due to a sharp decline in international prices of these commodities. The crisis to groundnut farmer is because of comparatively low prices of edible oils in the international market and also due to flooding of our domestic market with edible oil imports facilitated by the removal of quantitative restrictions on import of these commodities and also low import tariff.

Table 3: Opinion survey of farmers

Sl. No.	*Particulars*	*No. of farmers*
1	Declining demand for the product	22 (18.00)
2	Declining the prices for products	46 (39.00)
3	Both 1 & 2	52 (43.00)
	Total	120 (100.00)

Note: Figures in the brackets are percentages to the total.

The sample respondents have also felt the effect of these imports to the domestic market. Out of 120 households, 18 percent felt that the import of edible oils has been the main reason for the lack of demand for groundnut, 39 percent of respondents expressed their view that import of oils from the external market led to the crisis in the groundnut market. Remaining 43 percent of households felt that both the declines in the demand for the groundnut product and also the imports played a major role in the crisis of the domestic groundnut market. This led to a big crisis in oil industry and ultimately ruined the farmers engaged in the production of oilseeds. Naturally this had a great impact on the farmers engaged in the groundnut crop production. For this reason the groundnut farmer could not secure the remunerative prices. They could not even sell their groundnut due to lack of demand in the market.

Conclusion

The study reveals the basic fact that the ongoing economic reforms have adverse effect on the farming community of Anantapur district engaged in the production of groundnut. In the name of economic reforms, meagre financial allocations to the irrigation sector and the lack of credit facilities to the agriculture and the reduction of subsidies to the agricultural inputs have contributed to the crisis. Extension services i.e. pesticides, fertilisers, seeds, inadequate research and finally the removal of quantitative restrictions on agricultural products especially oil imports made the groundnut farmers more vulnerable to several problems. It is an obligation on the part of the government to seriously look into these aspects of economic reforms and review the net results so as to protect the interests of farming community.

REFERENCES

1. Samarendra N. Roy, 2000, Economics and Politics of Agricultural and Rural Development Policy in the era of Reforms, The institutional Structural Dimension.
2. R.C. Chowdary and R.P. Singh (Edited, 2000) Rural prosperity and Agriculture Policies and Strategies Economic Reforms and Agriculture, Hyderabad, NIRD, Foundation Series.
3. Dasgupta, Biplav, (1997), SAP: Issues and conditionalities—A Global Review, *Economic and Political Weekly,* May 17-24.
4. Government of India (1996), Planning Commission, Approach paper to the Ninth Five Year Plan, 1997-2002, New Delhi.
5. Government of India (1996), Planning Commission, New Delhi.
6. Hari Om Verma, Alternative Economic Survey, 2000-2001, Rainbow Publishers, New Delhi.
7. Alternative Economic Survey, 2000-2001, Rainbow Publisher, New Delhi.
8. Neelima M.Chandiramani, (2000) Indian Agricultural Under WTO Regime.
9. Vishal Rawat, A long way to go - *Agriculture Today,* February, 2002.
10. Vishal Rawat, A long way to go - *Agriculture Today,* February, 2002.
11. Hori Om Verma, Alternative Economic survey, 2000-2001, Rainbow Publishers, New Delhi.

12. V. Hanumanta Rao, (2001) Andhra Pradesh Arthika Vyavasta, Pratyamnaya Pariseelana, 1996-2001, Prajasakti Bock House, Hyderabad.

13. 2001 Andhra Pradesh Arthika Vyavasta, Pratyamnaya Pariseelana, 1996-2001 P.V. Prajasakti Book House, Hyderabad.

14. V. Hanumanta Rao (2001), Andhra Pradesh Arthika Vyavasta, Pratyamnaya Pariseelana, 1996-2001 P.V. Prajasakti Book House, Hyderabad.

15. The Indian Economy, 1999-2000, An alternative survey, New Delhi.

16. 1999-2000, An alternative survey, New Delhi.

17. Agriculture Statistics at glance (2002) Agriculture Statistics Division, Directorate of Economics and Statistics, Department of Agriculture Cooperation, Ministry of Agriculture, Government of India, Pushpak Printers.

18. Agriculture Research, Data Book (1999) Indian Agricultural Statistics Research Institute, Published by Directorate of Information and Publications of Agriculture, New Delhi.

19. K.N. Ninan (1999) Edible Oil Seeds, growth, Area Responses and Prospects, published by Oxford and IBA.

20. Seasons and corop report of Andhra Pradesh, (1999-2000) Directorate of Economics and statistics, Government of A.P., Hyderabad.

4

Economic Reforms and Coconut Economy

*Dr. K. Somasekhar**
Dr. V. Divyathejo Murthy

India is one of the leading coconut producing countries of the world. Its annual production is about 15,000 million nuts. The productivity of coconut in India is higher with 7,821 nuts/ha when compared with the world's average productivity of 4,294 nuts/ha. Coconut is essentially a small holder's crop, being mostly grown in homestead gardens and small holdings. About 5 million coconut holdings are reported with 98 percent of such holdings falling below 2 hectares. It is estimated that about 10 million people depend directly and indirectly on coconut culture and industry for their livelihood. It's contribution to GDP is about Rs.7,000 crore annually. It also earns foreign exchange to the tune of Rs.313 crore annually.

In India coconut is used for a variety of purposes. About 48 percent of coconut production is used for edible and religious purposes, 11 percent as tender coconut, roughly 31 percent for oil extraction, 8 percent for the manufacture of edible copra and balance is processed into products like desiccated coconut and coconut cream. Oil is

* Dr. K. Somasekhar and Dr. V. Divyathejo Murthy, Faculty Members, Department of Rural Development, Nagarjuna University, Andhra Pradesh.

the most important product of coconut in India. 40, 46 and 14 percent of coconut oil is used for edible purpose, toiletry use and industrial use, respectively. Coir and oil cake are the most important byproducts of coconut.

Trade generally takes place in international market in the products, such as coira, coconut oil, desiccated coconut, oil cake and coir products. The European Union and America are the major imports of coconut oil, coir products and desiccated coconut. However, export of coconut products from India declined sharply due to decline in the international prices of these commodities in the post-WTO period. The international prices of coconut products always rule lower than that of the domestic price. Further, the international prices of all vegetable oils showed a downward trend, which depressed the domestic prices of all oils including coconut to a very low level.

Analysis of price trends of coconut oil in the international market, compared to India's domestic market from 19991 onwards, reveals that the price of coconut oil in India was ruling around 185 to 310 percent higher than that of the International price. A similar trend is noticed in the case of milling of copra. A wide fluctuation in the exchange rate of rupee is one of the factors affecting the difference in price.

Furthermore, the declining prominence of coconut oil is mainly due to the increased production of other vegetable oils. Palmolein is the major oil that competes with coconut oil especially for edible uses. The other competing oils are soyabean oil, sunflower oil, rapeseed oil, and groundnut oil. The entry of palm oil in the vegetable oil sector was on a faster pace and now this oil holds its supremacy over other vegetable oils. This trend is expected to continue in the years to come.

An analysis of the prices of major vegetable oils for the last 4 years, revealed a steady declining trend. The average price of palmolein was US $ 646 per tonne in the year 1998. It declined to $437 in 1999 and further to $314 in 2000 and again to $244 in 2001. Similarly, the average price of soyabean oil was $625 in 1998, which slashed to $432 in 1999 and further to $347 in 2000 and again to $318 in 2001. In respect of all the above oils, the decline in prices was about 40 to 50 percent. However, in the case of groundnut oil the price which ruled around $ 911 in 1998 declined to $788 in 1999 and $718 in 2000 and to $692 in 2001, showing a comparatively low negative trend.

In the case of coconut oil, the average price was $658 in 1998. Although it improved to $738 in 1999, the price came down to $450 in 2000 and again to $402 in 2001. The net difference in this period was around 43 percent. The international price of coconut oil if compared with the domestic price, it could be seen that the latter was higher by about 62 percent in 1998, 71 percent in 1999, again 72 percent in 2000 and 117 percent in 2001.

As per the exim policy announced by the Government of India, all coconut products including fresh coconut could be imported into the country from April 2001 onwards. This caused worries among coconut farmers. The high domestic price of coconut oil led to import of cheaper vegetable oils from other countries.

If the present trend in prices of coconut products continues and the import policy remains unchanged, the ongoing trend in production may not be maintained in future. The excessive dependence on the imported edible oils and coconut products has already adversely affected domestic industry and thereby the coconut farmers.

Empirical Study

In order to assess the impact of economic reforms on coconut economy, an empirical study at micro-level is conducted. East Godavari district in Andhra Pradesh is purposively selected for the purpose. One mandal is selected based on the probability proportion of area cultivated under the drop, from each of revenue divisions of Kakinada, Amalarapuram and Rajahmundry. A sample of 120 coconut farm households are selected from the chosen mandals by adopting random sampling technique. 38 small, 59 medium and 23 large households constituted the total sample. 315 members from120 households were engaged in agriculture activity. The extent of land possessed by 120 households is 770 acres, consisting of 652 acres of wetland and 118 acres of dryland. 76 and 64 households cultivated the land through canal irrigation and wells/bore wells, respectively. Many of the farmers have more than one source of irrigation.

As per particulars provided in Table 1, the respondents owned 31 tractors, 24 power tillers, 57 seed drills, 95 ploughs, 53 harrows and 36 sprayers and dusters. Credit to coconut farmers is one of the most important production requisites affected adversely by the financial sector reforms as part of the economic reforms. The priority sector advances are lower when compared to rural deposits since 1991. Rural banking network and credit flows to rural areas have been affected negatively. This has created resource/ financial crunch to coconut farms.

Table 1: Particulars of Machinery and Implements owned by farmers

S.No	*Item*	*Small*	*Medium*	*Large*	*Total*	*No. of Implements possession*
1.	Tractor	1	14	16	31	31
2.	Power Tiller	-	10	14	24	24
3.	Seed Drills	13	25	19	57	79
4.	Ploughs	24	51	20	95	163
5.	Harrows	11	28	14	53	69
6.	Plant Protection Equipment	-	16	20	36	36

It is evident from Table 2, an amount of Rs.2,800/-, Rs.3100/- and Rs.6,900/- per acre are provided by the commercial banks, cooperative institutions and private sector, respectively. private sector lending with high rate of interest created many problems to coconut farmers. The non-availability of institutional finance has forced farmers to seek loans from private sources. The average loan amount per farmer worked out to Rs.12,800/-. This is grossly inadequate to those farmers growing coconut in more than one hectare. Shortage or lack of credit affected coconut cultivation.

Table 2: Particulars of Loan (Source wise in Rupees)

S.No	*Source*	*Total Amount Taken*
1.	Commercial Bank	2800-00
2.	Cooperative Institution	3100-00
3.	Private Source	6900-00
4.	Per farmer Average loan Taken	12800-00

According to the details presented in Table 3, the establishment and maintenance cost worked out to Rs.6,510/ - per acre and Rs.6,310 per acre respectively. thus the total cost of cultivation is estimated to be Rs.12,820/- acre. The cut in the subsides of agricultural inputs, increased cost of cultivation of coconut. Contrary to this the returns from coconut cultivation along with inter cropping worked out to Rs.13,825/- per acre, consisting of Rs.10,125 and Rs.3,700 from coconut and inter crops, respectively from one acre. The net returns are worked out to Rs.1000/- acre, which is a meagre amount.

The yield of coconut is also low due to pest attack and insufficient fertiliser application. It may be concluded that coconut cultivation, even together with intercultivation proved to be unremmunerative which has been causing distress to coconut farmers. About 8, 23 and 69 percent of

Table 3: Cost of Cultivation per Acre

S.No	*Establishment*	*Cost*	*Maintenance*	*Cost*	
1	Seedlings	3000-00	Irrigation	1500-00	
2	Land Preparation	900-00	Fertiliser	1800-00	
3	Digging of Pits	1200-00	Application	600-00	
4	Planting the seedlings	600-00	Inter cultural Operation	900-00	
5	Manure and Fetilisers	300-00	Harvesting	460-00	
6	Application of Manure & Fertilisers	60-00	Electricity	450-00	
7	Application of plant Protection chemicals	100-00	Watch & Ward	600-00	
8	Irrigation	450-00			
	Total	6510-00		6310-00	12,820/-

households sold coconuts in far-off places, nearby markets and their own coconut gardens, respectively. coconut processing factories are not available in this region. Further, the respondents reported that liberal imports of edible oils, such as palm oil and soyabean oil, reduced the demand for coconut oils in the domestic market and slashed coconut prices.

Conclusion

The implementation of economic reforms had affected adversely the coconut farmers. the cost of cultivation increased due to increase in input costs, such as, fertilisers, plant protection, chemicals, etc., Further, the credit facilities available are insufficient. These created adverse impact on the returns from coconut cultivation. Furthermore, the Exim policy of Government of India allowing liberal imports of coconut products into country reduced the demand for domestic products besides slashing the prices of coconut products. The economic reforms not only caused distress to coconut farmers but also to lakhs of labourers depending on coconut processing etc.

REFERENCES

1. Dr. P. Rethinam, (2001), Coconut Industry in India, Coconut Development Board of India, Kochi.
2. V.T. Markose, (1994), Coconut processing Sector in India. An overall perspective, Coconut Development Board, Kochi.
3. H. Kaushal, (1994), Processing and Marketing of Coconuts in India, Coconut Development Board, Kochi.
4. V.T. Markose, T.B. Nandakumar, (1998), Coconut Statistics (Ed) Coconut Development Board, Kochi.
5. Directorate of Economics and Statistics (1999-2000), Ministry of Agriculture, Government of India.
6. V. Hanumantha Rao, (2001), Andhra Pradesh Arthika Vyavasta, Pratyamnaya Pariseelana, 1996-2001 P.V. Prajasakti Book House, Hyderabad.

7. K.N. Ninan, (1999) Edible Oil Seeds, Growth, Area Responses and prospects, Oxford and IBA Publishing Co. Pvt. Ltd., New Delhi.

8. Season and Crop Report of Andhra Pradesh, (1999-2000), Directorate of Economics and Statistics, Government of Andhra Pradesh.

5

Reforms in Industrial Sector: Prospects of Indian Industry

*Prof. K. Nageswara Rao**

In order to accommodate the changes in the industrial environment some relaxations were introduced in the mid-seventies and mid-eighties in the functioning of Indian Industrial System. The New Economic Policy and the package of trade policy reforms aimed at (a) declining, deregulating, decontrolling and debureaucratisation of industrial licensing system, (b) encouraging private enterprise by reducing the reservation of priority areas of public sector mainly to promote efficiency and productivity of future industrial growth and (c) opening up Indian Economy to attract investment and technology.

These programmes aimed at access to high technology and world markets for strengthening export activity by the elimination of a substantial volume of import licencing and optimal import compression, of course, by protecting the essential imports of sensitive items like petroleum and fertilizers. However, India was compelled to accept some conditionalities which were reflected in the structural adjustment programme. As a result, Indian Industrial growth experienced a series of mixed trends during the period of liberalisation compared to earlier decades.

* Department of Economics, Sri Krishnadevaraya University, Anantapur-515003. Andhra Pradesh.

Purpose of the Study

In view of this dynamic scenario, an attempt is made in this paper to examine the changes in the industrial production, to analyse the trends in the industry-wise annual growth rate of industrial production, to explain the composition of industrial employment in public and private sectors, to estimate the effects of dis-investment in public sector units and to suggest some measures to sustain higher rate of industrial growth.

For this purpose, data relating to the industrial production for two decades 1980-90 and 1990-2000 are collected and the average annual values are estimated to describe and compare the industrial performance. Further, to analyse industrial growth during the period of liberalisation data relating to 1994-2001 with 1993-94 base year are used.

Industrial Performance during 1980-90

The rate of growth of industrial production was low during 1966-75 because India's planning strategy was conceived in the framework of a closed economy. It staged a smart recovery during 1975-79 and suffered a negative growth rate in 1979-80 due to the second oil shock, the drought conditions and the constant savings proportion to GDP at 16 percent. Hence, the period 1965-80 was treated as the period of industrial stagnation.

Industrial sector launched into a high growth phase during 1980-90. Table 1 shows the industry-wise index of industrial production and its annual growth rates. It is seen that the general index of industrial production increased significantly during 1985-90. This was mainly due to the higher growth performance of mining sector (40 percent), electricity (60 percent) and manufacturing sector (30 percent)

During 1990-94 the index of industrial production declined by (6 percent) every year. Due to the dismal

Table 1: Index of Industrial Production and Growth rates

Period/ Year	*Mining/ Quarrying*	*Annual growth Rate*	*Manufacturing*	*Annual growth rate*	*Electr city*	*Annual Growth rate*	*General*	*Annual growth rate*
1981-85	139.7	12.7	114.4	5.8	123.1	8.9	118.3	7.0
1985-90	188.1	5.7	146.7	8.8	183.9	9.4	167.9	8.5
1990-94	224.7	2.3	212.5	4.1	191.6	7.2	161.9	4.3
1994-99	121.9	3.3	139.9	6.3	130.8	9.0	137.1	6.0
1994-95	109.8	9.8	109.1	9.1	108.5	8.5	109.1	9.1
1995-96	120.5	9.7	124.5	14.1	117.3	8.1	123.3	13.0
1996-97	118.2	-1.9	133.6	7.3	122.0	4.0	130.8	6.1
1997-98	126.4	6.9	142.5	6.7	130.0	6.6	139.6	6.1
1998-99	125.4	-0.8	148.8	4.4	135.9	6.5	145.2	4.1
1999-00	126.7	1.0	159.4	7.1	141.8	6.6	154.7	6.6
2000-01*	126.6	4.0	162.0	6.2	152.8	4.6	157.3	5.7

Note: * April to December.
Growth rates in percentages.

Source: Govt. of India, Economic Survey, 2000-2001, S.37.

performance of manufacturing sector and severe import compression, it is reported that export industries suffered a recession and the industrial demand declined significantly. The depressed conditions of 1991-92 of the manufacturing sector were reversed and positive growth rate of 0.6 percent was recorded in the next year. Cement, machinery, ship-building, sugar, cloth, polyester, railway wagons etc, recorded a growth rate over 10 percent.

The general index of industrial production changed by 2.3 percent in 1992-93 over the preceding year because the intermediate goods, capital goods, consumer durables and basic industries achieved a positive growth. The mining sector also registered the same rate of growth while the growth rate of electricity sector was positive (5 percent) but less than the previous year.

During 1994-98 the general index of industrial production staggered because of the inconsistent performance of mining and electricity. Later, the performance of these sectors experienced ups and downs. The recession in the capital goods industries and a fall in the demand for exports due to international recession are responsible for the slower growth rate of industries.

The growth rate of general industrial production was 7 percent per annum during 1980-85 and increased to 8.5 percent per annum in the next five years. This was attributed to the high rate of growth of manufacturing and electricity industries.

The external debt and foreign exchange crisis of 1991 and the programme of stabilisation measures and structural adjustments led to severe import compression and hence industrial growth recorded a steep fall from 8.2 percent in 1990-91 to 0.6 percent in 1991-92. Thus, the period of economic reforms began with stagnation of industrial production.

Industrial production staged a steady recovery from 1992-93 and registered a high growth rate in 1994-95 and

1996-97 mainly due to better performance of mining and manufacturing industries. As a result of the positive measures like delicencing of several industries, simplification of procedures, opening-up of more areas to the private sector, steep reduction in personal and corporate income tax rates and customs and excise duties, industrial production recovered to 6 percent in 1993-94 and recorded a high of 9.8 percent in 1995-96. However, it suffered a setback in the following years due to infrastructural bottlenecks, demand recession for consumer durables etc.

Trends in Industrial Employment

Table 2: Industrial Employment in Public Sector

(Fig.in Lakhs)

Period/Year	*Central*	*State Govt.*	*Quasi-Govt.*	*Local Govt.*	*Total*
1981-85	32.75	60.37	50.72	21.11	164.94
Percentage	19.85	36.60	30.57	12.80	100.00
1985-90	39.74	67.46	59.18	22.15	183.91
Percentage	21.61	36.68	32.17	12.04	100.00
1990-94	33.95	72.33	64.05	22.18	192.51
Percentage	17.64	37.57	32.27	11.52	100.00
1994-99	31.69	74.18	64.45	22.23	194.55
Percentage	17.32	38.13	33.12	11.43	100.00
1994	33.92	73.37	65.14	22.02	194.45
1995	23.95	73.55	65.20	21.97	194.66
1996	33.66	74.14	64.58	21.94	194.29
1997	32.95	74.84	65.35	22.44	195.59
1998	32.53	74.58	64.61	22.66	194.18
1999	33.13	74.58	3.85	22.59	194.15

Source: Government of India, Economic Survey, 2000-2001, S. 52.

Table 2 shows the branch-wise employment in public sector industries during the pre and post-liberalisation periods. The annual average level of employment in public sector units was 164.94 lakh persons during 1981-85 and it increased to 183.91 lakhs persons during 1985-90. In other words, public sector employment registered an increase of 12 percent during the pre-liberalisation period. State Governments have been providing employment opportunities on a large scale followed by quasi-governmental units. Public sector annual average employment was nearly 40 lakhs before the phase of liberalisation.

A closer examination of Table 2 reveals that public sector employment showed a positive but very low rate of increase during 1990-99. In fact, it increased from 183.91 lakh persons in 1990 to 194.55 lakh persons in 1999. In spite of delicencing and liberalisation, the employment in public sector industries was a little more than 2 percent during 1990-99.

Further, it is noted that employment by state and quasi Governments accounted for 37 percent and 33 percent of the total employment after 1991. Except in 1994, the share of employment provided by Central Government was around 17 percent during 1991-99. The tempo of generating additional employment received a setback during the liberalisation phase and infact the average annual employment by Central Government in public sector units declined to 32.58 lakh persons compared to 39.74 lakh persons during 1986-90.

Industry-wise employment in public and private sectors during the pre and post-liberalisation periods is shown in Table 3. Manufacturing units have been the major source of industrial employment in public sector followed by mining and quarrying. Infact, the level of employment opportunities in manufacturing sector has been equal to the level of employment opportunities provided combined by the mining and electricity sectors.

It is noted that employment in mining and manufacturing sectors remained stagnant during 1990-93 and declined afterwards. On the contrary, the employment in electricity sector showed a marginal increase during 1994-99. In all, employment in mining and electricity accounted for 5 percent of the total employment during 1990-99 while that of manufacturing sector's share was around 10 percent.

Table 3: Industrial Wise-Employment in Public Sector

(Fig.in Lakhs)

Period / Year	*Mining / Quarrying*		*Manufac-turing*		*Electricity*		*Total*	
	Public	*Private*	*Public*	*Private*	*Public*	*Private*	*Public*	*Private*
1981-85	90.1	1.04	16.54	45.24	7.24	0.38	164.95	74.29
Percentage	5.46	1.40	10.03	60.90	4.39	0.51	-	-
1985-90	9.57	0.98	18.55	44.19	8.38	0.40	183.90	73.98
Percentage	5.20	1.32	10.08	59.73	4.56	0.54	-	-
1990-94	9.87	1.00	18.58	45.12	9.12	0.40	191.64	73.39
Percentage	5.15	1.29	9.70	58.30	4.76	0.51	-	-
1994-99	9.77	0.97	16.87	50.0	9.49	0.41	194.55	84.39
Percentage	5.02	1.15	8.67	59.25	4.88	0.49	-	-
1994	10.15	1.01	17.84	46.30	9.38	0.40	194.45	79.30
1995	10.16	1.03	17.56	47.06	9.35	0.40	194.66	80.59
1996	9.93	1.07	17.38	50.49	9.46	0.42	194.29	85.12
1997	9.78	0.92	16.61	52.39	9.58	0.41	195.59	86.86
1998	9.37	0.91	16.16	52.33	9.54	0.42	194.18	87.48
1999	9.26	0.87	15.69	51.78	9.62	0.41	194.15	86.90

Source: Government of India, Economic Survey, 2000-2001, S.52.

During 1991-99, the average annual employment level in manufacturing sector declined by 0.58 lakhs, it increased by the same rate in mining and electricity sectors. During the post-liberalisation phase, the performance of manufacturing sector has been fluctuating and discouraging while that of mining sector growth has been encouraging.

In the post-liberalisation period, the average annual employment in mining sector showed a gradual increase. Move towards privatisation resulted in an increase of employment in manufacturing sector from 44.57 lakh persons in 1990 to 52.39 lakh persons in 1999. On an average, manufacturing industry provided 58 percent of total employment in private sector. The level of employment in electricity remained unchanged while that of mining industry showed an increasing trend.

Dis-investment and Trends in Employment

The government strategy towards the public sector has been to encompass a judicious mix of strengthening strategic units, privatising non-strategic units through gradual dis-investment or sale of weak units. The main elements of the Government policy towards public sector undertakings are (a) to bring down or lower (b) close down public sector units that cannot be revived. On the recommendations of the disinvestment commission, thrust was given to the process of dis-Investment. The targets and achievements of dis-Investment in public sector undertakings during 1991-00 are shown in Table 4.

Though there was no clear strategy and a defined plan for finalising the level of dis-Investment amounts, at the beginning of liberalisation period the achievement exceeded the target of dis-investment in 1991-92. Surprisingly, no dis-investment took place in 1993-94. Later, less than 8 percent of the targeted amount was dis-invested during 1995-97. With an offer of voluntary retirement scheme, the level of dis-investment was placed at Rs.10,000 crore in 1999-00. However, the achievement was only 18 percent. It is interesting to note that for the period as a whole (1991-00) the size of dis-Investment was only 42.07 percent of the targeted amount.

The efforts of dis-investment resulted only in a slower pace of withdrawing capital from public sector units, mainly

Table 4: Disinvestment of Public Sector Undertakings

(Rs.in Crores)

Year	*Target*	*Achievement*	*Percentage of Total*
1991-92	2500	3038	121.52
1992-93	2500	1913	76.52
1993-94	3500	Nil	Nil
1994-95	4000	4843	121.07
1995-96	7000	362	5.17
1996-97	5000	380	7.60
1997-98	4800	902	18.79
1998-99	5000	5371	107.42
1999-2000	10000	1829	18.29
Total	**44300**	**18638**	**42.07**

Source: Govt of India, Economic Survey, 2000-2001, S. 135.

due to the non-cooperation of the bureaucrats. The policy of dis-Investment and the voluntary retirement scheme had their effects on the structure of industrial employment. Table 5 shows the sector-wise industrial employment during 1981-99.

Table 5: Sector-Wise Industrial Employment

Period / Year	*Public Sector*	*Percentage*	*Private Sector*	*Percentage*	*Total*
1981-85	164.95	68.95	74.29	31.05	239.24
1985-90	183.90	71.31	73.98	28.69	257.88
1990-94	191.64	71.23	77.39	28.77	269.03
1994-99	194.55	69.75	84.39	30.25	278.94
1994	194.45	71.03	79.30	28.97	273.75
1995	194.66	70.72	80.59	29.28	275.25
1996	194.29	69.54	85.12	30.46	279.41
1997	195.59	69.24	86.86	30.76	282.45
1998	194.18	68.94	87.48	31.06	281.66
1999	193.15	68.72	87.90	31.28	281.05

Source: Govt. of India, Economic Survey, 2000-2001, S. 52 & S. 53.

It is seen from the Table that more than two-thirds of industrial employment was in public sector and the rest was in private sector. The first four years of the liberalisation period itself experienced a shift in the share of employment from 'public sector to private sector. Later, this trend continued every year. This is mainly due to gradual dis-Investment in public sector units and encouragement for the scheme of voluntary retirement.

Conclusion

In its process of development, India adopted the import substitution strategy at the beginning and later on the strategy of self-reliance and minimum dependence on foreign resources for production. The performance of industrial sector was not bad and the economic growth was positive after 1966. As a result there was a shift from the import substitution industries strategy to export oriented industries strategy. The 1981 IMF loan and 1985-88 Exim policy confirmed the shift in this strategy. It was particularly during seventies and eighties that potential exporters got high export assistance from Government of India.

The industrial growth rates of some sectors, during 1991-95, slowed down indicating an industrial recession. Industrial output fluctuated in a cyclical pattern as a part of normal business cycle and dynamism of the development process. The slow down in the capital goods industry, and declining annual goods rates in mining industry were the causes of concern.

Since 1996-97 the industrial recovery was significant with accelerated growth rates in various sectors of the economy. A good harvest in 1998-99 resulting in greater consumer demand for industrial products, improved capacity utilisation, fiscal package including rationalisation industries, new programme of rural industrialisation and specific measures for the small scale sector are the major factors that are behind the industrial recovery.

However, the average annual industrial growth rate achieved after liberlisation is lower than that achieved in the decades before liberalisation. The following are some of the measures that sustain higher industrial growth rate.

1. Additional infrastructure facilities commensurate with the increasing requirements of industry are to be created at a faster rate.
2. Priority areas for foreign direct investment need to be clearly demarcated.
3. Enunciation of unambiguous policies and promotion of small scale and ancillary sector is the need of the hour.
4. Cut in the corporate and personal income tax may rejuvenate industrial demand.
5. Modification of excise duties on intermediate goods and reduction of customers duty on imported raw materials may promote the growth of manufacturing industry.
6. Drawing with restrictions on maximum permissible bank finance and granting little more freedom to banks in assessing credit requirements for borrowers may eliminate the shortages of investment funds in industrial sector.

REFERENCES

1. K.C.Sharma, Prospects in Industrial Sector Since Independence, Indian Economic Journal. Vol 46, Oct-Dec 1998. Bangalore.
2. Government of India, 1991 Indians New Economic Policies, New Delhi.
3. B.Majumdar, From Import Substitution to Open Door Industrilisation, An Evaluation, Productivity, Vol 33, No, 2, July-Sep.1992.

4. Ahluwalia, Isher Judge, "Industrial growth in India-Stagnation Since the Mid-Sixties". Oxford University Press New Delhi, 1985.

5. Government of India, Economics Survey 1997-98 New Delhi.

6. Kapila, U., Indian Economy Since Independence, 6th Edn., Academic, Foundation, New-Delhi, 1995.

6

Impact of Liberalisation on Rural Non-farm Sector

*P. Purushotham**

Introduction

The pattern of economic growth pursued in India during the last five decades of post-independence has given birth to several new, diverse and complex problems. While the country achieved remarkable progress in terms of bio, space and information technologies, the quality of life of a majority of rural masses has not been improve much. Illitercay, unemployment, poverty, lack of basic amenities such as drinking water, shelter, food security and higher rate of population growth—one of the prime causes as well as consequences of poverty—still challenge the planners. While these problems continue to demand the policy attention, the country could not be insulated against the economic changes sweeping across the world. Time has come for the country to revitalise the economy by identifying and correcting the structural deficiencies. This was the rationale for integrating the Indian economy with the global markets. So far, this process of integration has not been smooth and without causalities. In this paper, an attempt is made to review the challenges faced by the rural non-farm micro enterprises and the measures required to safeguard their interests.

* Professor in National Institute of Rural Development, Hyderabad.

Agro-Industries

Indian agriculture which livelihood to about 70 percent of the population in the country and contributes 30 percent to the national GDP is characterised by low productivity. This sector is not able to compete with the commodity imports from the world market. The threat of cheap agricultural imports from countries like China is turning out be real. The imported rice, edible oil, pulses, dairy products and dry fruits are cheaper by at least 10 to 30 percent. Very low productivity, high cost of production, lower base of technology, underdeveloped infrastructure, high cost of fuel and electricity, higher interest rates on capital, lack of processing and storage facility at the farmer level are rendering agriculture output less than competitive as compared to the farm output in developed countries. Thus, farm sector in India is not able to provide raw materials for agro-processing industry of international prices. Hence, most of the agro-industries in the country are ceasing to be competitive at the raw material stage itself. Several units of oilseeds processing industry in different parts of the country have turned out to be sick on this count. The case of cotton, sugar, copra, rubber, coco and cashew processing units is similar.

The Indian dairy industry is predominantly small farmer-oriented. It has been providing subsistence income to millions of rural households. With the exposure to the globalisation, cheap and low priced dairy products from Netherlands, Australia, Denmark, France and Spain are flooding the domestic market. This is causing serious concern. Milk and Milk products market provides one thousand billion rupees of cash flow to rural farmers every year. These small dairy farmers today are not getting any subsidies from the Government. This must be examined against the state subsidies of 52 percent in America and 55 percent in Europe provided to the dairy farmers. Although the world trade in milk products is US $ 10,000 million per annum, the Indian market share is less than US $10 million.

The international dairy market which is controlled by a few developed countries have been campaigning that the Indian dairy products contain higher levels of pesticide residue and undesirable bacteria which the Indian dairy farmers who have poor access to infrastructure, electricity and cold storage and processing facilities are not able to control the levels of supply, or add value to the dairy output through processing to suit the non-conventional markets. All these infrastructure and capacity are necessarily to be developed by the State which is not able to do sofar want of capital. Thus, Indian small dairy farmers are not able to benefit much from the globalisation by way of exports.

Handlooms

Next to agriculture, handloom industry is the most important economic activity in rural areas as it provides employment to over 12 million people. This industry utilises local raw materials and caters to the local markets which have a strong cultural character. In the Indian textile industry the share of handloom market has been in the range of 20 to 25 percent. Following the economic reforms, the government has withdrawn its assistance in terms of yarn subsidies, interest subsidy for working capital and development assistance for technology modernsation. The industry is not able to cope up with the new demands on quality and cost terms. Several handloom weavers are becoming sick and this is causing severe economic distress among the weaver households. Today, the weavers are expected to seek capital from market on competitive terms. Development agencies are redesigning their strategies in terms of project viability. The weavers are to compete on the strength of their craftsmanship, product quality and market acceptance. The cheap textile imports from other countries are indeed a threat and the handloom weaving industry in the country is settling down for a lower size of market and that too for fewer varieties of fabric. The industry is fold to sustain on its own competitive strength without any help from the government.

Next to agriculture and handlooms, the poultry industry has been a major employment-generating sector. This industry provides employment to about 1.6 million people. This industry has grown gradually with internal strength during the last 25 years and acquired some strength of its own. However, the current exposure to globalisation is threatening the industry. Cheap imports of poultry products from USA have been affecting the domestic poultry industry very seriously. The present duty level on poultry imports cannot safeguard the domestic poultry sector. There is a need to enhance the tariff level. As we see, this measure is not easy for the government as it is signatory to the WTO.

Other Rural Industries

The khadi and village industries sector, which has been providing full time and part time employment to over 1.5 million rural people right at their homes, too, is affected by the economic reforms process. Raw material subsidies, public fund support for technology up gradation, skill improvement, market development support from the government for the rural and small entrepreneurs are no longer coming forward. These enterprises are now required to operate on market viability considerations. The result is that hundreds of small and micro enterprises are getting closed. In some product lines such as soap, chemicals, cosmetics, edible oils, cotton and khadi, the incidence of sickness is very alarming. Of course, these products have strong eco-friendly character and as such are gradually winning the patronage of elite and mature consumer groups in urban areas. However, it will be a long time before the sector can complete on its own viability.

Another industry which is seeing disturbing changes is salt manufacturing which used to provide self-employment to over five hundred thousand households in coastal provinces and interior states such as Gujarat and

Rajasthan. With the exposure to the winds of globalisation, large scale, modern technology based plants have come up during the last five years. These units have been displacing the hundreds of thousands of self-employed salt workers who have at once become helpless to compete, in terms of technology, capital resources and entrepreneurship, with the large, modern and aggressive brand pushers.

Further, as a result of the free flow of capital and technology we see large scale mechanisation in the hitherto labour intensive rural industries such as oilseeds processing, papad-making, manufacture of leaf-cups and agarbathies (incense sticks). This has undermined the self-employment of hundreds of thousands of workers.

Marketing

The process of liberalisation is placing heavy demands on non-farm sector micro enterprises on their marketing abilities. In most sub sectors it is now becoming clear that they cannot face the competition from the large scale corporate sector which has the capital and access to media and highly professional marketing expertise to aggressively push their branded products in the market. Invariably, these products are attractively packaged and positioned in the market. Some of the marketing strategies pursued by the global players to penetrate into the thin and shallow rural markets where consumers have very low level of purchasing power includes positioning (retail packs of sachets) of products such as shampoos, toothpastes, tea powder, cosmetics etc. These well packaged and strategically positioned products are the ones with which the small scale/micro entrepreneurs cannot compete. To survive such competition the individual micro entrepreneurs can at best network themselves into market players so as to gain viability to market such consumer products in these highly advertisement sensitive markets. Experiments in such networking have been very few. As of now, no market innovations have been successfully attempted in such product groups. The experience of Khadi and Village Industry Commission, and INCOSERVE, a cooperative of small-scale tea producers in Oattacamund district, have not been successful. As a part of the liberalisation process the government has withdrawn market development assistance and support to the artisans in several industries. The notable example is the withdrawal of travel subsidy to the artisans which enables them to participate in the industrial exhibitions and trade fairs organised in large cities. Such participation is immensely useful to the artisans because it gives them an opportunity to know the pulse of the market (Jaya Jaitly).

Liberalisation coupled with the improvement in communication and infrastructure in rural areas is leading to the exposure of village economy to the urban styles of consumption. Consumers in the remote rural areas and tribal region as are effectively reached by the modern media technologies. Large corporate bodies with heavy media budget are spearheading this exercise, which is leading to the changes in consumption patterns in rural areas with long-term implications on the rural micro entrepreneurs. This can be understood by a simple observation, which the author made during one of the visits to a tribal village in Durg district of Chattisgad state. In this village, which has a population of about 8,000 of whom were adivasis, about 100 houses had black and white television sets which receive Doordarshan programmes. Two retailers also had these TV sets at the shop counters. The adivasis who do not own TV sets and have no access to electricity in their houses watch the programmes and the advertisements in the houses of village masters, traders and others with whom they transact. The retail shop owners who sell consumables which include low priced branded products as well as commodities shared with the author that about 65 percent of their sales are to the adivasis. Detailed enquiries with the adivasis revealed that they came to know about the products from the TV programmes as well as the radios and indent for them by describing the packaging. Most of the products bought this way are the result of influence by the advertisement media and they do not include in the core category of subsistence such as food, clothing and housing. These are branded tea, cosmetics, soap etc., which are viewed as vehicles to journey into "Civilisation".

In industries which are prone to high rate of technological obsolescence, it is the artisans and small entrepreneurs who having invested in equipment, tools and machinery run the risks of market rejection as well as technology by-passing. This phenomenon is noticed in handlooms, the powerlooms, oilseeds processing, footwear manufacturing, pottery and ceramic manufacturing, food processing and a host of subsectors. Field level investigation into the viability and operations of such enterprises in the context of liberalisation reveals that most of the entrepreneurs and artisans are to borrow from the moneylenders who do not in any case get exposed to technological obsolescence. The ultimate risk takers in such situations are the artisans and micro entrepreneurs. In order to minimise such risks, so far not much of entrepreneurship guidance and support have been taken up at the operator level in the rural economy. At the same time the writing on the wall is very clear. To survive in the markets which are exposed to liberalisation, the micro entrepreneurs have to acquire education, enterprise capability and professional skills apart from resources to invest in market infrastructure to minimise the incidence of such risks.

The liberalisation has led to the commercialisation of rural economy and put premium on several rural resources which were at one time owned by the community and were called common property resources. The working poor had access to these resources. Examples of these resources include clay, stone, fibers, sand, forest leaves etc., which now carry a market price and only those who can afford to buy them of these prices can stay in business.

Some of the rural based raw materials which are under the control of the government are priced in such a manner that the working poor and artisans are to pay higher rates as compared to the larger operators who pay much less for the same. The bamboo allotment is a typical example. While the artisans' cooperatives are allotted bamboo at prices which are almost equal to market price or sometimes even higher, the same are allotted to the corporate sector at far lower prices. Further, the corporate sector prices are fixed for longer tenures, while for the artisans the price terms are revised upwards annually. This discrimination is becoming too glaring in the post liberalisation era. Similar discriminatory pricing is noticed with regard to license fee level for traditional fishermen vias-a-vis mechanised boats too. Privatisation of raw material base has put the small operators and the micro enterprises at great disadvantage in terms of price negotiation.

For a major part, the prospects of rural non-farm livelihoods are linked to the viability of agriculture, particularly small farmer agriculture. With the liberalisation, the small former agriculture is loosing its viability and hence the prospects of the sections of the people who live on the rural non-form enterprises. Enterprises that come under this category include village based oilseeds processing, local seed manufacturing, puffed rice, jaggery manufacturing etc.,

Liberalisation, as it has been noted at the beginning of this paper, cannot be wished away at this time. However, there is a need to prepare the rural micro entrepreneurs to survive this process. It means equipping them with knowledge, skills, entrepreneurship abilities, technology, credit, organisation and innovative capabilities so as to stay in the market and if possible even benefit from the new opportunities if provides. Extensive and location specific micro level rural market study is required to identify such product lines where the rural non-farm and micro enterprises have identify such product lines where the rural non-farm and micro enterprises have competitive advantage. Such enterprises can be supported and sustained with reorientation of development support in terms of credit, technology and market. New and promising product lines such as bio-diesel from tree based non-edible oilseeds like karanji poongamia, glabras, kokam and sal seeds has to be developed. In this regard the technology is already available. What is necessary is the development of resource base in rural area. Similarly, the liberalisation process demands Indian agriculture to shift towards organic and chemical free farming in order to find acceptance in the markets of developed countries. Manufacture of natural pesticides such as neem extract, organic and bio-fertilisers and vermicompost offer promising alternative. Since the technology is simple and easily adoptable, it should not be difficult to build viable rural non-farm enterprises on this basis. Similarly, the agri-clinics and agri-business centers utilising the recent advances in information technology can be utilised to create viable enterprises for educated youth in the villages. The growing demand for natural products like vegetable dyes, ethnic textiles, medicinal and aromatic products and leather goods, handmade paper, and environment-friendly cotton textiles in world markets has to be appreciated and enterprise capabilities among the rural people to respond to such opportunities has to be improved. So far, we have not concentrated much on a major sub-sector which has great potential for rural development. This is the medicinal plants area. In fact, the economic value of aromatic and medicinal plants is something like Rs.10,000 crore per annum. While India is the home for over 8,000 varieties of medicinal plants, we have failed miserably in exploiting these resources for employment generation and earning foreign exchange, while the medicinal plants exported by us are being used by the countries importing them as high value inputs for manufacturing perfumes, soaps, medicines, cosmetics, etc. This is due to lack of technology for converting basic raw materials into high value inputs and products. Perhaps, we need a bit more enterprise for inventing appropriate technologies for producing high value inputs. Hence, there is a greater need to identify these potential areas and reallocate our resources, especially finance, technology and entrepreneurship, for achieving the desired results.

Technology

Today, the small and micro enterprises are required to reorient their production methods and organisation so as to cut down costs in order to gain hold in the competing markets. This means combining the advantages of mass production and customised demand. Unfortunately, no tested methodologies to access different models of technology innovation and transfer to rural small entrepreneurs are available. A large number of industry specific exercises to identify, diffuse and transfer technologies for rural industry is the need of the hour. R & D institutions, enterprises and technology transfer agents are to be coordinated to evolve synergy leading to effective and faster transfer of technologies.

Technologies concerning the wide spectrum of rural non-farm activities are yet to receive the attention of development institutions. Some of the rural activities even today have not acquired any technology breakthrough. Productivity in some of the horticulture crops and tree crops remains painfully low while the demand for the same has been increasing. Bamboo is one such example.

It is unfortunate that some of the by-products of agro-business could not be exploited properly for commercial utilisation which otherwise could have provided gainful employment to the rural people and at the same time contributed to the nutrition requirement of the rural population. The best example in this regard is the groundnut cake in western and southern India. A good part of this cake continues to be exported as raw material to other countries at low price. Such value adding technology is found wanting in case of by-products of soya industry too.

The liberalisation has also opened up new avenues for the micro enterprise sector. It has provided self-employment opportunities for over half a million youth in retailing telecommunications in rural areas. Similarly, it has also provided livelihood for about 60,000 Cable TV operators who are retailing modern recreation facilities through the wire in rural areas. These are no doubt today viable self-employment opportunities which have come up following the changes in information technology and telecommunication revolution.

The Policy Interventions

The reform process is irreversible, what is necessary is representation of national policies so that employment and income earning capacities of rural people are safeguarded to survive the challenges of liberalisation.

These imperatives dictate a few policy interventions and actions from the government. These, in order of priority, are:

(i) Develop rural infrastructure through massive public investment to enable the rural economic activity participate on competitive terms.

(ii) Provide internal subsidies to the rural micro-enterprises and targeting them better for effectiveness so that the enterprises will have level playing effect to compete with the new competitors.

(iii) Review the fiscal and tariff policy for differential tariff support to small enterprises so that the "dumping" of cheap foreign products could be checked.

(iv) Identify and encourage product lines which have inherent competitive strength in terms of cost, location, technological and market advantage and complete with the imported brands. In view of the disparity between costs of living in urban and rural areas, and increasing transport costs, our

rural development agencies are rediscovering that some of the rural enterprises using local resources for local markets are indeed viable. Products like neem cake, neem decoction and other low ended consumer products like candies, agarbathies, chalks and note-books are other examples in this regard. The rural infrastructure development should bestow focus on storage, transport, processing and marketing facilities, which go a long way in our overall development.

(v) Review the national development policy so as to encourage job creating capacity of the economy, subsidies, state support, public investment programmes for infrastructure development should be prioritised on this criteris.

(vi) Harness the new technologies such as bio-technology and information technology for enhancing the productivity of rural people vulnerable to the impact of globalisation. These sections include small and marginal farmers, artisans, women and small entrepreneurs.

Conclusion

Exposure of rural non-farm enterprises to the impact of liberalisation is placing a huge demand on the part of development institutions and government to equip the working poor and micro-enterprises with skills, knowledge, access to credit technology and all other requisite resources to enable them to operate, compete and survive in the competition against the large players. Development support for this sector has to be reviewed and redesigned in this context. This also requires large scale state investment for modernisation and expansion of infrastructure in terms of power, transport, communications, cold storage facilities etc. This is necessary to equip these industries with the necessary capacity to compete with the international products. Till such time, these appears to be no alternative for the government but provide a level playing field for the rural micro enterprises. This level-playing support, which has to be in terms of fiscal as well as tariff measures, has to become one of the core elements of the national strategy for the economic development whose priorities are removal of poverty, generation of productive employment and contribute to the livelihood security of majority of the population.

REFERENCES

1. Bhagwati, Jagdish and T.N. Srinivasan, (1993), India's Economic Reforms, Government of India.
2. Bhanu Pratap Singh (2001), "Why We Are Still Poor?", The Hindu, July 2.
3. Datt, Rudar, (1994), Industry and Employment: Recent Indian Experience, ISID Foundation Day Lecture, New Delhi.
4. Gupta, Ns.p., (1995), impact of Economic Reform on Poor, *Economic and Political Weekly,* Vol.XXX, No. 2, June.
5. Jaya Jaitly, Visavakarma's children–stories of India's Crafts People, Institute of Social Sciences and Concept Publishing Company, 2001.
6. Lal, Deepak and H. Myint, (1996), "The Political Economy of Poverty, Equity and Growth". Oxford, Clarendon Press.
7. Papola, T.S. (1992), Rural Non-Farm Employment: An Assessment of Recent trends, *The Indian Journal of Labour Economics,* Vol. 35, No. 3, July-September.
8. Sarkar, Prabirjit, (1995), Indian Economy since 1991: An Analysis of Trade, Price and Exchange Rate Behaviour; *Economic and Political Weekly,* May 20.
9. Singh, R.I., Prasad, V and Dangar, S.M. (1992), Indian Agricultural Policy in the Context of New Trade and Industrial Policy, *Indian Journal of Agricultural Economic,* Vol. 47, No. 3, July–September.

7

Impact of Economic Reforms on Powerloom Industry in Andhra Pradesh

*Dr. Y. Gangi Reddy**

Introduction

As a part of Industrial Revolution, the powerloom industry has transformed from an art of handlooms into a modern industry, producing around 60 percent of total cloth production of the country and employing about 10 million workers. The combination of traditional art and contemporary modern designs has given a unique character to the Indian Powerloom Textiles. The modernisation process of powerloom industry and the process of economic liberalisation has enabled the industry to widen the scope of product range and become globally competitive in terms of both price and quality. However, both the initiatives have also led the industry in selected places into a crisis particularly with reference to the worker weaver. Part of the handloom weaving industry artisans have started working on powerloom so as to survive and sustain in their traditional economic activity. The artisans, who belong to a few social caste groups, continued to depend on weaving as their family tradition and not able to diversify their

* Dr. Y. Gangi Reddy, Associate Professor, NIRD, Hyderabad. Faculty Member, Center for Rural Industries & Employment, National Institute of Rural Development, Rajendranagar, Hyderabad 500 030.

occupation. Hence, the weaving community remained as poor either as handloom weaver or as powerlooms weaver worker. Any reform or change that takes place in the industry has got a direct bearing on the livelihoods of poor artisans. Powerloom industry can survive or sustain only when the weavers conditions are good. Any threat to the welfare of weaver workers is bound to create problems for the industry as a whole. Hence, the present paper is prepared based on the research study conducted by the National Institute of Rural Development as part of its research endeavour. The study was conducted during 2001-2002 in four major powerloom centres in the state of Andhra Pradesh. The only objective of this paper is to examine as to what extent the implementation of Liberalisation, Privatisation and Globalisation (LPG) has affected Powerloom Industry (PLI) in general and weaver worker in particular in four different locations of powerloom centres in AP.

Status of Powerloom Industry

The powerloom sector attains lot of importance in the textile industry due to its widening scope of product range, production capacity and employability of workers. Of all other sectors such as mill, handlooms, hosiery, khadi, wool and silk, the share of powerlooms in terms of production of cloth is always significant. During 1990-91 the share of powerlooms in the total cloth production is about 57.21 percent and the same has increased to 59.13 percent during 2000-01 (Table 1). There are about 60 thousand traditional powerlooms in the state. About 40 thousand powerlooms are concentrated in the major centres of Karimnagar (Siricilla), Chittoor (Nagari), Nalgonda and Anantapur districts. However, over 60 percent of them in these centres have been lying idle since 1999. A comparative scenario of PLI in four districts revealed that the situation in Siricilla vis-à-vis Nalgonda, Nagari and Anantapur is bad in terms of the existing working environment and earnings. Data are presented in respect of weaver workers and job weavers who are crucial in the powerloom industry. There are two other categories of people i.e., master weavers and yarn and cloth merchants who are not immediately affected by the crisis in the industry.

Table 1: Sector-wise Production of Cloth

Year	*Mill*	*Handloom*	*Powerloom*	*Hosiery*	*Khadi, Wool & Silk*	*Total*
1990-91	2589	4295	13348	2696	402	23330
1991-92	2376	4123	13262	2827	390	22978
1992-93	2000	5219	14644	3182	430	25475
1993-94	1990	5851	15994	3637	426	27898
1994-95	2271*	6180	15976	3748	431	28606
1995-96	2019*	7202	17201	5038	498	31958
1996-97	1957*	7456	19352	5533	540	34838
1997-98	1948*	7603	20951	6364	545	37441
1998-99	1785*	6792	20689	6277	584	36127
1999-2000	1714*	7352	23187	6374	581	39208
2000-2001	1670*	7506	23803	6277	581	40256

* include weaving units.
Source: O/o the Textile Commissioner, Government of India.

In Siricilla alone, out of 12 thousand powerlooms only 6 thousand are working and less than 20 percent of their capacity (Frontline, 2001). The situation in Nagari, which has about 15,000 looms, is better than all the other three centres. An important factor for this situation is attributed to well knitted market support combined with vertical integration of different operations. A few of the manufacturers could also adopt improved technologies, which are imported from Switzerland, Germany and South Korea. Unlike in the state of Maharashtra, technology upgradation in Nagari is appropriate, limited to a fewer number of units and steady so as to equip the weavers with an updated operation. Anantapur is yet another important powerloom centre, which is involved in silk fabrics, with equal number of about 25,000 weaver families depending only on powerlooms. The slump in the market has pushed about 15,000 weaver workers to the adjoining areas of Karnataka state. Though the situation in Anantapur is equally bad, they are able to put up with the crisis, as demand for silk fabrics is yet to affect. Unlike in Siricilla, the weaver workers have an aptitude of diversifying their skills and activities so as to withstand from the immediate crisis. In Anantapur, women also supplement the weaving activity. Powerloom industry in Nalgonda is also undergoing a lot of changes, but as they are organised and able to get the support from people and officials, the situation is yet to reach to the level of Siricilla. There are a few advantages with PLI in Nalgonda compared to Siricilla. The district administration has responded positively to the credit needs of powerloom weavers during the recent crisis by advising all the bankers to extend the necessary support. The district level society, which has been active in acquiring and creating necessary market support, is actively associated with the crisis of powerloom industry in Nalgonda and Anantapur.

The number of artisans working on these looms are worked out to be two per loom, who are directly involved in the weaving activity. About a lakh weaver workers are surviving on this activity. Most of the looms are of second hand from Maharashtra. Except in Siricilla women also supplement the weaving activity on the powerlooms. Every powerloom centre is specialised in a selected fabric. A large number of people depend on dyeing, sizing and other related activities of weaving.

Though the powerloom industry has come up in the state during the seventies it has expanded to different locations and to different product lines. The artisans who have been working on handlooms have only turned on to the looms that work with the power over a period of time. By using power to run the looms the productivity has increased multifold and led to the increased incomes to the weaver workers and reduction of cost of the fabric. Though it has affected a few handloom weavers to some extent, the strength of traditional craftsmanship of handloom remain unchanged for all these years. However, during the recent past it is not only the handloom sector that is badly affected but also the powerloom sector, which is equally affected, the worker weaver being the focal point in both the cases.

The Crisis

The crisis that gripped the powerloom industry in Andhra Pradesh is attributed to the economic reforms initiated in 1991. Three major factors led the powerloom industry into a sudden crisis in Andhra Pradesh. The first factor being the power sector reforms, the second being technological changes followed by the third factor i.e., liberal import policy. All the three major factors are the result of new economic reforms. The government policies that focused on liberalisation, modernisation and globalisation of the industry by ignoring the livelihood issues pertaining to the lakhs of traditional handlooms and powerloom weavers are behind the tragedy of 50 suicide deaths in a small town called Siricilla (Srinivasulu, 2001). Though the crisis was serious and resulted into a phenomena, neither it was noticed by the concerned government departments nor by the industrialists who have been thriving on for the last three decades. A close study of the literature that has been built up after the crisis, interactions with all the stakeholders of the industry including officials and the people at large in selected locations of powerloom concentration reveal the following.

Power Sector Reforms

As part of liberalisation, privatisation and globalisation the government of Andhra Pradesh has taken the lead in taking measures to reform the power sector. The state has passed the state reforms act with effect from 1st February, 1999. The act facilitated the un-folding of AP State Electricity Board into AP Power Generation Corporation and AP Power Transformation and Distribution Corporation. With the assistance of World Bank loan under 'adaptable programme loan', the power sector has been reformed and restructured. DFID and CIDA have also extended the financial assistance as technical cooperation grant/assistance. As a result power sector is being handled by an Electricity Regulatory Commission, which is an independent advisory body.

The first and foremost impact of these reforms on power sector is high hike in power tariff. The increase in power tariff has also been repeated with frequent intervals. The increase is estimated to be around 200 percent between 1996 and 2001 (Table 2). Since the powerlooms primarily depend on power energy, the impact of hike in power tariff has been very serious. The cost of electricity in the total

Table 2: Cloth Composition of Powerloom Cloth

(Rs. Per Meter)

Element of Cost	*1996*	*2001*	*% Increase over 1996*
Weavers' wages	1.25(5)	2.25(6.5)	80
Job weavers' remuneration	3.60(14)	2.75(8)	24
Yarn	15.00(59)	20.00(57)	33
Power	0.15(0.6)	0.45(1)	200
Starching, dyeing, processing	3.35(13)	6.00(17)	79
Spare parts, misc., etc	1.15(5)	2.00(6)	74
Remuneration to master weaver	1.00(4)	1.10(3)	10
Total	**25.50(100)**	**34.55(100)**	**36**

Source: Computed with the primary data obtained from various sections of the powerloom industry in Nagari.

cost structure accounts for as much as 12.5 percent in the total value addition cost. An average two loom household is affected with an increase of Rs.1614/- from Rs.538/-. Different stakeholders of powerloom industry for its crisis single out the increase in power tariff. The weavers were of the unanimous view that the reduction of power tariff would alone save the industry from the crisis.

The reform process of the power sector is expected to provide timely and quality energy to the users. The whole objective of privatisation (unfolding) of APSEB is to minimise the inefficiency and losses so as to provide better supply of power to the users. Keeping this in view the power tariff has been increased. However, the power sector reforms has invited the large-scale hike in tariff, but failed in providing the quality power to the powerloom industry. The effects of these reforms have proved to be adverse without causing any positive results. Besides, interruptions in the power supply have also increased during the recent times, which has further affected not only the running of powerlooms but also the livelihoods of worker weavers. Since the wages are linked to the production of cloth, power-cut means cut in wages of worker weavers. This has further led to the crisis in the livelihood of weaver workers. During the power-cuts weaver workers tend to relax by consuming adulterated toddy or liquor. Having consumed the toddy they fail to return to work even after power is connected. There is a clear evidence that as soon as the power tariff was increased there is a reduction in wage rate as it would be expensive on the part of job weaver or master weaver. The weaver worker is the worst victim of both the hike in power tariff and the cut in power cuts. It is clear from this that any adverse change in the industry would immediately affect the weaver worker, who is at the bottom end.

Technological Changes

As part of modernisation of textile industry, the government has taken up the textile policy based on the recommendations of Satyam Committee Report to modernise the existing looms. The policy emphasises the productivity, efficiency and competition among the three sectors of handloom, powerlooms and mills that comprise the textile industry. One of the important aspects of this was declaration of bulk of weavers in both handloom and powerloom sectors as least skilled category. This means that a part of workforce needs to be shifted to semi-automatic powerlooms and jet-looms with a necessary training. The rate of displacement of these powerloom weavers reminds the displacement of handloom weavers during 1974, one powerloom weaver worker displaces 12 handloom weavers (Shivaraman Committee, 1974). The rate of displacement at the present technological level would be much more.

The crisis in PLI in Siricilla could be seen immediately as large number of weaver workers, who have migrated from Siricilla to different parts of Maharashtra (Satara and Sholapur), are displaced due to high technology upgradation. A few thousands of weaver workers returned from all these places during a short span of period to a small town, which could not absorb all of them and hence, the crisis intensified.

Though the Ministry of Textiles has come out with Technology Up-gradation Fund (TUF), it could not attract any of these powerloom industry owners as it invites large scale investment. None of the powerloom units in Siricilla are able to make use of this tuff scheme to their advantage. However, a few could appropriate their looms in Nagari and Anantapur without any support from any scheme or programme. Technology up-gradation that the TUF scheme envisages is not appropriate to the existing powerloom industry in the state.

Technological advancement brought out at the instance of New Economic Policies (NEP) has led to a serious crisis in powerloom industry in all the four major centres of PLI in Andhra Pradesh. The policy of Maharashtra in this regard is an indication that the thrust of GOI will not be appropriate to the existing powerloom industry in AP. It has been further observed that the effects of NEP are as follows.

(*a*) decrease in number of handlooms

(*b*) decrease in capacity utilisation of powerlooms

(*c*) closer of spinning mills

(*d*) disposal of powerlooms by weight

(*e*) increase in yarn price

(*f*) non-availability of quality yarn

(*g*) withdrawal of government purchase scheme

(*h*) de-reservation of powerlooms from the small sectors

(*i*) indiscriminate import of cheap fabrics

Liberal Import Policy

The intensified implementation of policies of liberalisation and globalisation has not only led the PLI into crisis but also few other related sectors such as textile sector as a whole and the agriculture. The policies of government are focused more on LPG rather than the livelihood issues pertaining to the lakhs of traditional handloom and powerloom weavers who are poor by birth, by nature and by profession. Further, the crisis was precipitated by a sharp increase in yarn prices, a steep rise in power tariff, concessions provided for technology upgradation which bypassed the small and traditional powerlooms and dumping by countries such as China and Thailand which led to a fall in the market for the textile products. The process of reforms is likely to invite the competitive strength of the weaver only when they are provided with basic infrastructure skills. Intensification of these policies without addressing the related issues would only lead to such crisis and disasters.

Table 3: Profile of Powerloom Industry in Andhra Pradesh

Particulars	*Siricilla*	*Nalgonda*	*Nagari*	*Anantapur*
Type of fabric	*Casement cloth*	*Dhoti*	*Dress materials*	*Silk fabrics*
Value of production				
Market network	Middlemen	Own Market	Chennai	Bangalore
Average literacy of workforce	39	39	31	45
Average weaving days	19	26	20	25
Average total income	2350	2847	3475	4033
Income - other sources	822	638	1525	1570
Average total expenditure	2434	3106	1601	2868
Expenditure on alcohol	173	131	26	100
Savings potential	-84	-259	1874	1165
Private loans	8250	7900	7526	11658
Bank debts	6000	200	0	1895
Size of the family	4	5	5	5

Source: Computed with the primary data obtained from various sections of the powerloom industry in Nagari.

Suggestions

The following are a few suggestions that emerged from the field study conducted in four major centres of PLI.

1. Government agencies should supply yarn at reasonable price and procure cloth under government purchase scheme. All departments of government use several products that are produced by both the handlooms and powerlooms. Hence, they should use only these products as long as they are useful. Government purchase programme is not just to provide market support

but to promote the products of this sector. There are several Government Orders to this effect. This has to be pursued by the Directorate of Handlooms and Textiles on priority basis.

2. Detailed inventory of each powerloom may be prepared, indicating the exact status of each component. Andhra Pradesh State Powerloom Industry Development Committee, which is constituted recently, could be entrusted with this task.

3. Conversion of existing over-pick looms to semi-automatic looms could be attempted, by enabling technical aspects like warp stop motion, weft feeler motion, cob changing mechanism, drop box motion, positive let off motion, positive take up motion, which is expected to require investment of about Rs. 25000 per loom, If 5000 looms are modernised in this manner, the investment would be to the tune of Rs. 12.5 crore.

4. Thousands of looms may not be fit enough for modernisation. They may have to be sold off as scrap. If half of such looms are replaced by new semi-automatic looms at a cost of Rs. 1 lakh each, the financial implications will be to the tune of few crores of rupees.

5. Primary emphasis could be given to semi-automatic looms, which will be adequate to meet the requirements of domestic market rather than shuttle-less looms like jet looms, gripper looms or rapier looms as they require huge investments

6. Limited modernisation would also render some members of the work force redundant. Careful identification of people who are likely to be rendered surplus and concrete action plan for their livelihood diversification needs to be done.

7. The spinning mills must be reopened. This will have the triple advantage of utilising cotton that is produced within the local areas, making yarn available for the powerlooms and handlooms, apart from absorbing some workforce.
8. Dealing with the manufacturing and marketing of products directly. Direct dealing with marketing demands immediate in-house manufacturing operations and vertical integration of as many operations as possible. Marketing through direct channeling will help to get to know the markets as well as technological changes so as to equip them better to deal with the rapid changes in the market.

Policy Issues

The powerlooms industry is in crisis not only in Siricilla or in Andhra Pradesh, where it is serious and immediate but also in all other centres and states. It is suggested that necessary precaution needs to be worked out based on the

Table 4: Profile of Powerloom Workforce in AP

Workforce		*1997*		*2001*	
No. of Weavers		*Total*	*Active*	*Total*	*Active*
A. Weaver Workers					
1	Karimnagar	12000	10000	6000	3000
2	Nalgonda	10000	6000	8000	4000
3	Chittoor	1450	1450	1350	1350
4	Anantapur	10000	3000	10400	3400
B. Job Weavers					
1	Karimnagar	2000	1200	1000	500
2	Nalgonda	4000	3000	3000	2000
3	Chittoor	1500	1500	1000	1000
4	Anantapur	600	400	800	600

Source: Assistant Director, Handlooms & Textiles, Karimnagar, Nalgonda, Chittoor, Anantapur.

isolated case (Siricilla) as it is symptomatic of the trend of such distress situations which could emerge in other industries in other locations, due to fluctuations in market conditions at a faster pace than the rate which the workers can cope up with by skill diversification or the management can upgrade machinery. It therefore, underscores the need for each Ministry/Department to develop a mechanism to study and anticipate impact of market changes on livelihoods of the poor and to make effective interventions to help the marginalised. With developments in information technology, it should be possible to collect market intelligence and use it effectively, for example, on loom-wise modernisation plan. Similarly, impact of power tariff should be analysed not from the books of Transco but its impact could be seen at the consumer's end. Siricilla crisis may be read as an alarm signal for the State to provide human face to the reform process. Finally, the old notion of adversarial relationship between powerloom and handloom sectors could be reviewed as recent developments like high yarn price hikes, difficulties in yarn availability, marketing difficulties, competition from jet looms etc seem to have pushed both the sectors into a similar situation. In any case the enforcement machinery now in place is actually ornamental as it has lost its utility. Areas where handloom sector has its own strength due to niche markets could be left without any support. In other areas where handlooms are facing acute competition from powerlooms due to imitation of designs, new ways of support could be considered like having a certification mechanism in place, which would certify a product to be a pure handloom product. An across-the board tax in textile industry for supporting the rich cultural heritage of handlooms could be considered.

Conclusion

The textile industry which employs about 1.5 crore people in handlooms, powerlooms and the mill sector and contributes about 20 percent of industrial output and a similar proportion to the total exports is facing an acute challenge of globalisation. In this backdrop all sectors of textile industry are being affected. In the absence of proper guidance and planned support from the state, micro entrepreneurs like powerloom operators, as in the case of Siricilla, cannot catch up with the reform process on their own. Threshold level of capital assistance, skill development, technology upgradation and tariff as well as input price-subsidies for the transitory period are required. This is because, the job weavers, who account for over 85 percent of the production in powerloom industry, have invested in looms and machinery which are prone to serious technological obsolescence and thus exposed themselves to risks associated with technological obsolescence. On average, they invested about Rs 20,000 on a single loom and related accessories. When the industry is exposed to the sudden and drastic changes in the market prices of critical inputs such as power, small operators like job weavers and the worker weavers could not cope up with such price hike. The extent of burden on this group of people has been so much that it led to financial distress, driving them to the extreme step of suicide in Siricilla. The incidence of suicides among the weaver population has mobilised the public and media pressure on the state to partially subsidise the power tariff for powerloom industry. This single measure has turned out to be effective in safeguarding the livelihood security of these groups of weavers. Thus the Siricilla experience shows two things. Firstly, that the suicides were caused by distress attributable to liberalisation. Secondly, that it is possible for the state to intervene and safeguard the livelihoods of the people who are vulnerable to the economic reforms. In view of this, we hold that even in the days of globalisation and liberalisation, it is possible for the state to foresee and assess the likely impact of reform process on employment and incomes of the working poor. The state must design and implement interventions to minimise the risk exposure to the workforce during the transition.

REFERENCES

1. Mukund Kanakalatha and Sundari B. Shyama, (2001), Traditional Industry in the New Market Economy: The Cotton Handlooms of Andhra Pradesh.
2. Sen Amartya, Human Development Report, 2000, UNDP.
3. All India Reporter 1981, 1985 and 1996 cited in Bakshi, PM (2000), the Constitution of India.
4. Bhavani. T.A., Small Scale Units in Era of Globalisation: Problems and Prospects, Economic and Political weekly, July 20, 2002.
5. Asha Krishna Kumar, Weavers in Distress, Front Line,, April 27, 2001.
6. Prof. Srinivasulu. K., Weavers' woes in Andhra Pradesh, The Hindu, April 26, 2001.
7. Crisis in Powerloom Industry in Sircilla, Andhra Pradesh, (Mimeo), National Institute of Rural Development, 2002.
8. Technology Upgradation Fund Scheme for Textile and Jute Industries, Textile Commissioner, 2000, Mumbai.
9. Sundaram. K., Employment—Unemployment Situation in the 1990s, Economic and Political Weekly, March 17, 2001.

8

Power Sector Reforms in Andhra Pradesh

*Dr. M.V.S Koteswara Rao**

The purpose of this work is three-fold. One, to present the growth of Andhra Pradesh State Electricity Board, which is spectacular, and serves as a model; two, to discuss the changes effected in the name of restructuring programme, which ultimately turned out to be unnecessary and anti-people; and third, to present an alternative. This paper is divided into three parts. The first part discusses the growth and characteristics of the Andhra Pradesh State Electricity Board (APSEB), the second part discusses the nature of the reforms and the last part bears some conclusions.

I

The Andhra Pradesh State Electricity Board (APSEB) was established in 1959 to take charge of generation and distribution. Prior to that, the Nizam State Electricity Board and composite Madras State's Department of Power and Energy used to cater to the power needs of the present Telangana districts, and Andhra and Rayalaseema districts, respectively. After the formation of Andhra State in 1953, this responsibility was directly carried by the State for three years. In 1956 the Telangana and Andhra regions

* Associate Professor, Department of Political Science and Public Administration, Nagarjuna University.

were united into a single state. After three years the State Government decided to establish a separate board to manage the power.

In 1959, power was a comfort of the elite. Only a few families in a town used to enjoy this luxury. Most of the villages around the cities and all the villages that were remote did not have the facility of electrification. In short, power installation was the costliest commodity available to few rich families of the urban India. The total power installation was a paltry 213 MW, against a population of almost four crores. Since then, the growth of **APSEB** was spectacular and sounds like a folklore story. By 1999, the installation capacity rose to 5612 MW i.e., a rise by 27.5 times. There was a corresponding growth in each and every related area. To crown the achievement, power was taken to each and every village and to around 90 percent of the backward localities. The operational side of the Board was governed by the 1948 Electricity (Supply) Act. Section 59 of the Act stipulates that the power generation and distribution shall be so managed by the states that the Boards must earn 3 percent of profit on net assets value. **If any state government is not in a position to fix the tariff to ensure the 3 percent, profit, it shall meet that amount as subsidy to the Electricity Boards.** Thus it is mandatory on the part of state government to ensure 3 percent per year.

As already mentioned, the installation capacity of the power rose to 5612 MW in 1999. In addition, it received 897 and 273 MW share from the Central and joint sectors, respectively (besides it got 495 MW from the Private Sector). So, the installed capacity of the State was 6782 MW–a rise by 34 times. The APSEB's capacity to meet the peak demand rose from 146 MW in 1959 to 6480 MW in 1999-a rise by 44 times. The number of service connections rose from 2.7 lakhs in 1959 to one crore and ten lakhs by

1999–a rise by 36.7 times. The number of agricultural connections rose from 18,000 in 1959 to 18.85 lakhs in 1999 –a phenomenal rise by 100 times. The supply of power rose from 686 million units in 1959 to 40,574 million units in 1999–a rise by 59 times. The length of the transmission

Table 1: The Details of Power Sector in Andhra Pradesh by 31-11-1999

Sl. No.		
1.	Installed capacity	6782 MW
2.	Maximum needs fulfilled	6,480 MW
3.	Production in 1998	2796 Mu
4.	Electricity purchase—Import (1998-99)	13.569 Mu
5.	Total Current (5+60)	40.615 Mu
6.	Units Handled by the System	38.788 Mu
7.	Sold, Utilised Units total	26.168 Mu
8.	Utilization per head	475 KWH
9.	Transformers Distribution	1,67,908 Numbers
10.	Electrified Cities	264 Numbers(100%)
11.	Electrified Villages	26,565 Numbers(100%)
12.	Electrified Satellite Villages (65.34%)	21,450Numbers
13.	Electrified S.C& S.T. Colonies 39,874Numbers(92.52%)	
14.	Electrified Minority Colonies	12,955 Numbers
15.	Agricultural Pump sets (including Rescos)	18,84,678Numbers
16.	Consumers total (including Rescos)	1,09,69,615 Numbers
17.	Total Employees	74,980 Numbers
18.	Earnings	Rs. 4,824.68 crore
19.	Investments	Rs. 1,832.28 crore
20.	Total Properties	Rs. 5,180.00 crore

Source: Computed from the Table provided by APSEB, Power Development in A.P. (Statistics), 1996-97 and 1997-98.

and distribution lines was 6,08,000 km in 1999. The total number of consumers was about eleven millions of which 1.8 millions were agricultural consumers (Government of Andhra Pradesh, 2002 and **APSEB,** 1998.)

Contrary to the public belief mostly created by the Gobels propaganda by the interested sections, that "public sector" is a symbol of inefficiency and drain on public exchequer, the performance of the **APSEB** was enviable. The following Table explains the spectacular growth and its service to the society, particularly to backward sections.

This growth was achieved despite the failure of monsoons, 'Almattis' resulting in a nosedive in Hydel generation, negligence in modernising the power plants by the State and most important, with highly subsidised tariff to domestic, local government, agricultural services and deprived communities. In terms of Plant Load Factor, which reflects upon the efficiency of power generating units in utilising the installed capacity, the APSEB units showed an extraordinary performance as is shown in Table 2.

Table 2

Year	*Plant Load Factor*		*Rank among SEBs*
	APGENCO	*All India Average*	
1992-1993	64.9	57.1	III
1993-94	68.7	61.0	III
1994-95	70.1	60.0	II
1995-96	78.2	63.0	I
1996-97	78.1	64.4	I
1997-98	82.3	64.7	I
1998-99	77.6	64.6	III
1999-2000	83.2	67.3	II
2000-2001	85.1	69.0	I
2001-2002	86.3	69.9	I

Y: Highest PLF achieved by APGENCO, APSEB till 1998.
Source: APGENCO, A Decade of Performance (1992-2002), p. 3.

However, the active persuasion of Rural Electrical Programme (REP) from early 1970's started straining the resources of **APSEB.** The importance of rural electrification in the socio-economic development of a country with a predominant rural area and agriculture-oriented economy was unanimously accepted. It offers not only promising means of raising incomes, but also generates employment. But the problem is in extending the network to remote areas, which lie thousands of kilometers away from cities. Rural electrification means extending the power lines, establishing a number of substations, transformers and employing additional staff. To quote the report of the Institute of Public Enterprises, "the transmission problem which India faces is that of rapidly electrifying vast rural areas. In fact, every MW of installed capacity in India has over 4 Km of transmission lines with voltages of 66KU and above. This may be contrasted with the situation in UK has about 0.3 Kms of HV lines per MW of installed capacity; U.S.A. which adds 0.6 HV lines for each added MW of capacity; and 1.5 KM/KW of added capacity in Canada". In Andhra Pradesh, the total length of the power lines in terms of circuit Kms reached a figure of 1,55,877 by 1978(IPE:131).

Since, the rural India is very poor, the decision to extend the electrical facility implied subsidised supply to agricultural sector. The average cost of delivering one unit of low Tension Power was paise 27.60 and paise 33.90 against a return of paise 15.20 and paise 13.55 in 70-71 and 72-73, respectively. The power supply to agricultural consumers has become a perpetual source of losses for not only APSEB but also to all Power Boards of South India. To quote from IPE(p.181) "...the power supply to agricultural consumers has become a perpetual source of vast losses for the four SEB's, since the profits earned on account of the supply to the rest to the consumers do not balance out when compared with the losses incurred in supplying to this sector. The State Electricity Boards are finally left with marginal profits and many times pushed deep into the red". As Dayal (1980) rightly said:

"Howsoever efficiently an electricity board may function organisationally, and howsoever economically its affairs may be managed and howsoever cost-conscious it may be and cost-oriented its rate structure may be for the non-rural sector consumers, as long as it expected to assume the expanding obligations of rural electricity with the inevitable concomitant implication of a subsidised or concessional tariff structure for rural consumers, the Board cannot avoid incurring losses, mounting arrears of interest charges and continued inability to build up the various prescribed reserves, the receding prospects of its being able to repay the principal amounts borrowed from State governments or of generating any worthwhile internal surpluses to financé expansion plans. Therefore, the question for restructuring the electricity tariffs...assumes urgency and important if it is not to prove a perpetual milestone round the neck of State Electricity Board" (H.V. Dayal, 1980: 252-53).

The losses incurred by APSEB because of the Rural Electrification Programme were very high. In 1976-77 APSEB lost Rs 1170 lakh. Though it earned Rs 1066 lakh from other sectors, its year-end balance was on the negative side with Rs104 lakh loss, before subsidy. The trend was an all India one. Because of Rural Electrification programme, there was a sudden spurt in the consumption in the agrarian sector. The electricity consumption was only 6 percent of the total electricity consumption in India. The figure jumped upto 10.2 percent in 1970-71 14.4 percent in 1975-76 and reached 31.2 percent 1998-99 (Economic Survey, 2000-2001, Government of India)

The decision of the State Government to give up the metering system in the early 1980's made the situation much worse and proved to be a short sighted one. It had affected the whole system on two fronts. First, it deprived the State Government of any mechanism to know how much power was consumed by the agriculture sector and second, it led to the misuse of the facility by a number of people. It is common in many places to supply water to others by charging money from them on 'per hour' basis. With the connivance of the staff of the Electricity Department, the theft of power became a regular feature. The affluence of the staff who are posted in rural area lured others to teach the other consumers the methods of pilferage and to protect them for a 'Charge'.

The crisis was accelerated by non-investment of money in the power sector by the Telugu Desam Government under N.T. Rama Rao.If we accept that it takes at least four years to commission a project, the Telugu Desam Government contributed (from 1987 to 1993) only 560 MW of Power to total Installation (For details on Installation see, APGENCO, 2003 and APSEB 96-97 and 97-98). On one hand there was a spurt in the consumption by the agricultural sector, particularly after 1983 and on the other hand, there was no corresponding investment to meet the demand. In 1981-82, 942 million units of energy was consumed by the agriculture sector. It jumped to 1393 million units in 1982-83 and to 1540 in

Table 3: Consumption of Electricity by the Agricultural sector

S.No.	*Year*	*Million Units Consumed*
1	1970-71	394
2	1981-82	942
3	1982-83	1393
4	1985-86	2569
5	1990-91	6285
6	1997-98	9336*

Source: APSEB, Power Development in Andhra Pradesh (Statistics) 1997-98).

* The figures were inflated to a large extent to cover the commercial losses. Still the fact is, the consumption in agricultural sector had been on higher side. The subsidy provided to the agricultural sector was utilised by well off sections among the peasantry (see World Bank, 2001, Chapter 2 & 3)

1983-84 and finally to 936 in 1997-98. The following Table shows the quantum to growth in the consumption of electricity by the agricultural sector.

Added to this, the problem of declining volume of cheaper Hydel Electricity and increase in the utilisation of costly Thermal Electricity imposed enormous burden on the Board. The following Table presents the changing ratio of Hydel and Thermal Power during 1990-1998.

Table 4: Details of Power Generation in MW

Power Gen	*1990-91*	*1991-92*	*1992-93*	*1993-94*	*1994-95*	*1995-96*	*1996-97*	*1997-98*
Hydel	10017	9516	8758	9633	9687	6662	7970	7245.13
Thermal	8102	8726	9114	9639	10842	15103	16719.76	19019.49
APSEB	18119	18242	17872	19272	20529	21765	24689.76	26264.62

Source: APSEB, 1998: 41.

Further, the rising prices in coal and railway tariff also put burden on the finances of APSEB. In fact, there was a 100 percent increase in the prices (see Murthy, 2001:42). Even under these highly adverse circumstances, the APSEB never faced unmanageable financial crisis. It not only regularly met its debt servicing commitments but also earned profits till 1996-97. For the first time, the APSEB faced a financial loss of Rs.1134 crore in 1997-98. This was prior to subsidy component calculation. After the subsidy from the State Government, the loss would come down to manageable levels. The following Table gives the details of Revenue receipts and Expenditure (Rs. in crore).

The State Government which was bound by the 1948 Act to give subsidy to ensure 3 percent profit, if the State Electricity Board does not earn this amount on its own, never bothered to meet this obligation. For example, the net assets of the APSEB were Rs.2547 crore during 1985-1990 (APSEB 98:8). The net profit after expenditure including debt servicing must be Rs.76.5 crore. But the

State Government bothered to keep the profit rate at Rs.76.5 crore. The following Table gives the details of profit of APSEB and the subsidy given by the State Government from 1985 to 1995.

The frustrating problem for the APSEB had been the power theft. It was estimated that the transmission and distribution losses were 33.33 percent, 33.15 percent, 32.94 percent, 32.47 percent and 35.40 percent of the total power handled by the APSEB during 1996-97 to 2000-01, respectively. Of this around 20 percent losses had been because of theft. The situation was so worse that only 41 percent of the energy distributed was billed. The rest 59 percent could not be accounted (TRANSCO, 2001, Table-5). The puzzle being, the initiation of reforms saw alarming growth in the loss of energy. (Transco, 2001 Table.4). Since

Table 5

Sl. No.	*Category*	*1983-84*	*1990-91*	*1991-92*	*1992-93*	*1993-94*	*1994-95*	*1996-97*
1.	Revenue Receipts	409.25	1301.70	1633.38	1935.50	2303.15	3220.44	4408.94
2.	Revenue Expenditure	277.55	914.76	1182.19	1395.94	1741.84	2310.57	3205.97
3.	Gross operating results	131.70	386.94	451.19	539.56	561.31	909.87	1202.97
4.	Other expenses like depreciation, interests	75.54	211.71	251.5	313.36	302.02	535.80	654.79
5.	Net surplus/ loss	9.45	80.99	84.44	79.45	86.99	87.25	129.19

Source: APSEB, Power development in Andhra Pradesh (Statistics) 1997-98 p.105.

Table 6

Details	*1985-86*	*1986-87*	*1987-88*	*1989-90*	*1991-92*	*1993-94*	*1994-95*
Income/loss of APSEB	-9.65	-54.37	+29.3	+2.52	+14.9	86.08	-836.86
Subsidy by the Government	24.01	62.83	0.00	0.00	69.54	0.13	944.11
Mandatory profit to the APSEB 3 percent of Rs. 2547 crore	76.5	76.5	76.5	76.5	105[1]	132[2]	186[3]
Net loss to APSEB	62.14	67.69	47.2	73.48	20.50	45.79	107.25

Source: APSEB, 97: 105 and 98: 105

Income: Sales of Power + miscellaneous – Revenue Expenditure + Depreciation + Interest charges.

Net Loss: Net Income + Subsidy – 3 per cent of Assests.
(1) 3 per cent Profit on Rs.3500 crore of Net Assests, *(2)* 3 per cent Profit on Rs.4403 Crore of Net Assests, *(3)* 3 per cent Profit on Rs.6190 Core of Net Assets

1995 the power purchase was increased by 33 percent and the power losses increased by 173 percent (TRANSCO, 2001, para 6). A very moderate official estimate put the value of the stolen power at Rs.48 crore and 63 lakh during a single financial year, 1997-98(APSEB, 1998:94).

II

It is in this background that the State Government decided to reform or privatise the Power Sector. The reasons like bridging the gap between demand and supply, need of improvise the financial performance of the APSEB, to control the commercial losses etc., were offered as the immediate reasons for privatisation (w.w.w.andhrapradesh.com./07/16/2002). Also see Government of Andhra Pradesh, 2001, IBRD, 1999, TRANSCO, 2000, and World Bank 1997 and 1999). To rationalise the process, the State Government appointed a committee called "High Level Committee on Reconstruction of Power Sector" to suggest the alternatives to reform the Power Sector in January 1995 and the committee shattered all the records of India by submitting its report in April 1995. The committee, popularly known as Hiten Bhaya Committee after the name of its Chairman, it has calculated that the demand for power will increase by 10 percent every year and a total of 18051 MW capacity installation is needed to meet the growing demand for power by 2005. The Government estimated that an amount of Rs.32,000 crore of rupees at the rate of Rs.4 crore investment per Mega Watt were necessary to install the extra capacity. The Government also estimated that Rs.20,000 cores to extend the distribution network and Rs.17,000 to modernize the present distribution system were necessary. So, an amount of Rs.53,000 crore were projected as minimum requirement to make power available to every one (Murthy, 2001:38).

The Hiten Bhaya Committee made the following important recommendations: (1) The power sector must be privatised to bring additional investment leading to efficiency and competitive structure. (2) By inviting interested investors an atmosphere of effective competition shall be created. No monopoly shall be allowed for it would make the situation worse. (3) An independent judicial regulatory system shall be created to protect the interests of both the consumers and the developers. (4) By the end of the Ninth Plan a competitive atmosphere should be created with the prospective generators competing to sell the power and prospective distributors competing to distribute power to consumers. (5) The PSEB will confine itself to the role of facilitator instead of remaining the monopoly structure to generate and distribute the power. The functions of generation and distribution will have to be separated and assigned to different organisations (Government of Andhra Pradesh, 1995).

The World Bank, which has to finance the restructuring programme in Andhra Pradesh, was not satisfied with the recommendations and added the following.

1. The proposal that APSEB continue as a holdings company for the new companies would continue to expose **APSEB** and consequently its subsidiaries to political pressure, and the power sector would not be insulated from short-term political expediencies. This world undermines the main objective of the reform programme.

2. The committee defines the role of the regulatory commission narrowly: to deal with retail tariff. The responsibility of the commission should be broadened to include regulation of the bulk supply tariffs, distribution tariffs, and connection charges. In addition, it should also grant licenses to all transmission and distribution companies and enforce them.

3. Unbundling **APSEB** and creating separate companies are major changes that could be achieved only through new legislation dealing also with transfer of assets, staff and interests.

4. A suitable structure must be clearly defined that suits the privatisation of distribution and generation. The power facilities must be privatisation of ensure that they operate without any interference.

5. The tariff rate to the agriculture must be increased to at least 50 paise/kwh and the tariffs must be adjusted to cover the costs and reduce the cross subsidies (World Bank: 1997).

Once the stand of the financier was clear, the government of Andhra Pradesh released its power sector policy statement of June, 14, 1997, to officialise the opinion of the World Bank. According to it, the aims of the State Government are:

1. Providing operational, managerial and functional autonomy to APSEB/ other successor utilities to enable it/them to operate along commercial lines.
2. Besides separating policy and regulatory functions from the management functions of the APSEB, ensures the establishment of a regulatory framework that would look after the cost-optimisation by securing operational efficiencies in generation,
3. Transmission and distribution and collection of related revenues.
4. Ensuring that while Government will continue to determine the overall policy framework for the power sector, it withdraws from regulatory functions.
5. Promoting and supporting the increasing participation of the private sector in power industry, under sustainable conditions.
6. Removing dependence of electricity utilities on Government budgetary assistance for achieving prescribed statutory financial returns,

The process of privatisation gained momentum. The State Government had the Andhra Pradesh Electricity Reform Bill, 1998 approved within a record time. This was done at the cost of suspending all the opposition members from the house. Their mistake was to demand for a select committee on the Bill. The Act came into effect from 01-02-1999. The main provisions of the bill are:

1. The creation for an independent regulatory commission to be called AP Electricity Regulatory Commission (APERC).

2. The facilitation of the reorganisation of the Electricity Supply Industry on functional basis through creation of separate corporation for transmission and generation under the Indian Companies Act.

3. The defining of the respective roles of the various players in the power sector (www.andhrapradesh.com/07/16/2002).

Everything would have been fine if a number of distribution and generation companies had competed for licenses. It atleast theoretically, would have given an opportunity to the consumers to select a highly economic and effective power company to cater to their power needs, as in the case in television channels or radio stations or detergents etc. Exactly here everything went awry, leading to capitulation of the state to the private promoters in the name of privatisation.

Immediately after enacting the Electricity Reforms Act, in February 1999 the APSEB was bifurcated into Power Generation Corporation (APGENCO) and Transmission Corporation (APTRANSCO). AP Electricity Regulatory Commission (APERC), to decide the tariff every year, was created in April 1999. A little later four distribution companies (DISCOM) were set up, and the state was divided into four distributive zones.

Salient Features of the Reforms:

1. The State Government withdrew from power sector and independent bodies were created to decide the issues related to generation, distribution and pricing. The Government is supposed to be an on looker.

2. Regulatory Commission emerged as key player and supposed to insulate the power sector from external forces.

3. Any transmission or distribution company is free to generate or distribute power after getting a license. The customers are free to choose their own distribution. This is expected to improve efficiency and power supply at a cheaper price.
4. Every action of the GENCO, TRANSCO and APERC will be transparent and people enjoy the right of information. Thus, the exercise becomes more open and democratic.
5. Every year the GENCO has to file an Annual Revenue Report (ARR) and seek the permission from APERC to hike the price, if there is gap between expenditure and income. The decision taken by APERC will be final.

Some important questions were overlooked in the euphoria of reforms. Foremost among them was who will pay the unaccounted consumption, which results from subsidy, theft and line losses. Do the distributing companies or generation companies forego that amount? Certainly no. Then who has to pay? The government has to pay for it. Then why not pay that to APSEB, instead of paying to private parities? What happens if the power produced by private companies becomes excess? Who will supply power to the disadvantaged sections?

The practical side of the reforms was a rude shock including to those who saw privatisation as a penacea. Each and every imagined and propagated advantage was evaporated within no time. Instead of free competition, both Government and consumers become captive in the hands of generators. Government was forced/gratified to sign on the dotted lines. Power hike had become a regular feature. The very word ARR by the TRANSCO became synonymous with extra burden. The proposed transparency was proved to be a myth. No power purchasing agreement was made public.

The Indian public money ultimately financed the Independent Power Projects (IPPs) what they have invested was less compared to what they get from Indian Financial Institutions as loans. For example, the BPL was given Rs.1929 crore as debt and the debt–equity ratio was approved as 70:30 percent by the Central Electrical Authority. The equity of the BPL being a paltry RS.819 crore (APERC, 2001 and V.K.Srinivasan, 2003).

The IPPs were not asked to give guarantee for the debt, an essential banker's rule. Instead the TRANSCO stood as the guarantor. In case the IPPs wind up their business, it was the TRANSCO, which has to pay the loans to banks. Much worse on the demand of IPPs that the State and Central Governments became counter guarantors. When the IPPs failed to complete the projects in time, the time was extended at their will. The earlier agreements, which call for the imposition of fines for delay, were simply ignored and fresh agreements were signed.

The cost of the project and value of the power that was to be generated is linked to the value of US dollar. Whenever the dollar appreciates, value of the power and cost of the project automatically get appreciated. The implication being, the power becomes costlier regularly. Firms like BPL were given the undue advantage by allowing them to inflate the cost of the project at their will.

For example cost of the power generated by 100 MW Simhadri Thermal Power Station of NTPC was fixed at Rs.4.18 crore per MW and the cost of the power generated by Rayalaseema Thermal Power Project (420 MW) of APGENCO was fixed at Rs.3.57 crore per MW. But the BPL's power rate was fixed at Rs.5.28 crore, and this is subject to further raise depending upon the appreciation of the dollar.

The State Government, which never gave 3 percent return for its own organisation generously, committed itself to pay 16 percent return on equity to private companies. It is to be recalled that had the State Government respected the mandate of 1948 Act and duly paid 3 percent return, the APSEB would have accumulated thousands of crores as reserve fund.

As we have seen already, the Thermal Projects in Andhra Pradesh consistently turned out 80+ PLF. But in case of IPPs, the PLF is fixed around 68 percent (65 to 68 percent). The surrender to the IPPs is so complete that, the Government accepted to pay 0.525 percent on equity to the BPL as incentive for every 1 percent of PLF over 68.49 percent up to 85 percent. This works out to be Rs.82 crore for every one percent raise in the PLF. If the same 'affection' were showered on APSEB units, thousands of crores of rupees would have been earned by them every year. This nakedly unjust agreement naturally creates doubts on the motive of the Government in accepting these terms.

More mysterious is the clause that the APTRANSCO shall buy the power generated by the IPPs, whether it needs it or not. Even if TRANSCO does not draw any power from IPPs it has to pay the full value of the power. What happens if Hydel Centers start generation with full capacity? The Government is too busy to think about these sundry details.

Escrow facility is one of the many unjustified clauses of the agreements. This clause enables the IPPs to have first charge on the money earned by the APTRANSCO. The TRANSCO accepted to hypothecate all its present and future receivables till it opens an "escrow" account.

The power supplied by the APGENCO is much cheaper compared to the power "Imposed" by the IPPs. The average unit cost of the Power supplied by the APGENCO is Rs.1.43. But the cost of power supplied by GVK is Rs.2.20 per unit, Spectrum's is Rs.2.14 per unit, Lanco Kondapalli Power

Plant is 4.10 per unit and the BSES is 5.47 per unit (APERC, 2001, Chapter II and III).

Perhaps the following extracts from the Report of the Comptroller and Auditor General of India on GVK, and Spectrum power plant reflect upon the intentions and motives of the people responsible for the reforms.

Due to delay in completion of the project and the consequent exchange rate variations, the project cost may go up Rs.113.62 crore. This increase entails an additional burden in the shape of higher tariff on the Board by Rs.17.76 crore per annum.

The PPA provide for recovery of a maximum of Rs.30 crore by way of liquidated damages (LD) for the period of delay in commissioning of the individual units. However, on the basis of time allowed for commissioning for the second and subsequent units., the Board became entitled for levy of LD of Rs.23.20 lakh. But this was not recovered so far.

Unlike in the case of payment of taxes on income to the Developer, the Board agreed for payment of return on equity (ROE) on monthly basis instead of on annual basis. Payment of OE monthly at 16 percent per annum (Rs.39.17 crore) thus would work out of 17.17 percent per annum (Rs.42.03 crore).

Depreciation charges were computed for payment of fixed charges on the entire project cost without excluding the cost of land. Since land does not attract depreciation provision, failure to exclude it for computation of depreciation results in an over payment of Rs.78.40 lakh to the developer per annum.

The PPA stipulated for computation of incentive for achieving higher PLF (above 68.49 percent) on the equity instead of ROE. This results in undue benefit of Rs.1.07 crore per annum to the developer for every one percent increase in PLF above 68.5 percent. At 90 percent PLF the undue benefit would be Rs.66.81 crore.

In deviation to PPA conditions, the Developer reduced the proposed equity in Indian currency by Rs.61.20 crore with a corresponding increase in the equity in foreign currency. This results in increase in the Board's liability towards foreign exchange variations on the return on foreign equity, which would be around Rs.1.35 crore per annum.

The foreign currency component of the total debt for project financing was fixed in Indian rupees at November 1993 rates of exchange. As this value in Indian rupees if fixed and does not undergo change and vary with exchange rate variations, the Developer had an undue benefit due to exchange rate variations between November 1993 and actual dates of drawl of loans. On the loans drawn till May 1996, such gain amounted to Rs.23.38 crore and there would be a further gain of Rs.56.06 crore with reference to the prevailing exchange rates on the loans yet to be drawn. The PPA was silent as to the treatment of such gain to the Developer due to exchange variations.

The Board so far purchased 432.13 MU of energy from the Developer on payment of Rs.94.69 core. As against the projected unit rate of Rs.2.06, the actual purchase cost per unit worked out to Rs.2.19 resulting in an extra expenditure of Rs.5.62 crore on the energy so far purchased.

In contravention to the PPA terms providing for fixation of variable cost (cost of fuel) duly taking into account, the transportation charges of gas, the Board paid transportation charges separately without any regard to actual quantity of gas used. This resulted in over payment of transportation charges by Rs.3.84 crore related to the gas not used for the period from July 1996 to April 1997.

The land costing Rs.10 crore acquired by the Developer was adequate for two stages of the project. But, the entire cost of land was loaded into the project cost of first stage

(216 MW). Non-apportionment of the cost of land equally between the two stages of the project, results in undue benefit of Rs.1.13 crore per annum to the Developer.

CAG's observations on Spectrum's Kakinada Power Plant

With a view to encouraging private investment in power sector, the State Government selected Spectrum Power Corporation Limited (Developer) who had initially agreed to set up 400 MW gas based power plant at an outlay of Rs.780 crore but it was scaled down to 208 MW. As a follow-up, the Board and the Developer entered into a Power Purchase Agreement (PPA) according to which the former agreed to buy the entire power generated on payment of fixed and variable charges at rates mutually agreed upon.

Due to postponement of combined cycle commercial operation date of the Board had to bear the extra burden of Rs.17.05 crore towards higher fuel cost (Rs.11.71 crore) and additional fixed charges (Rs.5.34 crore) during the period from 29 September 1997 to 18 th April 1998.

By agreeing for payment of ROE monthly on pro rata basis instead of annually, the Board extended additional benefit of Rs.2.63 core per annum to the Developer.

As the foreign exchange component of total debt of the project was fixed in Indian rupees at December 1993 rates of exchange, there was an exchange gain of Rs.38.94 crore to the Developer and further exchange gain of Rs.1.27 crore on the balance debt yet to be drawn. But the PPA was silent on the treatment of such favourable gains in arriving at the final project cost.

In contravention to the PPA terms providing for fixation of variable cost (cost of fuel) duly taking into account the transportation charges of gas, the Board paid transportation charges separately without any regard to actual quantity of gas used. This resulted in over payment of transportation charges by Rs.6.63 crore related to the gas not used for the period from 9 January 1997 to 31 December 1997.

The minimum PLF to be achieved during the stabilisation period was fixed at 51.37 percent. This was low when compared to the PLF of 68.49 percent fixed in respect of another project implemented around the same time. The fixation of PLF on lower side during stabilisation period resulted in foregoing recovery of Rs.9.50 crore from the Developer by way of disincentive.

The Threshold level of PLF at 68.5 percent fixed for computation of incentive was not realistic as the O & M contractors of the Developer guaranteed operation of the plant at an annual PLF of 85.6 percent and agreed to pay penalty for every 1 percent fall in PLF below 85.6 percent. As 85.5 percent of PLF the incentive payable to the Developer by the Board would be Rs.19.08 crore per annum while the PLF at this level was assured by the O & M contractors to the Developer without any extra payment.

As against the projected unit cost of Rs.2.2, the actual cost per unit of energy purchased was Rs.2.46. The resulted in an extra financial burden of Rs.18.51 crore in respect of 771.33 MW of energy purchased during the period from 11 February 1997 to 18 April 1998 (Government of Andhra Pradesh, 2001).

As People's Democracy rightly commented, "If the Financial Institutions are giving the money on the basis of AP Transco's guarantees, why should the IPPs own the projects? Text book capitalism tells us capitalists get profits as they take risks. Apparently, this is not true for capitalism in India and certainly not in the Power Sector. Gone also is the argument that IPPs being in additionally of resources" (PD Vol. 26, no.2. Also, see, Pukayastha Prabhir, Delhi Science Forum). Also gone were the much-trumpeted opportunities like chance of competition, efficiency, economy and consumer facility.

III

The above discussion shows that the attempt at privatisation is totally uncalled for. The criminal negligence by the State was the primary reason for the crisis in Power Sector. A progressive Subsidy Tariff system, where the subsidy is given to the poor must have brought more positive results. The subsidy to rich, both in agrarian and domestic sectors, is not necessary. This class can afford to pay the tariff. A Government, which cannot even minimise the power theft, inspite of an army of officials its control, has little moral right to tax the people with unreasonable agreements.

1.	Required Installation capacity by 2005	12854.00 MW
2.	Power Available by 31-03-1999	7276.00 MW
3.	Target for 2005(2-1)	5578.00 MW
4.	Extra Installation between 1999-2005	
	a APGENCO	1725 MW
	b Share from Central Pool	1846 MW
	c Share from Joint Sector	560 MW
	Total	**4131.00 MW**
5.	Net Requirement 2005(4-3)	1447.00 MW
6.	Power Available from IPPs Including Short Gestation Projects	4397.00 MW
7.	Net Excess of Power by 2005 (6-5)	3450.00 MW

Source: 1. Parthasarathi 1997 and 1998.
2. GENCO Bulletins.
3. Secretariat of Andhra Pradesh Legislatures 2001.
4. M.Thimma Reddy, 2000.
5. P.N.V.Nair, 2002.

The Hiten Bhaya Committee estimates about the rise in the power consumption proved to be an exaggeration. As the House Committee of the Legislative Assembly on Power Tariff estimated, required installed capacity would be 12,854 MW by 2005. Surprising fact is that the estimated capacity is not only available in the State, but also it is available in abundant. The following Table gives the break-up of installation details in the State.

The million-dollar question is what to do with 345.00 MW excess capacity? Why the public finance should be drained out, for no reason? These are the two of scores of questions that are purposefully unanswered by the Government.

It may be concluded that figures were cooked up, manipulated and the people were given wrong information. Gobelian techniques were employed to project the otherwise highly efficient APSEB as bankrupt and inefficient. What was provided was much worse, much inefficient and anti-people.

END NOTES

1. The State of Andhra Pradesh comprises three regions-Coastal Andhra Pradesh,Rayalaseema, and Telangana. At the time of Independence, the first two regions were a part of Madras Presidency under he British India and the last one was a part of Nizam State. After a prolonged struggle the first two regions were separated from Madras State and Andhra State was created in; 1953. The people of Telangana and the newly created Andhra State people agitated for three years for a separate state to Telugu speaking people. As a result the State of Andhra Pradesh enveloping all three regions was created in 1956.
2. Even within a small period of 5 years i.e. 1991-92 to 1996-97, APSEB achieved a remarkable success in transmission and distribution. On the transmission side the APSEB augmented its network by 26.4 percent and thus achieved the highest network expansion among SEBs in the country. The total length of T &D lines was expanded from 1,55,000 in 1978 (Institute of Public Enterprises (IPE): 131) to 6,08,000 kms by 1999. The distribution system was expanded at a brisk pace during the same period. The number of substations increased substantially from 1135 in '90-91 to 1844 in '98-99'. The number of distribution transformers increased from

88,000 in '90-91 to 1,71,083 in '98-99 Government of Andhra Pradesh 2002.Also see, Arun Ghosh, 1997; Srihari, 1997 and Hanumanth Rao 1997 and 2002.

3. It is a superstition among intellectuals that the public sector had become a white elephant and a major reason for the fiscal crisis in our country. However, the statistics speak otherwise. Though a good number of public sector units are sick and dozen of sick units in the private sector were forced on the public sector by the government of India, the overall performance of the public sector is not that discouraging. It earned a profit of Rs.13,700, 13,200 and 14,600 crore in 197-98,1998-99 and 1999-2000, respectively (Government of India 2003 and 2001. For a detailed analysis of public sector contribution to Indian Society and Economy, see, Alternative, Delhi Science Forum, 2003.)

4. The VTPS has been turning out a sterling performance every year. It stood **First** in the country during 1994-95, 1995-96, 1996-97, 1997-98 and 2001-02 by achieving the highest Plant Load Factor. This Station has been the recipient of many prestigious Awards from various organisations including Meritorious Awards instituted by the Government of India. The Station has received Meritorious Productivity Award for **nineteen consecutive years** totaling to an amount of Rs. 252.34 lakh. The Station also got the incentive Award for **ten consecutive years** totaling to an amount of Rs. 94.55 lakh. The Station has bagged a Gold Medal for 2001-02. **8th time** in a row since 1994-95. The Rayalaseema Thermal Power Plant stood first in the country in terms of PLF in 1998-99 and 2000-01. It won Meritorious Productivity Awards for five consecutive years and Incentive Awards also for six consecutive years. Kothagudem Thermal Power Station V won Meritorious Productivity Awards for **three consecutive years** and Incentive Awards also for **three consecutive years.** The Ramagundam 'B' Thermal Power Station achieved the **Highest PLF for four times at all India level.**

5. The **REP** was a revolutionary programme aimed at taking the electricity to the villages and rural people, particularly to the rural poor, who cannot afford to enjoy the benefits of power. Even the section 18 of the 1948 Act says that, the board should be charged with the general duty of promoting the coordinated development by taking electricity to those areas which were not given this benefit adequately

(Government of India. Third Five Year Plan:405-6). Since the First Five Year Plan, the Government of India had been giving top priority for rural electrification without much success. The number of electrified villages and towns with a population of below 5,000 was only 3,687(out of 5,61,107). It was decided to electrify 43,000 villages or small towns by 1996. For this purpose a "Rural Electrification Corporation " was set up during the third plan, However, it was during IV Plan that rural electrification was taken up on the large scale.(IV Five Year Plan: 270-281).

6. The cost of Hydel and Thermal powers from 1990 to '97.

Category	*1990-91*	*1991-92*	*1992-93*	*1993-94*	*1994-95*	*1995-96*	*1996-97*
Hydel	9.41	10.34	11.05	8.97	13.28	21.69	17.92
Thermal	58.14	69.46	81.91	91.02	110.72	116.43	121.98

Source: APSEB, 1998 P. 107.

7. Subsidy is not a favour. It is mandatory on the part of all State Governments. The State governments as subsidy must meet the gap between revenues and 3 percent of total Assests value. Still, the AP Government repeatedly projected the subsidy as a favour to the APSEB.

8. So far no perfect mechanism is available to identify the different components of power loss, agriculture consumption, technical loss and theft are included under the single category, i.e. power loss. Before the reforms i.e.1996-97 much loss was attributed to agriculture by deliberately inflating the power consumption by agriculture. After reforms much of the loss was attributed to technical loss theft (see APTRANSCO, first five tables and Ajay Pandey 2001:128.)

9. According to World Bank, the value of energy loss if India is equivalent to 3 Billion US Dollars or to 1 percent India's GDP (World Bank, 1999[2])

10. The State Government in its attempts to convince the people about the necessity of privatisation of power sector, completely manipulated the figures propagated that the APSEB was in red, despite huge subsidies since 1989-90 (www.AndhraPradesh. com/07-16-2002 and http://ercap.org/apprtrstruc/annexure/htm). The World Bank News Release No. 99/2103/SAS dt. 19 February 1999 maintains that ".....AP's

power sector has imposed a heavy burden on the state's finances and power sector reforms are urgently needed".

REFERENCES

1. Ajay Pandey, 2003, "Power Sector Reforms: A Long Road Ahead" in *Survey of Indian Industry 2003, Madras,* The Hindu.
2. APGENCO, 2003. *A Decade of performance (1992-2002),* Hyderabad, APSEB.
3. APSEB, 1997, *power Development in Andhra Pradesh (Statistics) 1996-97,* Hyderabad, APSEB
4. APSEB 1998, *Power Development in Andhra Pradesh (Statistics) 1997-98,* Hyderabad, APSEB.
5. Dayal, H.V. 1980, "Analysis of power sector", in Rajendra K.Pachuri (ed.) *Energy Policy for India,* Delhi, Macmillan.
6. Delhi Science Forum, 2003,*Alternative Economic survey 2001-02,* Delhi, Delhi Science Forum.
7. Ghosh Arun,1997, "Break-up and Privatisation of SEB in Andhra Pradesh: An Upcoming Scam", *Economic and Political Weekly, I Vol. 32, no, 29.*
8. Government of Andhra Pradesh, 1995, *Report of the High Level Committee, 'Guidelines on Restructuring and Privatisation of Power Sector an Power Tariff",* Hyderabad.
9. Government of Andhra Pradesh, 2000, *Report of the Comptroller and Auditor General of India, 1966 to 2000.*
10. Government of Andhra Pradesh, 2001, *Strategy paper on Power, Hyderabad.*
11. Government of Andhra Pradesh, 2002, *Reforms and Restructuring of Andhra Pradesh Power Sector (India),* www.andhrapradesh.com 07/16/2002.
12. Government of India, 2001, *Public Enterprises Survey 1999-2000.*
13. Government of India, 2002, *Economic Survey 2000-2001.*
14. Government of India, 2003, *The Economic Survey 2001-2002.*
15. IBRD, 1999, *Andhra Pradesh Power Sector Restructuring Programme*, New Delhi, IBR.
16. Institute of Public Enterprises, 1982, *Organisational Structure and Financial Policies of the State Electricity Boards (Study sponsored by Planning Commission),* Hyderabad, IPE.

17. Murthy, Ramachanra K. 2001, *Vidyut Valayam: Samskaranala Visleshana (in Telugu). Hyderabad, Lifeline* Communications.

18. Nair, P.N.V. 2002, *AP Reform Pays*, w.w.w.projectsmonitor.com

19. Purkayastha, Prabhir, *The Andhra Electricity Tariff Hikes: The Real Face of Reforms*, www. Delhiscienceforum.org/power.

20. Purkayastha, Prabhir, *The Power Sector; Crisis of the Reforms*, www.delhiscienceforum.org/power.

21. Rao, Hanumantha, V. 1998, *Veluthurunundi Cheekatiloki: Vidyuth Rangamupi Pariseelana (in Telugu)*, Guntur, Prajapandha Publications.

22. Rao, Hanumantha, V. 2002, *Economy of Andhra Pradesh 1996-2001: An Alternative Survey* (in Telugu), Hyderabad: Prajasakti Book House.

23. Reddy Thimma. M.2000, *Development in the Power Sector in Andhra Pradesh*, www.prayaspune.org/energy/32_india_reformsupdates.

24. Srihari, V.1997, "Is Restructuring of APSEB Inevitable:", *Economics and Political Weekly, Vol.32, no. 39.*

25. Srinivasan, V.K., 2003, "Achilles Heel of Economy" *in Survey of Indian Industry 2003*, Madras, The Hindu.

26. Transco, 2000, *Andhra Pradesh Power Sector Reforms, "Powering the New Millenium, Hyderabad.*

27. TRANSCO, *2001 Power Sector Status & Tariff in Andhra Pradesh*. http://ercap.org.apprtrstruc/annexure.

28. World Bank, 1997, *Andhra Pradesh: Agenda for Economic Reforms.*

29. World Bank, 1999, *Project Appraisal Document on Andhra Pradesh Power Sector Restructuring Programme, Report No. 18849.*

30. World Bank, 1999 *World Bank to Support Power Sector Overhaul in Andhra Pradesh.*

31. World Bank, 2001, *India, Power Supply to Agriculture, Vol. I, Summary Report No. 22171-in.*

32. Parthasarathi, 1998, *"foreword" Power Generation in Andhra Pradesh.*

33. TRANSCO, (Statistics) 1997-1998, Hyderabad.

9

Power Sector Reforms: A Case Study of Andhra Pradesh

*Dr. N.V. Madhuri**

Introduction

India embarked upon the economic reform programme in 1991 more out of compulsion than conviction. The widening fiscal deficit, depletion of foreign exchange reserves, balance of payments crisis, and the impending default on foreign debt repayment forced the government to take the plunge. The steps taken have certainly improved the strength of the economy in short and medium term. Foreign exchange reserves improved and economic growth saw a moderate spurt. Fiscal deficit showed a declining trend for sometime, only to increase later. The fiscal deficit of Union and State Governments put together, is estimated in the current year to about Rs.1800 billion, equivalent to about 12 percent GDP. About 48 percent union's tax revenues are spent on debt servicing. Real improvement is possible only if tax revenue increases significantly, subsidies are cut down drastically, and government is reduced in size, eliminating redundancies.

Each of these results is possible, but cannot be achieved in a vacuum. Tax revenues cannot be improved without rapid economic growth. The first flush of economic reform

* Assistant Professor (CHRD), National Institute of Rural Development, Hyderabad.

resulted in higher growth, largely because some of the artificial constraints imposed on the entrepreneurial energy of the Nation were removed. It was like a dam blocking the natural course of a river. As the dam is breached, water flows down. But as the reservoir is emptied, mere demolition of the obstruction cannot improve the flow of water downstream. We must replenish the reservoir through the more difficult operation of catchments treatment. Infrastructure bottlenecks in various sectors – energy, ports, roads and railroads–are formidable and need to be addressed with vigour and clarity. The only sector which has been sustained improvement is communications, since new technology can be transplanted in this sector with relative ease. Once government allows private initiative, no major governance reform is needed for improvement in communications. In case of energy, ports, roads and railroads however, significant public investments, policy initiatives and the will and capacity to mobilise public opinion in favour of growth-oriented polices are needed.

It is well recognised that energy services play a critical role in enhancing human and economic development. Accordingly, since Independence, the central thrust of India's energy policy has been on augmenting the country's energy system. As a result of significant planning and public investment, there has been a substantial expansion of, and shift in, the country's energy sector. Yet India still suffers from energy shortages. This situation has been increasingly viewed as a bottleneck to India's Industrial Growth that inturn is seen as critical to stimulating the country's economic and social development. The perceived urgency of the need to add to energy supplies combined with the paucity of public sector funds available to do this, was a major rationale underlying the promotion of private sector participation in the energy sector's development during the initiation of economic reforms. This led, in the following decade or so, to a number of policy developments such as encouragement of private power generation projects, restructuring of the state electricity boards to make the power sector more attractive to private investors, opening up hydrocarbon exploration to the private sector, and attracting private investments in coal.

The power situation in the country is extremely bad and appears to be worsening. The addition of installed capacity during the Eighth Plan period was originally planned for 30538 MW but due to shortfall in the first three years of the Plan, actual likely capacity addition is estimated at only 180232 MW. The main reasons for shortfall are deficiencies in project management, problems related to externally aided projects, resource constraints and law and order problems. Shortage in peaking and energy at the end of the eighth Plan are projected to be as much as 29 percent and 15 percent, respectively. Therefore, there is an urgent need to accelerate investment in power in both public and private sectors.

So far, the prospects of power sufficiency in the Ninth Plan do not appear to be very encouraging. The generation and consumption figures since 1973-74 are given in Table 1.

Table 1: Generation and Consumption of Power

Year	*Installed Capacity (MW)*	*Generation (Bus)*	*Consumption (KW) Total*	*Agricultural*	*Others*
1973-74	16664	4002	3015	378	2637
1978-79	26680	3842	2897	451	2446
1984-85	42585	3683	2679	492	2187
1989-90	63636	3857	2756	692	2064
1994-95	81171	4372	2596	793	1803
1996-97	85795	3948	2800	840	1960
1997-98	89060	4206	3903	912	2991
1998-99	93253	4480	4202	943*	3359*

*Estimate

In the energy sector, the key reforms advocated are unbundling and corporalisation of State electricity boards, privatisation of generation and eventually distribution, investments in T & D sector to minimise technical losses, effective mechanisms to eliminate corruption and theft, demand-side management to improve efficiency of end use and minimise wastage, elimination of redundancies in work force, and most of all, realisation of more economical user-charges. All these require fundamental changes in our governance process. For instance, endless delays in statutory clearances, arbitrary decision-making, and corruption are retarding private investment in generation. Even as many projects are approved, the energy boards do not have the capacity to buy power from all. Most States have failed to evolve simple fair, economical norms for power purchase. The capital costs and tariffs approved vary significantly, and the high-cost and high-tariff projects are often preferred to low-cost projects while finalising power purchase agreements, and providing escrow mechanism. Obviously such predatory behavior hurts consumer interests, and adversely affects the financial health of the already ailing electricity boards, and gives economic reform a bad name.

Andhra Pradesh Electricity: More Heat than Light

The recent electricity tariff increases have raised difficult and disturbing questions about the management of power sector in Andhra Pradesh over the years. Huge system losses unchecked over a period of time have led to deep crisis. This was compounded by the Governments failure to provide subsidies to meet the deficits arising out of the agricultural service connections at uneconomical rate. Nor were rational policies adopted to encourage energy saving in agriculture. As a net result of several years of criminal neglect, rampant corruption and rank incompetence, the once much acclaimed APSEB and its successor organisations are now facing severe financial crisis.

Unfortunately, reliable statistics on the performance of APSEB/AP Transco are not available. The claims of Transmission and Distribution (T & D) losses of power for instance, have been frequently revised.

Table 2: T & D Losses Estimated

Year	*T & D losses %*
1994-95	18.94
1995-96	18.85
1996-97	32.04
1997-98	33.06
1998-99	31.80 (later revised to 38.1)
1999-2000	36.90
2000-2001	35.40 (estimated)

As seen from these figures, the T & D losses have been growing alarmingly over the years.

These estimates have been charged at will. For instance, the T & D losses for the year 1998-99 were initially shown to be 31.8 percent. However this figure was later revised upwards to 38.1 percent.

The amount of energy metered and billed is a more accurate indication to the efficiency of the T & D system.

Table 3: Percentage of Energy Metered and Billed

Year	*Percentage*
1998-99	43
1999-2000	42.72
2000-2001	41.58

Unacceptable Line Losses

The above figures indicate that only about 40 percent of the power into the system is actually metered and billed. That means only about 2 units out of 5 units supplied to AP Transco are metered and billed. An appalling three-fifths of the power loss in the system means a loss of revenue to the tune of nearly Rs.100 crore. In a well managed system about 10-12 percent losses are permissible. These losses occur at various levels of transformers and conductors. Giving allowance for a certain degree of inefficiency, these T & D losses should not exceed 16 percent. However, AP Transco estimated system losses are as follows:

Nature of loss	*AP Transco*	*International Standard %*
Transmission	4.5	2-3
Distribution	18	7-9
Commercial losses estimated (thefts)	14.4	Nil
Total	**36.99-12**	

These statistics clearly show that at least 20 percent of the power supplied to the system is being stolen or lost because of incompetent management, corruption and poor infrastructure. The purchase cost of this 20 percent power (after giving allowance to 16 percent acceptable system losses) would be in the order of Rs.1680 crore. If an average tariff of Rs.3 per unit is realised from this energy unnecessarily lost, the revenue lost would be a staggering Rs.2500 crore.

Agricultural Consumption

APSEB and AP Transco have also been showing grossly varying figures of agricultural consumption over the years.

As agricultural power is not metered, farmers are charged a flat rate on the basis of load irrespective of consumption. Various assumptions have been made from time to time effectively transferring the system losses to agricultural consumption. As sample metering showed that agricultural consumption may be lower, the figures are being revised now, showing correspondingly higher system losses. However, there is evidence to suggest that the flat

Table 4: Agricultural Consumption

Years	*% of Agriculture Consumption*	*% of energy*
1994-95		47.3
1995-96	38.7	48.7
1996-97	24.4	37.4
1997-98	25.7	39.3
1998-99	25.5	39.2
1999-2000	–	–
2000-2001	23	35.6

rate of power charged for agricultural sector encouraged sale of low efficiency pumps and motors, excessive use of power and needless withdrawal of water depleting groundwater reserves. It is generally accepted that farm sector needs to be partially subsidised for lifting water. However, all efforts should be made to save power and groundwater, even as reasonable subsidies are continued. Despite the mounting crisis in the power sector no effective steps have been taken to conserve groundwater and save energy. Even now no rational policy for farm sector power has been evolved.

Revenue Deficits

On account of the mounting inefficiencies, rampant corruption and theft and unsustainable subsidies, APSEB and AP Transco have been claiming huge revenue deficits. As Electricity Supply Act 1948 makes it mandatory for the government to ensure 3 percent rate of return to the utilities, the Government has been transferring resources to the sector over the years. However, in reality these have been only book transfers or writing-off of loans and as of now there have been no real cash transfers.

These figures clearly show that there have been no real cash transfers to APSEB/AP Transco from Government. Over the years equity and loans have been written off

Table 5: Revenue Deficit

Year	*Revenue Deficit Rs. in Crore*	*Govt. Payments*
1994-95	857	Equity written off to a tune of Rs.944 crore
1995-96	1128	Loans written off to a tune of Rs.1259 crore
1996-97	721	Loans written off to a tune of Rs.850 crore
1997-98	1134	Subsidies to a tune of Rs.1255 crore due from government
1998-99	2038	Rs.2519 crore due from government
1999-2000	3600	–
2000-2001	3558	Rs.1626 crore promised

merely reducing requirement of return on reduced equity, or reducing the burden of debt servicing. The control of Government on APSEB/AP Transco has been total in terms of policy, tariffs and personnel. In addition, there has been interference in day-to-day functioning and routine executive decision. Pilferage, thefts and corruption continued unchecked on account of political patronage and lack of political will to improve the system. The power sector became the proverbial goose that laid golden eggs, and public interest suffered grievously. Endemic power shortages, voltage fluctuations, frequent tripping, tremendous corruption, harassment and extortion, populism, unreliable power and high tariffs have become the order of the day.

Disproportionate Rise of Domestic Tariffs

In this backdrop, the AP Electricity Regulation Commission (APERC) was created under AP State Electricity Reform Act, 1998 in order to insulate tariffs and licensing decisions from partisan political control. On May 27, 2000 APERC gave this orders on the tariff revision proposals of AP TRANSCO for the year 2000-2001. The resulting higher tariffs affected the domestic sector disproportionately. This distortion was largely a result of the high estimates of cost to serve. Most of the thefts (95 percent) are assumed in LT sector alone; the burden of thefts is thus disproportionately borne by domestic sector. In addition, as domestic consumption is largely during the peak hours between 6 PM and 10 PM, AP Transco charged most of the domestic sector. Both these assumptions of high losses and thefts in domestic sector, and additional cost on account of peak hour load are flawed. It is unlikely that most thefts are in domestic sector, and in any case thefts are a result of incompetence, connivance and corruption in AP Transco. It is unreasonable to transfer the burden of the utilities follies to the honest consumers who pay bills. In a situation of endemic scarcity and power cuts, it is not reasonable to transfer the burden of additional power generation entirely onto the domestic sector. In addition, nearly half of the power generation capacity in the State is in hydroelectric stations, in which cost of generation is very low. These stations can be switched on and off at will, and ought to be operate when the load peaks. Given these facts, the assumption of 496ps as cost to serve in domestic sector is highly exaggerated. Unfortunately APERC has largely relied on these unscientific estimates while revising tariffs.

Table 6: Domestic Tariff Comparison

No. of	*Old*		*ERC*			*Revised*		
units	*Rate*	*Amount*	*Rate*	*Amount*	*%incr*	*Rate*	*Amount*	*%incr*
50	0.80	40.00	1.45	72.50	81%	1.35	67.50	69%
100	1.20	120.00	3.90	267.50	123%	2.95	215.00	79%
200	1.65	330.00	3.90	657.50	99%	2.95	510.00	55%
300	2.10	630.00	6.15	1272.50	102%	4.50	960.00	52%
400	2.90	1160.00	6.15	1887.50	63%	4.50	1410.00	22%
500	3.40	1700.00	7.05	2592.50	53%	5.25	1935.00	14%

From the above Table it can be seen that the burden of tariff increase has disproportionately been on the domestic sector. In particular, greater hardship is felt by the steep increase in 50-200 units slab and reduction of the earlier six slabs into four. Given the public concern and the steep hike, there is a strong case to reintroduce the earlier six slabs, and to provide relief in 50-200 units slab. However, relief to the small domestic consumer may pacify the public, but the crisis in power sector will need to be addressed squarely to protect consumer interests.

Real Issue: Better Management, not Revenues

However, the real issues in Electricity sector are camouflaged in the current debate arising out of tariff revision. If our whole emphasis in on increasing revenues to meet the expenditure, then the burden of tariffs will be unsustainable. If AP Transco is suffering losses, then someone has to pay. The only way of maintaining tariffs table even as losses are mounting is by huge government subsidies to AP Transco. The government itself is showing huge fiscal deficits and all development expenditure has been stopped.

The real answer to the crisis lies in addressing three fundamental issues to improve system efficiency, reduce corruption and minimise future expenditure.

1. T and D losses
2. Power Purchase Agreements(PPAs)
3. Distribution privatisation.

As the Table above shows, improvement of efficiency and reduction of technical losses and elimination of thefts alone will significantly improve the financial health of AP Transco and the four distribution companies. Increase in non-agricultural billing by 10 percent in the current year, 5 percent in 2001-2002, and 4 percent in 2002-2003 is both practical and vital for the future of electricity sector. As the Table shows, if these improvements are made, it will be possible to significantly reduce revenue deficits even at the

Table 7: Financial Position of AP Power Sector

1 Demand projection (MU)		27500	30000	33000	36000
2 Energy Losses (MU)		15000	10500	8750	7500
3 Energy Purchases		35%	26%	21%	17%
4 Revenue Requirement		8365	8200	8500	9000
PP Costs		7042	6745	6900	7200
Other costs (10% increase)		1323	1455	1600	1800
5 Revenue Realisation (Rs in crore)	5448	6521	7110	7821	8532
	(As per old tariff)	(As per revised tariff)			
6 Revenue Deficit (Rs in crore)	2917	1844	1090	679	468
7 To be covered by					
Subsidy	2417	1344	890	579	368
Efficiency improvement	500	500	200	100	100
Ave. purchase cost/unit		1.66	1.66	1.66	1.66
Ave. Selling cost/unit		2.37	2.37	2.37	2.37

Note:
It is assumed that
1. Demand will increase 10% per annum.
2. Power Purchase Cost will be stable during the period 2000-2001
3. Average sale price of power will be as per APERC order for the year 2000-01
4. Reduction of T&D losses will be 10% in the year 2000-2001, 5% in the year 2001-2002 and 4% in the year 2002-2003.

current tariff levels. Tariff increase will not be necessary for the next three years. Simultaneously, the subsidy burden on Government will fall significantly to a nominal Rs.368 crore by 2003-04. Clearly, genuine improvements in distribution and elimination of thefts and corruption are the most vital requirements to safeguard the future of the power sector.

Power Purchases Agreements (PPAs)

As APSEB's financial health declined over the years, there has been no investment in new generating stations to meet the increasing demand. The APSEB/AP Transco has entered into power purchase agreements (PPAs) with several private companies, foreign as well as domestic. There are two serious problems with these projects. Firstly, the realistic capacity of AP Transco to buy power from private sector in the next five years does not exceed about 2500 MW. However, the State has entered into PPAs with projects with a total capacity of over 5600 MW. There are no objective and verifiable norms as to which project will be promoted, and which will be sidelined. This arbitrariness led to enormous scope for corruption and delays. Secondly, as power plants have been promised returns on 'cost plus' basis, capital costs of these plants have been escalated and are highly variable. Plants with similar fuel and in the same locality cost a lot more than other comparable projects, resulting in higher tariffs. Added to this, there has been no proper planning and foresight in promoting plants with appropriate fuel mix keeping in view economy, availability and reliability. As a result, naphtha-based short gestation projects have been promoted, and the rising cost of naphtha has led to unaffordable tariffs. While gas-based power is clean and cheap, there is limitation of gas availability, which may not exceed 1000 MW. Also gas has greater value as a chemical than as a fuel, and therefore, the limited gas reserves cannot be used exclusively for power generation.

Given these facts, unless a transparent and fair policy is evolved and implemented, there is a real danger of enormous escalation of tariffs as private projects become operational. The Kondapalli project which is already commissioned will have to be kept idle on account of high cost of naphtha, and AP Transco will have to pay about Rs.300 crore per annum as fixed costs until gas supplies are available. In Maharastra, Enron is similarly being paid about Rs.1000 crore per annum as fixed costs.

Decentralisation of Distribution

The Government has repeatedly declared its policy of privatisation of distribution network. People are unconcerned about ownership and management of distribution companies, as long as abundant, affordable, high quality power is available to meet our consumption needs and fuel economic growth. When the Government and management of AP Transco proclaim their inability to mange the distribution system, reduce line losses, and eliminate thefts and corruption, competitive private management is one option.

The electricity generation, transmission and distribution network shows that about 4.5 percent of power is lost in high tension transmission. While there is room for reduction of these losses by about 1.5 percent of the investments needed are relatively high. Also there are no thefts possible in transmission. The real area of concern is distribution, in which losses are of the order of 32-33 percent. About 14 percent of the power is estimated to be lost by thefts alone. Elimination of thefts requires political will, legal enforcement, and local strength and influence to counter political pressures and small mafias. Technical improvements in distribution do require infusion of technology and investments.

Unless Government and AP Transco address these basic issues of T and D losses, power purchase agreements and decentralised and transparent transfer of distribution rights, the electricity sector is bound to sink deeper into financial crisis and collapse sooner, than later.

Conclusion

The immediate challenge for the power sector is to narrow down the gap between demand and supply. The energy shortage is approaching 10-11 percent and the peak-demand shortfall is in the range of 20 percent. This has bottlenecked economic growth. According to an estimate, the opportunity cost of the energy shortage and the peak demand shortfall is 1.5 percent of the GDP. The country needs over 55,000 MW of new capacity during the Ninth Plan. But the feasible addition may be in the range of only 20,000 MW—25,000 MW. Even this may be mostly in the form of base-load stations, which are not needed.

While India needs a rich infusion of foreign investment in power sector, it will have to attract domestic investors too in a big way. The Rakesh Mohan Committee's infrastructure Report also says that the lion's share of investment in the infrastructure sector, including power, has to come from the domestic market. To make investors interested in the power sector, a wide range of steps beginning wih power sector reforms have to be taken.

Reforming and ultimately 'privatising' distribution and transmission will help infuse money and vibrancy. The sensitive, yet essential step of rationalising tariffs to make SEBs viable and credit worthy will have to be taken. Special tax incentives have to be considered for small investors subscribing to 'power bonds' of SEBs. Faster clearance of projects should also be ensured. The idea is to make investment attractive and power projects viable and bankable. The frequent policy-shifts tend to increase the perceived risk and therefore, the risk premium. Hence, there is a need for stabilised and enabling environment conducive to investments.

Investment alone would not bring in the necessary results. The following measures would have to be taken to improve performance.

- Removal of corruption and inefficiencies
- Improvement in capacity utilisation;
- Raising end use efficiency through programmes is effect industrial agriculture and lighting efficiencies; and
- Co-generation and captive generation of electricity.

These measures would also reduce the need for investment in capacity addition.

Reforms need to be pursued aggressively to ensure viability of the sector by improving efficiency in investment and operations, creating a level playing field and obtaining clarity in demand estimates. Privatisation of distribution zones like the ones that have been implemented in Orissa and U.P. are expected to bring in efficiency and the establishment of regulatory authorities will only further help transperancy. The other constituent in the reform process is the establishment of fair and competitive power market. The promulgation of availability based tariff order by CERC is expected to facilitate trading in power and better rates for consumers.

The establishment of competitive markets would ensure freedom of choice to the consumers to buy power from efficient procedures and to producers to supply power to credit-worthy consumers. This would certainly take some time but, ultimately, the consumer will be the king.

REFERENCES

1. CMIE, (2001), Economic Intelligence Service: Energy Centre for Monitoring the Indian Economy, Mumbai.
2. IEA, (2000), Energy Balances of Non-OECD Countries, 1997-98, International Energy Agency, Paris.

3. TERI, (2000), Tata Energy Data Directory and Year book 1999-2000, Tata Energy Research Institute, New Delhi.

4. NRC, (2001), Energy Research at DOE: it Worth Its Energy efficiency? And Fossil Energy Research 1978 to 2000, US National Research Council, National Academy Press, Washington, DC.

5. "Plight of Power Sector in India-II" by Kannan and Pillai, EPW, January 20, 2001.

6. The Indian Electricity Act, 1910.

7. Loksatta Times, Vol. 1, No. 2 October 2000.

10

Whether Financial Sector Reforms?

*Prof. K. Aravindakshan**

India has gone through more than a decade of economic reforms. And the Indian economy as of now, is said to witness what has come to be called "the second generation reforms". What is really means is more free markets, more monetary policy, more foreign capital, more and more attempts at de-reservation of small enterprises and more and more doses of hire and fire policies and so on. Along with these anti-people and anti-labour policies to expedite the process of marketisation and globalisation, crucial changes have also been taking place in the financial sector as well. When the budget for 2000-01 was announced by the former Finance Minister Yashwant Sinha, it was claimed by the protagonists of reform as the open expression of the "successful" decade of economic reform measures that has passed by. It was also described as the signal for the kick-starting of the second phase of reforms or second generation reforms. The budget for 2002-03 prepared and presented by the new Finance Minister Jaswant Singh has also been moulded along the earlier pattern set by his predecessor. The present analysis is restricted to the first decade of economic reforms (1991-2001) with particular accent on reforms in the financial sector.

* Prof. K. Aravanidakshan, Kochi-682036.

A Decade of Financial Sector Reforms(FSRs)—In Retrospect

The decade covering the period 1991-2001, witnessed a series of sweeping reforms in the banking sector, in the money, securities and capital markets, as well as foreign exchange markets. The salient features of these reforms can be analysed and reviewed two broad heads:(a)banking sector and (b) financial markets.

Banking Sector Reforms

Since monetary policy, which has its inevitable impact on the banking sector, has been subjected to the dictates of "Neo-liberal" prescriptions relating to "market based" or "market-determined" rate of interest, there arose the urgent need for restructuring the Indian Banking system as a whole. Thus, a series of measures were taken to reform the banking sector so as to align Indian banks to the 'best' global standards and practices existing in industrially developed countries.

Before going into the reforms of the banking sector in tune with the liberalisation, privatisation and globalisation(LPG) policies, we may have to make a quick survey of the trends in the banking sector in India in the pre- and post- nationalisation periods. For instance, in June 1969, there were only 1443 rural branches of scheduled commercial banks in India – just 17.6 percent of the total number of bank branches. The total credit advanced to the clients in the rural sector was not more than Rs.11.5 crore or 3.3 percent of total bank credit. By June 1991, the number of rural bank branches had gone up to 35216 or 58.1 percent of total number of Bank branches. And, rural credit had expanded to Rs.3316 crore or 15.1 percent of total bank credit. Under pressure of "reforms" this trend has been totally reversed. By June 1999, many rural bank branches have been closed down and their number declined to 32850 or 50.35 percent of total bank branches. Rural credit too naturally declined to 10.7 percent of total bank credit. What about the trend in "priority sector" lending ? After nationalisation, there was an uptrend in lending to this sector comprising agriculture, small industries, job-generating new 'services' sectors. The increase recorded in lending to these areas was from 14 percent of the total credit in 1969 to 42.6 percent of total credit by June 1989. It was this higher percentage or uptrend that fell to 32.8 percent by June, 1996. It is true that there has been a revival of this trend to 37.3 percent of total credit by June 1999. How ? That was only after extending the definition of "priority sector lending" to embrace lending to food processing industries which, strangely enough, included MNCs like Kelloggs, Pepsi, Hindustan Lever and the like besides advances made to infrastructure funds. What does it really imply ? Priority sector lending in the reform era extends to loans availed of by MNCs which, in no way, offer any help or relief to either small farmers or small industries or self-employment generating sectors as was the case in the pre-reform period.

What has been the nature of reform measures undertaken during the reform decade of 1991-2001? The Statutory Liquidity Ratio(SLR) has been progressively brought down from 38.5 percent before to 25 percent as on 22-10-1997. The Cash Reserve Ratio (CRR) which was as high as 16.5 percent was brought down to 9.75 percent earlier and it stands at 4.75 percent as on 16-11-2002. Bank rate effective from 22-10-2002 has been placed at 6.25 percent. What about Investment Deposit Ratio? As on 25-10-2002 it is 41.30 percent. Selective credit controls have been practically done away with. The administered rates of interest have been virtually dismantled. Globally accepted prudential norms of capital adequacy, income recognition, assigning risk weights to government approved securities etc., have been adopted. Competition is being encouraged in the banking sector by permitting the setting up of a new generation of private sector banks, Indian as well as foreign. With effect from May 10, 2001 the foreign investment limit in banks has been raised to 49 percent. An Independent

Board for Financial Supervision under the RBI has been established. The Board has already incorporated all the known principles of bank supervision prevailing in the West. Banking sector reforms, visualized a part of economic reforms, are still incomplete, though the present NDA Government is evidently committed to carry them forward as expeditiously as possible. The dilution of government equity in public sector bank to 33 percent, leaving 67 percent to private sector, decided upon by the previous Cong(1) led Government, still stands. The announcement of a further reduction in government equity by the NDA is yet to be implemented. Irrespective of what the present government ultimately does or not, what is really relevant today is whether under the new reforms atmosphere of globalisation, some of the social goals expected of the banking sector in the wake of nationalisation will be kept in tact or not, or whether they will be thrown to the winds. In the light of the present pace of gloabalisation which has gathered a new momentum, one can legitimately expect that social goals will be at a discount in the days to come.

Let us, for a break, recapitulate the happenings prior to the period of mad rush for LPG policies. Despite the reduction in SLR in the 1990s, more than 36 percent of incremental deposits were deployed in government securities as against 25 percent in the 1980s. What this trend indicates is clear–banks have shifted an increasing share of their funds in favour of financial investments than credit. The average credit deposit ratio(CDR) declined from 67 percent in 1980s to 55 percent in 1990s. Still later as on December 29, 2000, the ratio came down to just 35 percent. But with effect from 25-10-2002 it is 54.25 percent. What about the growth of commercial bank credit? Its average annual growth which stood at more than 18.2 percent in the earlier decade fell to 15.2 percent in the 1990s.

And, what is the present state of affairs? The era of priority sector lending, subsidized interest rates, differential interest rates and so on, has virtually come to an end. Even the definition of priority sector has been subtly changed so that it no longer serves the interests of agriculture, agri-based industries and the small-scale sector or self-employed or self-employable categories. It is for these sections that priority sector lending was expected to cater to. What have the banks done instead? They have gone to the other extreme, that is, lending for speculative activities through the pumping of money against collateral security of stocks and shares. It is little wonder, therefore, that stock market scams have become a regular feature during the post-reform period.

The share of agriculture in the total credit advanced by commercial banks has come down from amount 18 percent in the 1980s to 10.6 percent in 1998-99. According to the figures given in the IBA Bulletin published in December 2002, the outstanding priority sector advances of public sector banks increased by 16.8 percent and thus priority sector advances formed 43.1 percent of the net bank credit. At the same time advances to agricultural sector as a whole formed only 15.7 percent of the net bank credit as in March 2002. As for private sector banks, their total advances to the entire priority sector constituted 40.9 percent of net bank credit whereas the share of agriculture taken alone was just 8.5 percent. The implications of these figures are clear. That is, among the priority sectors, agriculture has not been receiving its due either from public sector or private sector banks. Similar has been the experience of small-scale industries sector as well as that of the ST/SCs and other weaker sections of society. Many impartial studies and analysis have shown that rural branch banking system, effectively blocked and destroyed by the champions of reform, is nothing but a costly misadventure from the point of view of agriculture and small-scale industries.

Stranger still is the remarkable increase in the personal loan content of bank credit from 5 percent of total credit in 1988-89 to 10.4 percent in 1998-99. This is a clear reflection of a shift from rural to urban clients in the metropolitan areas. Regional disparities and imbalances in credit disbursements have also deepened and widened. So too have class disparities with the upper middle-class and the urban elite swallowing a big chunk of bank credit, not to speak of the corporate sector borrowers who have so far accumulated NPAs to about Rs.1,10,000 crore which is inclusive of the principal and interest. And, it is this group of corporate sharks and the organisations sponsoring them, such as FICCI and CII, who demand privatisation of public sector banks, so that they can write off all the dues in course of time.

There is little wonder that economic reforms in the banking sector are proceeding along these lines. These are days when global finance capital has assumed remarkable proportions and grown to a dominant position in the world order with unipolarism ruling the roost. The USA, the citadel of global capitalism, decides everything on own, without taking counsels from any quarter. And finance capital which is a combination of industrial capital and banking capital, is madly in search of new pastures for investment. It is in this context that global finance capital is attracted to developing countries like India where labour is cheap, physical and natural resources are abundant. What is needed further is banking capital over which there can be total control provided banks are privatized. Native industrial capitalists also want the same facility for their own unimpaired growth. In order to speed up the process of privatsation of public sector banks, the provisions of the Basle Accord of 1988 are being imposed upon the Indian banking system. This accord was designed by the USA and UK in order to contain the growth of Japanese finance capital which was rapidly spreading its tentacles and expanding its might around the world. The main provision of the Basle Accord was Income Recognition and Capital Adequacy Ratio (IRCAR). Since the Japanese banks had only a thin capital base, it was easy for US Capital to force upon these banks the principle of capital adequacy. But any attempt to impose this norm on the Indian public sector banks is totally unwarranted because it is the Government which has 100% control over them. If at all there is any need for it, it is merely a matter of procedure. And, in case the capital base of public sector banks in India is weak, it is the result of accumulation of bad debts or NPAs for which the big corporate borrowers are responsible. What does the Government do? Instead of trying to recover loans not repaid in time by willful defaulters by suitable legal measures, what the RBI and the Government have been doing is to devise such clever means as 'One Time Settlement,' 'Compromise Settlement', which mean writing off of crores of rupees to the benefit of the defaulters and at the cost of national interest. It is necessary and instructive to remember that in March 2001 alone public sector banks had written off Rs.8000 crore in this way. Where has this much of money come from? From the hard-earned savings of hundreds of common people. The huge loss to the exchequer incurred in this way, is ultimately a loss to these people. More than this aspect, if there is no attempt to penalize the defaulters for their deliberate act, it will set a bad precedent for all future borrowers.

In spite of all these, the Government has been going ahead with the adoption of new measures to salvage the guilty such as the settings up of an Asset Reconstruction Company (ARC) in order to handle the so–called Asset Reconstruction Fund (ARF). This measure, first suggested by the Narasimham Committee and supported by the Verma Committee as a permanent institutional arrangement, is aimed at cutting the very roots of the banking system in India. In India, unlike in many other countries, where the banking system collapsed due to the accumulation for NPAs there is no urgency, provided the defaulters are persuaded to honour their commitments.

However, what is really relevant in this context is that the formation for ARC is not aimed at saving loss-making banks, but to make their bottom line clean before privatsation. And this is what exactly our corporate borrowers also want. The RBI and the Government of India are dancing to the tunes of the corporate sector, by refusing to simplify the procedure for NPA recovery through the Debt Recovery Tribunals (DRTs) which follow procedures that are practically ineffective and time-consuming in nature.

The setting up of the DRTs followed by that of the ARC has not at all helped the process of NPA recovery. And it is naturally so, because the real intention of the Government is not to save public sector banks, but to expedite the process of their privatisation which is an essential ingredient of financial and banking sector reforms. The new generation private banks which are coming up in big cities are madly mergers and acquisitions of well-established banks both in the public and the private sectors, so as to be of help to the interests of big business and traders who make quick money and profits and accumulate black money through stock market scams. They provide all modern facilities such as credit card facilities, ATM arrangements and internet transfers as part of hitech culture, with no interest in priority sector lending and promotional activities.

Financial Market Reforms

The most important segments of financial markets are the money market, securities market and foreign exchange market. It is true that the Indian financial system is dominated by the banking sector. But, ever since the commencement of the "reforms" phase, and permission was granted to foreign institution investors (FIIs)from early 1993 to register with the SEBI and operate freely in India, several measures have been initiated to open up the financial markets as much as possible. The basic objective of monetary policy under the era of reforms has been to make the financial markets more autonomous by eliminating all forms of control. The monetary and credit policies announced by the RBI in April 2001 have clearly demonstrated this strategy.

Banks which are an integral part of the financial sectors, are now free to invest any amount in PSU bonds. Many of the nationalised banks like the Union Bank of India and the Canara Bank have issued bonds in the open market to raise capital. A wide net work of money market institutions such as the SEBI, the National Stock Exchange (NSE), Over the Country Exchange of India (OTCEI) have started functioning in full steam. The Budgets for the two years 2000-01 and 2001-02 have been clearly "reform-oriented".

Along with the reforms in the money and debt markets in the domestic sector, several measures have been taken to integrate the Indian foreign exchange market with the well-organised global financial systems. Banks in India are allowed to borrow from and invest in other countries. But integration is not yet complete. Full capital account convertibility which is the essence of full integration with the global market has so far been kept in abeyance, largely due to the fear of a repetition of the East Asian crisis of 1997-99. Still, the objective remains, that is, keeping capital account convertibility as the ultimate goal of the second generation for financial reforms. The RBI, on its part, as part of second generation reforms, has generously liberalized the erstwhile policy on investments abroad by Indian business houses, individual and firms so that they could expand globally. The so-called auto-matic route has been significantly liberalized. All Indian companies are now permitted to acquire has permitted the Indian partner ship firms to invest abroad. The role of the RBI has been substantially diluted. It is now more a regulator than a controller.

Now that India has completed a decade of reforms, it is the right time for us to recollect some the experiences in the past so as to plan further changes in the pattern and content of reforms in the future. While the protagonists of reform claim that FSRs are on the right track, the critics of reform have a different view of the whole process. They are tempted to raise several doubts about the direction which the FSR s has been taking. One of them is related to the flow of FDI to various countries. Those who demand the opening of the economies of developing countries insist of 'transparency' as a pre-condition for flow of capital. But out of the 850 billion dollars of capital flow to developing countries in 2000, the share of India was only $2 billion and that too mainly by way of mergers and acquisitions. What about China, where there is 'Zero' transparency? The FDI flow to China was as high as $ 40 billion. What this trend indicates is clear-FDI is unwilling to flow into developing countries except under guarantee of profits as in the case of ENRON. The result is that the "servicing costs" of external capital for India are very much higher than the higher output and employment generated through FDI. Investment of foreign capital by way of acquisition of domestic enterprise merely results increases in external payments burden. In short, profit expectations of foreign capital are higher than higher productivity. Still, there is no decline in profit earnings. How does it come about ? Managers of foreign capital are adopting a clever way of manipulating higher profits through acquisition of low valued 'assets' in developing countries. Thus, foreign capital flows in recent times, are largely through 'trade in assets ' which hardly adds anything to GDP.

The integration of 'financial markets' has brought in many serious dangers and pitfalls for developing countries in general, and for India, in particular. First, it becomes impossible for them to formulate and pursue fiscal and monetary policies in their own national interests. Secondly both interest rates and profit levels will have to kept at high levels in order to attract external capital. Naturally, as we have already seen, the serving costs will be more than gains from productivity. Thirdly, the policies of liberalisation and globalisation have been a costly experiment especially since it has meant the implementation of WYO provisions since 1995. As a result, the prices of consumer durables have declined so that the middle classes have fallen victims to a spending spree while at the same time, import liberalisation and removal of QRs on imports have made the farmers and small scale industrialists totally pauper because of the fall in the prices of their products. Both these developments have depressed the savings rate of the community in general. India's domestic savings declined from 25.3% in 1998-99 and it has come down to 22% in 200-01. Fourthly, the evolution of new financial instruments like share price indices have driven domestic savers towards speculative investment rather than productive investments.

Please look at the figures given in the Table below.

Total New Equity Issues in India and Market Capitalisation on the Bombay Stock Exchanges

	1994-95	*1998-99*	*1999-2000*
1. New Equity raised by private sector	349	125	228
2. Market capitalisation on BSE	4334	5429	9128
3. Trading volumes on BSE	677	3108	6850

The figures given in the Table are self-revealing. With the added momentum of everyday speculative purchases and sales, the 'players' in the speculative share market must keep more cash. This cash, a major part of which comes from savings, goes to bolster the cash balances of speculators and brokers. As the late Prof. Arun Ghosh has rightly put it, "This is a typical Keynesian scenario of 'ex-ante' savings being lost to 'ex-post' in the from of hoards".

It is little wonder that since the process of liberalisation and globalisation of the Indian economy was initiated since

1991, the country has come across at least a dozen major frauds and crimes in the financial sector. In fact, throughout the 90s, India has witnessed major financial frauds, occurring almost every year. And, regulatory authorities such as the SEBI and RBI have been mute witnesses to these crimes on the helpless people of India. Starting from the securities problems facing financial markets in India. Then TNCs allotted shares to themselves at prices far below the prevailing market rates, profiting thereby to the tune of Rs.5000 crore. All this happened due to the eagerness of the then Finance Minister Dr. Manmohan Singh, to quickly deregulate and liberalise the Indian economy. SEBI ought to have taken urgent measure to re-regulate the preferential price norms. But it was not done and, by the time SEBI had acted, the TNCs had their way.

The period between 1992 and 1996 had witnessed a series of frauds especially the so-called vanishing companies fraud. For wan of strict guide lines and regulations, fly-by- night operators could float as many as 4069 public issues and collect over Rs.4,500 crore from the public of fictitious grounds. Once they got the money they wanted, these unscrupulous operators vanished into this air, as it were. What is surprising is that SEBI took notice of this fraud on the people only after two years. Many of the vanished companies are yet to be traced and their promoters brought to book.

The sordid story continued through the mid–90s, when the country witnessed the Plantation Companies fraud when dubious investment companies mobilised from the public, quite openly, a fabulous amount of RS.50,000 crore for various well-orchestrated plantation schemes. 'Money grows on trees' was the theme they advertised and many unsuspected people, especially small savers fell into this trap. And the promoters vanished as quickly as they had stormed the financial market. Then came the Non-Banking Finance

Companies fraud in which many more small investors were trapped by the offer of high returns on fixed deposits. Here too, action came too late.

In 1998, Indian financial markets were rocked by a phenomenal case of share price rigging racket, involving industrial groups for standing and reputation such as BPL, Sterlite group for a pittance when Arun Shourie launched his ambition plan of privatisation of PSUs under the pretext of disinvestments. The CAG has now charged the Government of India with having undervalued the shares of this PSU to the extent of nearly of RS.500 crore and caused loss to the exchequer. So far no punitive action has been taken against any of these companies and the main offenders including Harshad Mehta who in not alive today. Consequent on the fraud, the Sensex recorded a steep fall of 224 points on a single day. The international institutional investor, Morgan Stanley, lost no time in indulging in heavy short selling in close association with global bear cartels. This joint and organized onslaught hit the government-owned UTI which had substantial stake in the companies. This day is known as "Black Monday" in the Indian financial markets.

It is true that SEBI had promised to investigate the clash. But nobody has any idea as to what action has been taken given against Morgan Stanley and the global bear cartel who conspired against the domestic investors.

The country, as you know, was under grip of IT mania with the dawn of the year 1999. In order to deceive ordinary investors, who were ignorant of the tricky ways of financial market dealings, a number of private Companies changed their names to dotcom. Just two examples would suffice to bring home the point. Oriented Paper Ltd. Changed its name to Oriented Software Ltd. And Aftek Business Machines Ltd. Changed its name to Aftek Infosys. The value of the shares issued by the newly named companies suddenly shot up and there was a mad rush for them in the share market. Once the job had been done, the promoters closed down their shops and just vanished. Another major fraud is likely to Cyberspace Infosys Ltd. Which changed its original name from century Finance. The promoters of the company who had strong political connections could easily make good their escape from the country along with the money robbed off numerous innocent small investors who were left to fend for themselves. There was none to bring them relief; nor to shed tears for them. The innocent and helpless investors were condemned to fall victims of market fundamentalism.

This was not end of the story either. The Indian financial markets were in for another serious panicky situation of April 3,200. Then the Sensex lost 361 points when then slerths in the Union IT Departments served notices on several FIIs operating in the Indian financial markets for income tax non –payment issues. As a result, nearly Rs.6000 crore were lost by investors at one go. And, this was the second biggest single-day market crash, since the dawn of the era of free market economic reforms. Everybody in the media who was in the know of things, was aware of the fact that several Mauritius-based corporate giants with huge amounts of cash had been operating sub-accounts of FIIs. The money thus accumulated, was finding their way back into the country through illegal routed. This money was actively involved in price rigging operations of bulls and bears in the financial markets in India. What happened thereafter is interesting story? Global financial capital was all rage against the Government of India for having thought of initiating penal action by just sending notices. Global investors stood as one man, put pressure on the Government and finally, the then Finance Minister, Mr.Yashwant Singh was forced to relent. The notices issued by his officials were summarily with-drawn and Mr. Sinha, of all persons, had virtually to apologise for the proper and timely action taken by his subordinates in the Finance Ministry, in such matters. Many more similar instances can be cited. But for want of time and due to time and due to constraints dictated propriety, the scribe is forced to conclude this section at this point.

Indian Financial Sector–in Prospect

We have already examined the various dimensions of the financial sector in India in the post-reforms decade. This examination in retrospect can never be claimed as exhaustive and full. But from what we have gone through so far, we have been able to gain some insight into the major ailments of the sector after its integration with the financial markets with their global counterparts. Despite the introduction of sophisticated investments and gadgets as well as electrònic trading devices, Indian financial markets still remain highly inefficient and amenable to manipulations by a handful of rogue traders and speculators. The nexus of big institutional investors, business lobbies, bankers, bureaucrats as well as opportunist and self–seeking politicians is a formidable force to manipulate financial markets to their advantage. Pitted against this powerful alliance, the small investors are always the losers. The speculative investors enter the market only where the time is ripe, that is, dark as to what is happening. And, by the time they know what the game is all about, the big and unscrupulous market operators move out and the share prices start falling steeply and the small investors end up as the only long-term players in the Indian financial markets, but with no financial gains worth the name.

Why has this state of affairs come about? It is due to frequent frauds and market manipulations which has wiped out the interests of the small investors in retail investment and equity markets. No wonder, the gap created in this way has paved the way for the smooth entry of big operators and institutional fund managers and their total domination over the entire financial sector. What we find today is this domination except, of course, for the presence of domestic institutional investors such as the UTI. And, as for the UTI, we know very well, what its present plight, is due to the frauds and irregularities committed by those at the top the then Chairman, M.P. Subramaniam, N.M. Kapur, the Excetive Director and other top bureaucrats, besides the then Finance Secretary, Ajith Kumar while sparing the then Finance Minster Yashwant Sinha. The SEBI and RBI have also been indicted. The JPC headed by Prakash Mani Tripathi which enquired into the UTI fiasco, has brought out the nexus between the notorious stock broker ketan Parekh, banks, financial institutions and corporate houses. It passes Muster how the JPC, which unanimously approved the findings of the 435 page report, decided to spare the Finance Minister who had the responsibility to keep himself informed of the happenings in his Ministry. In this respect, there is a repetition of the recommendations of the JPC report on the 1992 headed by Ram Niwas Mirdha involving big bull, the late Harshad Mehta stock brokers Hiten Dalal, Bhupen Dalal, Finance and Banking and Economic Affairs Ministry top officials like K.P. Geethakrishnan, Montek Singh Ahluwalia, S.Venkitaramanan, former Governor of RBI, V, Krishnamoorthy, former Member of Planning Commission, among others. The 1992 JPC Report had spared the then Finance Minister Dr. Manmohan Singh just as the present JPC Report has spared Yashwant Sinha. In 1992, however. Gurudas Das Gupta, the CPI MP of Rajya Sabha who was a member of the JPC had the guts and moral responsibility to publish a parallel report, "The Securities Scam—A Report to the Nation" expressing his opinion that the responsibility for the scam should be shared by all. Consequently, Dr.Manmohan Singh had at least expressed his willingness to tender his resignation. But this time, neither of these has so far been reported. The more interesting fact is that the Action Taken Report (ATR) submitted to Parliament still remains unattended. In the meantime Harshad Mehta is no more, whereas many other allegedy involved, have either retired or rehabilitated in plump posts, Montek Singh Ahluwalia having been made a Member of the Planning Commision.

The irony of the situation in the Indian financial sector is that successive governments in India have been promoting the financial casino as part of the economic reforms imposed upon by the IMF-World Bank–WTO trio. It is a fact that under the scenario created by economic reforms more than 500 FIIs have registered themselves in India. But out of this, only 5 top FIIs contribute over 40% of the total portfolio investments. Overall, their role has been mainly to orgainse frequent bull and bear runs in order to maximize their speculative gains while causing incalculable hardships to thousands of small investors. Instead of punishing the big sharks and controlling the volatile and speculative pro-pensities of the financial market operators, the successive governments whether led by the Cong(I) or the BJP, have been providing incentives for their nefarious activities. The flow of the external capital is still on the increase, with forex reserves having crossed 65 billion dollars. There reserves do not find any reflection in the productive investment sectors, but are only a shield to maintain high growth of the GDP, which is more artificial than real. Reforms were initiated with the promise that the GDP growth will be substantial so as to serve as the sheet anchor to benefit all. But since 1997-98, this measure of prosperity has not been successful. The Eighth plan target of 8% growth rate in GDP does not at all sound convincing in view of the past record. During the reform decade of 1991-2001, the average GDP growth was only 5.59% lower than the 5.62% growth rate in the preceding decade. During the Ninth Plan the overall growth rate targeted was 6.5% though the actual was lower than 5.62%. What does this trend indicate? The achievement statistics betrays the reformers' claims in this regard.

The facts and figures stated in the above paragraphs reveal the sordid state of the Indian financial sector, despite a decade of reforms. Unless some radical measures are taken, the situation will certainly worsen. Therefore, in order to prevent a bleaker future from emerging, the need of the hour is total overhaul of the entire financial and banking system, some what on the following pattern.

1. Adoption of suitable regulatory measures to prevent volatiltity in the stock markets.
2. Measures to strengthen the banking sector are essential due to the following reasons:-
   (a) The practice of private banks in lending huge amounts to traders and speculators against shares is not to be encouraged. In this respect, the worst offenders have been Global Trust Bank, Standard Chartered Grindlays Bank (formerly Stanchart Bank), and Citibank. In times of a massive stock market crashes, banks with heavy exposure to stock markets will suffer most;

   (b) This can be done by the further strengthing of the Prudential norms and regulations relating to bank lending;

   (c) There should be better coordination between the RBI and the SEBI to monitor the developments in the financial markets on a regular basis. After the initiation of the reforms process the traditional walls between the stock markets and the banking sector have broken down. The concept of 'Universal banking' which has been introduced, has also eliminated the distinction between development banks (eg. IDBI) and commercial banks (eg. SBI), besides changing the nature of the Indian capital market.

(*d*) The Non-Banking Finance Companies (NBFCs) which have become widely prevalent in the Indian financial sector, must be brought under the responsibility of the RBI in regard to supervision and surveillance.

3. The government of India must take a decision that it will no longer pursue the path of encouraging the process of transforming the entire financial system into a speculative market-based system on the pattern of European industrialised nations. In these nations banks with surplus funds at their disposal look for opportunities for investments in order to make higher returns by purchasing under-valued shares and stocks in the stock markets. Instead, the banks and financial institutions, both public and priavate, must invest in productive ventures which are of benefit to the national economy as a whole. The present policy will only promote speculation, real estate dealings and such other risky ventures with unsettling consequences for the national economy through unstable financial market conditions.

4. Financial sector management must be totally divorced from all political interference. For this managers of financial institutions must be empowered to assume risks and grant rewards in the appropriate manner. Such an arrangement has to be built into the system. Excessive politicisation has caused more harm than good.

To conclude, we must state that the first generation 'reforms' is over. The economy is said to have managed the initial 'hiccups and hurdles', if the words of official spokesmen of reform are to be believed. And, the second generation reform policy is on its way. Once this phase gathers momentum through the gradual and steady adoption of the proclaimed package of greater liberalisation and privatisation policies, the key role is to revolve round monetary policy rather than fiscal policy. Naturally, in the new scenario that will emerge, the economy is to lean almost totally on foreign savings or foreign capital. But, given the level of corruption is high places and lack of transparency in administration, weak human development index, poor infrastructure and so on, the manner in which foreign capital will be utilised, still remains a moot question. It is, therefore, time for us to pose certain pertinent questions growth for whom and at what social cost? How far is it realistic to expect and unscrupulous and profit-hungry FDI to act as over saviour? It is not time for India to re-think our soft approach towards the tempting offers of the IMF-World Bank-WTO trio working in tandem with the US Government and the MNCs?

REFERNCES

1. Abusaleh Shariff and Anil Gumber, (1991), "Employment and Wages in India" Pre and Post-Reform Scenario", Indian Journal of Labour Economics Vol.42(2).
2. Bhalla GS and G.Singh, (2000), "Indian Agriculture: four Decades of Development" Sage Publications, New Delhi.
3. Datt Gaurav, (1999), "Has Poverty Declined since Economic Reforms?" Economic and Political Weekly, December 11-17.
4. Datta KL and Savita Sharma, (2002), "Facets of Indian Poverty" concept Publishing Co. New Delhi.
5. Deaton A and Jean Dreze, (2002), "Poverty and Inequality in India: A Re-examination, "Economic and Political Weekly" September 7.
6. Gupta, SP, (1999), "Trikle Down Theory Revisited: The Role of Employment and poverty", V.B.Singh Memorial Lecture, 41st Annual Conference of the Indian Society of Labour Economics, November 18-20, Mumbai.
7. Hanumantha Rao K and K.Rajya Lakshmi, (2002)., "Structure of Employment and Causualisation in Rural India during Pre and Post-Reforms Regime", Journal of Rural Development Vol. 21 (1).

8. Hanumantha Rao K, (2000), "Changes in the structure of Employment in RuralAreas" NIRD, Hyderabad.

9. National Sample Survey Organisation, Reports Nos.461, 457, 458.

10. Sundaram, K (2001a), "Employment-Unemployment Situation in the Nineties: Some Results from NSS 55th Round Survey", Economic and Political Weekly, March 17.

11. Sundaram, K (2001b), "Employment and Poverty in 1990s" Further Results from NSS 55th Round Employment—Unemployment Survey, 1999-2000, Economic and Political Weekly, August 11.

11

Banking Sector Reforms–The Challenges Ahead

*Dr. D. Dakshina Murthy**
*Dr. B.K.S. Prakasa Rao***

Introduction

Today, the entire world is undergoing a transition. The fall of Soviet Union, the merger of East Germany with West Germany amply proves the same. Another important aspect of this transition is that, various economics in the world are moving towards capitalism either from their present Communism or Socialism. During this transition process, structural disturbances naturally take place resulting in severe losses to the economies concerned. Besides this, various countries in the world started reforms process during the late eighties. As a part of reform processes, the developed and developing nations like—USA, Canada, Japan, India opened up their economies to the market forces resulting in free flow of trade among countries. India also in tune with the global trends undertook reform processes popularly known as liberalisation, privatisation and globalisation in the early nineties. With the introduction and implementation of

* Professor & Head, Department of Management Sciences, RVR & JC College of Engineering, Guntur-522 019. Andhra Pradesh.

** Reader, Department of Management, RVR & JC College of Engineering, Guntur-522 019, Andhra Pradesh.

these reforms, the Indian Industries and in particular the Public Sector Banks (PSBs) have been witnessing keen competition from private sector banks. This paper examines some of the consequences of the banking sector reforms in India, which were an integral part of the liberalisation process of the economy initiated by the Government in 1991.

A vibrant, efficient and competitive banking system is necessary to support the structural reforms in the real economy. Over the years, the Indian Banking and the financial system has made impressive progress in terms of both geographical spread and functional reach[1].

The Eight Five Year Plan document points out, "The balance sheet of the performance of the financial sector is thus mixed, strong in achieving certain socio-economic goals and in general widening the credit coverage but weak in viability".[2]

There have been significant changes in the flow of credit to various groups and sectors within the economy, some of which might be thought not to be inconformity with the stated social goals of the Government.

Geneses of Public Sector Banks (PSBs)

The year 1969 was not just man setting foot on the moon, it was also the year Indira Gandhi nationalised 14 private sector banks in July and it is a historic and momentous event in the history of India.[3] Prior to that, most banks like Central Bank (owned by Tatas,) United Commercial Bank (Birlas) and Syndicate Bank (Pais) were owned and managed by business houses. The only exception was the State Bank of India, known as Imperial Bank of India before 1955, this had been nationalised in July 1955 under the SBI Act of 1955.Nationalisation was resorted to on the ground that the commercial banking system often ignored the Government's focus area, agriculture and small scale industries.[4] That neglect was one reason for the nationalisation of banks and also Indira Gandhi's desire to spread the banking habit in rural and semi-urban areas, freeing farmers from the clutches of usurious money lenders. In 1980 again the Government took over another six commercial banks- altogether 20 nationalised banks excluding SBI and its seven associate banks. At present 27 banks (19 PSBs, SBI and 7 SBI Associate Banks) are existing in India.

Post-Nationalisation of Indian Banking up to Reforms

Today banks cater to the entire mass of the Indian population, offering them diverse service. No wonder, banks now constitute the largest chunk of the service industry. In post-nationalisation era, banks have ceased to be the institution of the privileged. They have become truly broad based with their customer profile ranging from a multimillionaire industrialist on the one end of the spectrum to a humble farmer, vegetable vendor or a small garage owner at the other.

Rapid economic development pre-supposes tremendous expansion of commercial banks. Initially the banks were conservative and opened branches mainly in metropolitan cities and other major cities. Branch expansion gained momentum after the nationalisation of major commercial banks and the introduction of the lead bank scheme. Table-1 presents the progress of branch expansion, deposit mobilisation, bank credit and credit deposit ratio.

Table:1 Progress of Banking (1969, 1990-91 to 2000-01)

As on 31st March	*Total No. of Branches*	*Rural Branches*	*Rural branches as % of total*	*Bank deposits*	*Bank credit*	*Credit Deposit ratio*
1969	8187	1443	17.6	4822	3467	
1990-91	60597	35216	58.1	219539	133745	

From Table 1 it is clear that in a matter of 22 years after bank nationalisation, there was 740 percent increase in number of branches, the most spectacular progress was in rural areas i.e. about 2440 percent increase. M. Gopalakrishnan, a Professional Banker states, "The single striking feature of the post-nationalisation banking scene is the rapidity with which the branch network has multiplied itself. The rate of branch expansion has been unparalleled anywhere else in the world.[6]

Since 1969 deposit mobilisation and supply of credit by banks were growing at a rapid rate. 22 years after the bank nationalisation bank deposit had increased by 46 times i.e. from Rs.4822 crore in 1969 to over Rs. 219539 crore in 1990-91 and the same trend was noticed with bank credit also i.e. around 39 times.

Banking Sector Reforms—A Backdrop

India had witnessed a phenomenal expansion in the geographical coverage and functional spread over banking and financial system since bank nationalisation 1969 and 1980. Despite impressive quantitative achievements in resource mobilisation and in extending the credit reach, several distortions had, over the years, crept into the banking and financial system. As a result, productivity and efficiency of the system had suffered; its portfolio quality had badly deteriorated and profitability had been eroded. Several public sector banks have been incurring losses year after year due to many reasons.

Indian banks are obliged to satisfy the cash reserve ratio (CRR) and the statutory liquidity ratio (SLR). The CRR requires the banks to hold part of their deposits in the form of cash balances with the Central Bank, the RBI. In the 1950s and 1960s the CRR was around 5 percent but thereafter it progressively increased. In early 1991, the CRR stood at its legal upper limit for 15 percent. In 1991, there was an incremental CRR of 10 percent in addition to the average CRR of 15 percent. While all banking systems in the world stipulate some reserves for prudential purposes, they are less than 8 percent in developing countries taken as a whole and only 2-3 percent of deposits in the developed countries. The SLR stipulates the proportion of deposits that banks must hold in the form of Government and other approved securities. The SLR steadily increased upwards, the statutory upper limit being 40 percent. Thus, in 1991, a staggering 63.5 percent of bank deposits were compulsorily impounded by the RBI. Both the impounded cash balances and the government securities earned considerable advances. After the banks had satisfied the SLR and CRR requirements, they were obliged to lend around 40 percent of the remaining funds to priority sectors comprising agriculture, small scale industries and weaker sections of the society. In addition, there were sub-targets for each of the sub groups- 18 percent of the credit for agriculture and 10 percent for weaker sections. The priority sector loans were given at concessional rates of interest.

In India, the financial sector, particularly banking, was the only organised sector, how-so-ever weak, it may have been, in terms of economic base and financial structure. It therefore became backbone in the strategy of growth, rather than being a follower of growth. In the process, the autonomy and profitability of the banking system seriously compromised and importantly, rather than acting as a conduct of intermediation, the banking system acted as the 'engine ' as opposed to being the 'wheel' of economic growth. These shortcomings, coupled with the crisis of 1990s forced reckoning of the imperative for financial sector strengthening. India faced a serious economic crisis in 1991. There was a steep fall in the country's foreign exchange reserves to about $ 1 billion, equal to the value of only two week's imports. There was a large fiscal deficit close to 10 percent of GDP and an unsustainable external balance with current account deficit at 3 percent of GDP.

In tune with the changes in economic policies and with the implementation of financial sector reforms, the banking sector in India has undergone a sea change over the last ten years.

The landmarks in banking reforms were the introduction of prudential norms, partial deregulation of interest rates, reduction in directed lending, SLR and CRR and also the entry of private sector banks. The recommendations of the Narasimham Committee-1 in 1991 provided the printblue for the first generation reforms of the financial sector. The period 1992-97 witnessed the laying of the foundations for reforms in the banking system.[7] The initial reforms in 1992-93 aimed at bringing in transparency in banking system. Introduced in April 1992, the prudential norms involved a new look at asset classification, income recognition, provisioning of bad debts, capital adequacy etc. Income is now viewed in terms of realisation rather than on accrual basis.

Progress of Banking Sector in Post-Reforms Period 1991-2001

The major recommendations of Narasimham Committee are accepted and implementation was started straight away by the Government, inspite of stiff opposition from bank unions and political parties in the country. Some of them were implemented in a phased manner i.e., reduction in CRR and SLR, setting up on new private sector banks and deregulation of interest rates and others.

Bank deposit mobilisation and expansion of credit were growing at a high rate. For instance, since the last three decades after bank nationalisation, bank deposits had increased by about 178 times and bank credit increased by around 120 time. The number of branches were continuously increased up to 1991-92. The share of rural branches as percentage of total branches has declined from 58.1 percent in 1990-91 to 1999-2000. The following Table provides the No. of branches, rural branches, bank deposits, bank credit and credit deposit ratio.

Table 2: Progress of Banking (1969, 1990-91, to 2000-01)

As on 31st March	*Total No. of Branches*	*Rural Branches*	*Rural Branches as % of total*	*Bank deposits*	*Bank Credit*	*Credit Deposit ratio*
1969	8187	1443	17.6	4822	3467	0.72
1990-91	60597	35216	58.1	219539	133745	0.61
1991-92	60690	35218	58.0	233086	142211	0.61
1992-93	61235	35301	57.6	27068	165836	0.61
1993-94	61852	35379	57.2	317918	180017	0.57
1994-95	62264	35008	56.2	375864	222507	0.59
1995-96	62849	33092	52.7	426073	263533	0.62
1996-97	63534	33008	52.0	492227	282237	0.57
1997-98	64267	32890	51.2	592068	328637	0.56
1998-99	65118	32856	50.5	7011871	389460	0.55
1999-2000	65521	32719	49.9	822133	469032	0.57
2000-01	–	–	–	859380	414630	0.48

Source: RBI Website on Report on Trend and Progress of Banking in India.

The reserve pre-emotions have been gradually brought down to boost profitability of banks. The CRR, which was 15 percent in 1991-92 has been gradually reduced over the years and was at 11 percent in August, 1998, and it was further reduced to 5 percent from 15th June, 2002 onwards. The base SLR, which stood at 38.5 percent in 1991-92 has been reduced to a statutory level of 25 percent, which is the minimum stipulated under the Banking Regulation Act 1949. The following Table gives the movement of CRR and SLE. The RBI has been pursuing its medium term objective of reducing CRR to the statutory minimum level of 3 percent.

Table 3: Movement of CRR & SLR

Period	*CRR*	*SLR*
1990-91	15	38.5
Aug.1998	11	25
March, 1999	09	25
March,2001	08	25
May,2001	7.5	25
October,2001	5.5	25
June,2002	5.0	25

Source: RBI Website on Report on Trend and Progress of Banking of India.

While the pre-emption of inevitable funds in common among the banking systems, the rates have been comparatively higher in India. Nevertheless, the reduction have been reduced to the levels recommended by the Narasimham Committee. To ensure the level playing field among the players in the banking sector the branch expansion norms were issued by RBI. In April 1992, branch licensing policy was liberalised, giving freedom to banks to set up specialised branches, and relocate or spin off branches.

As per the Basle Committee norms, the internationally accepted prudential norms relating to income recognition, asset classification, provisioning and capital adequacy have been introduced by the commercial banks. The commercial banks should maintain a capital to risky assets ratio. (CRAR = Capital + Reserves ÷ Risk Weighted Assets x 100) of not less than 8 percent. Very few banks in India had a capital adequacy ratio of 8 percent prior to 1991. By March 2001, out of 27 public sector banks, as many as 25 had CRAR exceeded the stipulated minimum of 9 percent, only two PSBs had CRAR below the stipulated minimum, but they accounted for 4.3 percent of total assets of PSBs at the end of March, 2001. Accordingly, the RBI has revised the CRAR upwards and

Table 4: Performance of Public Sector Banks(%)

As on March 31st	*Gross Profit/ loss as % of total assets*	*Net profit/ loss as % of total assets*	*Interest Income as % of total assets*	*Net interest income(spread) as % of total assets*	*Provisions and contingencies as % of total assets*	*Interest expense as % of total assets*
1991-92	1.84	0.28	10.18	3.22	1.57	6.96
1992-93	0.94	-0.99	9.55	2.39	1.92	7.16
1993-94	0.99	-1.15	8.56	2.36	2.14	6.20
1994-95	1.41	0.25	8.61	2.92	1.16	5.69
1995-96	1.49	-0.07	9.20	3.08	1.56	6.12
1996-97	1.60	0.57	9.69	3.16	1.03	6.53
1997-98	1.58	0.77	9.10	2.91	0.81	6.19
1998-99	1.37	0.42	9.01	2.80	0.95	6.21
1999-00	1.46	0.57	8.92	2.70	0.89	6.22
2000-01	1.34	0.42	8.84	2.84	0.92	5.99

Source: RBI Website on Report on Trend and Progress of Banking of India.

the banks have to achieve a minimum capital adequacy ratio of 9 percent by March, 2001 an d10 percent by 2002.

The New Capital Accord was released by the Basle Committee on Banking Supervision (BCBS) in January, 2001, which is expected to be more sensitive to the level of underlying economic risks.

The New Capital Accord rests on three major points, the first one sets out the minimum capital requirements, the second one of supervisory review process and the third one of market discipline.[8]

RBI announces detailed guidelines on asset classification from time to time. In the earlier guidelines, on asset was classified as NPA if the amounts due in the account remained past due for more than two quarters. It was clarified on December 17, 1992 that an account should be considered past due when it remains outstanding for 30 days beyond the due date.Due to the improvements in the payment and settlement system, recovery climate, up-gradation for technology in the banking system etc, it was decided to dispose with past due concept, with effect from March, 31, 2001. Accordingly, with effect from that date, an advance has to be classified as NPA, if interest and/ or installment of principle remain overdue for a period of more than 180 days in respect of a term loan, and the account remains out of order for a period of more than 180 days with respect to an overdraft/cash credit (OD/CC).

The present day situation regarding gross NPAs of the 27 PSBs shot up to Rs. 54,773 crore in September, 2001. This staggering number not only reduces the yield on advances but also has an advance impact on the profitability of banks. The stratagem of using Debt Recovery Tribunals recovers dues has failed miserably.[10] The root problem is that here is a sizeable overhang component arising from the weak debt recovery processes, inadequate legal structure, weakness in underlying security, inadequate risk management techniques etc.[11] The following Table provides NPA of PSBs during 1993 and 2001.

Table 5: Gross and Net NPs of Public Sector Banks during 1993-2001

Year	*Amount*	*% to gross advances*	*% to total assets*	*Amount*	*% to gross advances*	*% to total assets*
1993	392253	23.2	11.8	–	–	–
1994	41041	24.8	10.8	–	–	–
1995	38385	19.5	8.7	17567	10.7	4.0
1996	41661	18.0	8.2	18297	8.9	3.6
1997	43577	17.8	7.8	20285	9.2	3.6
1998	45653	16.0	7.0	21,232	8.2	3.3
1999	51710	15.9	6.7	24211	8.1	3.1
2000	53033	14.0	6.0	26187	7.4	2.9
2001	54773	12.4	5.3	27969	6.7	2.7

Source: RBI Website on Report on Trend and Progress of Banking of India.

The quantum of gross as well as Net NPAs are continuously increasing from Rs.39,253 crore in 1993 to Rs. 54, 773 crore in 2001 and from Rs. 17, 567 crore in 1995 to Rs. 27,969 crore in 2001, respectively. The gross NPAs as a percentage of advances of PSBs declined from 23.2 percent in 1993 to 12.4 percent in 2001. The Net NPAs and percent of net advances also declined from 10.7 percent in 1995 to 6.7 percent in 2001. The net NPAs to total assets declined from 4.0 percent in 1995 to 2.7 percent in 2001.

Broadly, all non-performing assets (NPAs) can be categorized as loans to agricultural sector, directed lending, loans to small enterprises and loans to corporate sector. Many of the directed loans are subsistence loans, where default rates are high and recovery prospects not bright. In case of loans to agricultural borrowers, legal impediments often prove to be a challenging proposition for banks to recover their dues. Loans to small enterprise become difficult to recover due to in ordinate judicial delays. As regards corporate loans, suits pending/referred to Board for Industrial and Financial Reconstruction leaves little headroom for banks to effect recovery.

The NPAs movement in 27 PSBs ranges between 1.98 percent in Corporation Bank and 18.37 percent of advances in Dena Bank. The gross NPAs as well as net NPAs are continuously increasing in absolute terms. While the gross and net NPAs as percentage of gross advances and net advances in relative terms declined from 16 percent to 12.4 percent and 8.2 percent to 6.7 percent. Further, reduction is quite possible with the help of new ordinance – securitisation and reconstruction of financial assets and enforcement of security interest, which was issued on June 21, 2002 may make bankers life easier and change the way he does business. The new ordinance allows secured lender to sell or lease assets which are charged with them by defaulting borrower without a protracted legal tussle.

New Private Banks

RBI announces norms for setting up new banks in the private sector in January,1993, governing the entry of new private banks—a minimum paid up capital of Rs. 100 crore among others. This was the first time, following the nationalisation of banks in 1969. At present eight new private banks that have emerged on the Indian financial topography since 1993 are clear outperformers in an otherwise troubled sector. In eight year, these banks have grown to account for six percent of the total assets and 10 percent of the total profits of the banking industry.

Mergers and Acquisitions in the Banking Sector

The banking system in many emerging economics in terms of the number and size of institutions, ownership, profitability and competitiveness of banks, use of modern technology and other related structural features. In view of the global phenomenon of consolidation and convergence, the Narasimham Committee, 1991 had suggested a substantial reduction in the number of banks, both in the public and private sector through mergers and acquisitions. The phenomenon of mergers in the banking sector is a relatively recent one in India. The following Table presents the number of mergers in the banking sector in India since 1990.

Table 6: Mergers in Banking Sector in India: 1990-2001

Name of the merging bank	*Date of merger*	*Name of the merged bank*
Purbachal Bank	1990	Central Bank of India
New Bank of India	1993	Punjab National Bank
BCCI	1993	SBI
Bank of Karad	1994	Bank of India
Kashinath Seth Bank	1995	SBI
Bari Doab Bank	1997	Oriental Bank of Commerce
Punjab Cooperative Bank	1997	-do-
20th Century Finance	1998	Centurion Bank
Bareily Corporation Bank	1999	Bank of India
Sikkim Bank	1999	Union Bank of India
Times Bank	2000	HDFC (Bank)
Bank of Madura	2001	ICICI Bank

Source: Website RBI—Trends and Progress in Banking.

Mergers and Acquisitions alone would not give much benefit to the Banking industry. What is important is that the system for internal controls and risk management are put in place in order to take speedy decisions for offering a wide range of products through multiply delivery channels. The success of consolidation efforts will depend on how effectively the banking industry is able to put in place firewalls against financial crisis, while blending risks with returns.

Voluntary Retirement Scheme

As per the recommendations of the Narasimham Committee, the banks have the authority of redeployment of staff, cut in operating cost and reduction of manpower. It is estimated that, out of the 8.83 lakh employees in 27 Public Sector Banks, 2.5 lakh are surplus. The Federation of Indian Chambers of Commerce and Industry, said that the banking industry was over staffed by 25 percent. The Governments own estimate put the figure at around 30 percent. Faced with the problem of surplus manpower resources, several public sector banks introduced a voluntary retirement scheme(VRS) as a measure of cost reduction. The scheme brought to the fore certain accounting issues relating to booking of VRS, related expenditure such as ex-gratia payment and other terminal benefits. Consequently, the accounting treatment of VRS expenditure was specified in consultation with the Institute of Chartered Accountants of India (ICAI). In particular, the banks were advised that unless expenses are in the same period, the entire ex-gratia amount as a result of VRS could be treated as an extra-ordinary item and as Deferred Revenue Expenditure (DRE) and in view of the extra-ordinary nature of the event, VRS related DRE would not be reduced from tier I capital. The banks are required to disclose in the balance sheet the accounting policies followed in respect of VRS expenditure. The DRE would be restricted to a maximum of 5 years.

Round one VRS has led to major benefits for the bank's balance sheet. For instance a study of Business India finds that employee's costs in banks have largely fallen after VRS. The highest reduction in employee's cost was shown in 2001-02 by Dena Bank, which clocked a 25.76percent in such costs, with the outgo declining to Rs.322.57 crore from Rs.434.50 crore in 2000-01. The next steep fall came from Bank of Maharastra, which recorded a 20.77 percent decline. The third slot was taken by Bank of India, which saw a 19 percent and SBI showed a healthy decline of 14.29 percent in employee costs.

Table 7: VRS in Public Sector Banks

Name of bank	*Total Strength*	*VRS opts*	*%*
State Bank of India	237504	35380	14.90
State Bank of Travancore	13137	920	7.00
State Bank of Bknr & Jaipur	14400	1250	8.68
State Bank of Mysore	9163	17675	19.26
State Bank of Indore	680	706	10.38
State Bank of Hyderabad	14766	2798	18.95
State Bank of Saurashtra	10300	1130	10.97
State Bank of Patiala	13200	1185	8.98
Allahabad Bank	22345	1571	7.03
Andhra Bank	14603	1793	12.28
Bank of Baroda	47054	6762	14.37
Bank of India	51962	7600	14.63
Bank of Maharastra	16908	2797	17.37
Central Bank	55464	8566	15.44
Central Bank	48260	8500	17.61
Corporation Bank	10162	–	–
Dena Bank	14546	3534	24.30
Indian Bank	25935	3988	15.38
Indian Overseas Bank	28347	3988	14.07
Oriental Bank	14398	640	4.45
Punjab National Bank	65705	5800	8.83
Punjab & Sind Bank	12192	2072	16.99
Syndicate Bank	33883	7157	21.12
UCO Bank	31223	5479	17.55
Union Bank of India	30834	4321	14.01
United Bank of India	21757	2800	12.87
Vijaya Bank	14420	1582	17.91
Total	**878478**	**125084**	**14.24**

While some bankers agree that it is difficult to arrive at a direct relation between a decline in employee costs and an in increase in profitability, they concede that the fallout of VRS had a major role in the higher profits posted by a number of banks. For example, A Bank recorded a hefty 104 percent jump in net profit, making a huge turn around from a loss of Rs.266.12 crore to a profit of Rs.11.36 crore in 2001-02. Bank of Maharastra, on the other hand recorded a steep rise in net profits, which grew 222 percent, while SBIs was up by 52 percent.

Conclusions

Many people have different opinions on the reforms process in India. Why are reforms in India so halting and hesitant? GDP growth has decelerated from 6.7 % annually in 1992-2002. The weak and worsening economic performance since 1997 must raise the question in some minds; Do the reforms have some lasting damage to the growth process? To syncopate, the reform process cannot be entirely painless. While there are achievements, there are pitfalls as well. First, there have been an increase in the ratio of deposits to national income in the post-reform period. Second, there has occurred a structural break in the movements of bank deposits, bank credit and bank investments in the rate of growth of both bank deposits the pre-reform period. There has been an increase in the rate of growth of bank credit. The third, the banks have invested in government securities a much larger portion of their deposits than is warranted by the prescribed SLR. This has mainly been due to the persistently large budget deficits run by the Central and State Government. There is no doubt that the reform of the banking system has not been accompanied by a decline in government borrowings rather a substantial increase. Large public sector deficits, in general, tend to be in compatible with financial liberalisation and development. Commenting on the emergence of the banks preference for government securities, the RBI in its Report on the trend and progress of banking in India for 1996-97, noted that assets. The deregulated environment has not resulted in any marked improvements in the efficiency of PSBs with the exception of a few. Government and political interference in the decision making of banks are the problems that plague the PSBs. Bailouts and recapitalisations by Government have become incentives for inefficiency. Further, the proposed gradual increase in capital adequacy ratio of 10 percent by the year 2002 may compel some banks to raise additional money. The available option is raising funds enroute capital market. Absence of functional autonomy and freedom to attract professional talent continue to remain with their adverse impact on the banking sector. Transparency of prudential norms in banks financial reporting is still a far cry. Multiplicity and incompatibility o flaws compound the inefficiency of the banking system. Until these problems are solved, Indian Banking Sector continues to remain a specimen of shackled liberalisation.

REFERENCE

1. Misra S.K. and Puri V.K.(2000) Economic Environment of Business, Himalaya Publishing House.
2. Eighth Five Year Plan—1992-97, Volume–1, p. 89.
3. Ashish Gupta, Business Today, Tenth Anniversary Issue, Jan. 2002.
4. Ruddar Datt and Sundaram, Indian Economy, Millennium Edition, 2000. S.Chand & Co. Ltd., New Delhi, p. 765.
5. Basu. M.G. Facts For You, June, 1999. p. 35.
6. M.Gopalakrishnan in the Hindu, Survey of India, 1989.
7. Rangarajan, C,1998, Banking Sector Reforms; Rationale and Relevance, SICOM. Silver Jubilee Memorial Lecture, Mumbai.
8. Basel Committee on Banking Supervision (2001), RBI Annual Report, 2001.
9. Monitory and Credit Policy for the year 2001-2002, RBI Report.
10. Ashish Gupta, Business Today, Anniversary Issue. 2002, p. 88.

11. M.G. Bhide, A. Prasad, Saibal Ghosh, Economic and Political Weekly, Feb. 2002, p. 403.

12. Hawkins, J. and P. Tumer (1999) Bank Restructuring in Practice.

13. Dabir Sign, (Chairman, IBA & CMD, Central Bank) Business India, July 22-Aug 4, 2002.

12

Indian Banking Sector Reforms: An Appraisal

*Dr. Noor Basha Abdul**

The banking sector reforms were started in India in 1992 as a part of liberalisation of Indian economy, with an intent of providing "a vibrant, diversified and competitive financial system"[1]. Besides, the Narasimham Committee, also added that these reforms in the banking sector would "better serve the emerging needs of the real economy in which the spirit of competitive efficiency is being ignited". The Narasimham Committee in fact had set the stage for far-reaching changes in the financial system, by making several key recommendations relevant to monetary management; including reduction of statutory reserve requirements, regulation of interest rates, cutting down directed lending, promoting competitiveness, etc.

No doubt, the deregulation and liberalisation have opened up new opportunities for the Indian banks, but at the same time, the pressures of competition from the foreign banks have led to the narrowing spreads, shrinking margins, down sizing of the manpower, and consolidation and restructuring. In this process, banks are led to focus on core competencies, synerging strength and shedding activities like directed credit and subsidies and swapping

* Dr. Noor Basha Abdul, M.Com., Ph.D., Professor of Commerce, Special Officer, NUPG Centre, Ongole.

of branch offices that are not remunerative[2]. However, several prominent studies have observed that the Indian financial sector reforms have failed in achieving their goal of making the banking sector more vibrant and efficient.[3] For instance, there has been a hardening of interest rates instead of the cheaper credit that was promised and the privatisation and the VRS have also not yielded back the desired results. The banks during the post-reforms period were also observed to have undermined the sector's social commitments.[4] A few such implications of the reforms that were proved neither useful to banks nor to the general customers and people at large are discussed here under.

Privatisation of PSBs and Myth of Healthy Competition

With the passing, in the Parliament, of the Banking Companies Bill, a couple of years back, the stage is all set for privatisation of the nationalised banks. Of course, the Government has maintained that it holds atleast 33 percent stake in the banks and thus, the public sector character of the banks will remain and the Government retains the right to appoint the top management.

The hollowness and the unfairly contradictory dimension of this Government's story, however, has now come out in true colours. For instance, once their stake falls below 50 percent and they are brought under the purview of Companies Act, from the existing Banking Companies Act. the banks would automatically lose their public sector character. The intention of the Government therefore, is clearly of privatisation. Further, even though the maximum holdings of shares with an individual corporate does not exceed one percent, for the purpose of voting rights, the individuals/corporates can accumulate shares at the time of public issue in anticipation of privatisation further. All this pruning down is only meant for facilitating the free entry of foreign banks into the Indian banking industry.

Similarly one of the widely publicised purposes of the banking sector reforms was to introduce a healthy competition among the banks. However, according to several critical studies, the experiences are proved totally different. For instance, if the banks are thrown open to fair competition from stronger banks both from within or outside the country, they might trigger a systemic crisis as they would surrender profitable avenues to their superior competitors. To force them to raise capital to the viable is risky when profits are down. If they reduce credit, especially when the real economy is on a downward slope, the recession may be aggravated. On the other hand, if banks are allowed to continue in competition with stronger banks, they would be tempted to follow unsound banking practices[5].

However, competition has been infused in the Indian banking industry by allowing new private sector banks and more liberal entry of foreign banks. As at the end of March, 2001, there were 8 new private sector banks such as ICICI Bank Ltd., HDFC Bank Ltd., and UTI Bank Ltd., 23 old private sectors banks besides 42 foreign banks working in India. Besides, measures have also been taken to broaden the ownership base of the PSBs, Consequently, the private share holding in PSBs has gone up, ranging from 23 percent in Bank of India to 43.7 percent in State Bank of India[6].

The entry of New Private Sector Banks (NPSBs) and the foreign banks have ushered in more competitiveness in the banking industry. The foreign banks have been opening more branches. They have got at their command the systems, both technical and operational, to be put to the best and stand to the times. The birth of NPSBs in the era of deregulation in the banking system has changed the context and the way the bankers do the business of banking. The public sector banks are working in-conditioned atmosphere. The autonomy and the freedom of management has enabled them to strip their excess fat and trim to size[7].

Public sector banks long seen as unchallengeable, are slowly but surely losing out to the more aggressive new private sector banks which have increased their market share during the year ending March, 31, 2000. The profitability of the new banks also remains the highest. The net profit margin of these banks improved to 10.5 percent from 9.7 percent in 1998-99. While the margin of PSU banks improved to 5.62 percent from 4.12 percent, the net margin of foreign banks increased to 9.32 percent (6.07 percent) while that of old private banks was at 7.48 percent (4.26 percent)[8].

They are at different stages of technology adoption partly due to their different legacies as much as the differences in their strategic approaches to computerisation and technology absorption. With increasing competition as well as changes in the regulatory environment, the gap may narrow in the coming years. The agenda for the different constituents will vary due to organisational differences, the spread and nature of operations. A look at some of the indicators of banking operations of these segments in the banking industry reveals the highest growth rates in deposits, advances, and net profits of the PVSBs reflecting amongst other things aggressive customer centric policies and adoption of technology driven solutions.[9] All this indicates, that the Indian Public Sector Banks could not to gain in competition against the private and foreign banks in the deregulated environment. Moreover, it is not wise to make a comparison between the public sector banks with wider branch network including in the rural areas and the foreign banks with only a few urban branches.

Voluntary Retirement Scheme (VRS)

The announcement of VRS in Indian Banking industry was backed by the Government strong intention of making the PSBs slim before they are put for sale/privatisation. Following the recommendations of the Narasimham

Committee, on the need for pruning down the operating losses, all public sector banks, except Corporation Bank, have carried out VRS between November 15, 2000 and March, 31, 2001. Out of the total 8,63,117 employees in the 26 public sector banks, around 1,00,810 (11.7 percent) employees opted and took the offer before March, 2001. Consequently all the 26 Public Sector Banks had to pay an unreasonably hefty amount of Rs.7,500 crore for VRS optees. For the State Bank of India alone, the cost of VRS had exceeded Rs.2,000 crore[10]. Table 1 presents a bank-wise implementation of VRS by March, 2002.

The VRS being offered by the public sector banks has left many employees and customers disgruntled and disappointed. The banks had to face an abrupt pressure on their cash resources and liquidity for the heavy payments towards VRS package, which has strained the cash position of the banks, and their profitability. Mr. V.K. Chopra, Executive Director, Oriental Bank of Commerce while commenting this resultant financial load as the first challenge for the banks, had cautioned that its impact on the Capital Adequacy Ratio will have to be kept under watch[11].

Another significant challenge that surfaced during the post—VRS period was some imbalance in staff availability in certain regions or in certain categories of staff. For instance, in the case of State Bank of India, which had shed down 20,784 staff including 6,694 officers and 11,271 clerical staff, the banks managerial staff had to share some clerical functions, which led to inordinate delay in the clearance process, thus impairing on the efficiency of the bank as a whole[12]. The impact of manpower reduction has been strictly heavy during the post-VRS scenario, especially in the light of the fact that most of the banks functions had not been automated or computerised.

The SBI also faced flak not only for customer service but also for interest lost on money transferred from various

Table 1: VRS in Public Sector Banks

Banks	*Number of Applications*	
	Received Under VRS	*Accepted Under VRS*
State Bank of India	35,380	20,784
Associates of SBI		
State Bank of Bikaner & Jaipur	2,044	1,231
State Bank of Hyderabad	2,566	1,545
State Bank of Indore	819	359
State Bank of Mysore	1,829	1,374
State Bank of Patiala	1,199	925
State Bank of Saurashtra	1,183	965
State Bank of Travancore	1,069	915
Total of SBI and associates	46,089	28,098
Nationalised Banks		
Allahabad Bank	1,503	1,503
Andhra Bank	1,797	1,602
Bank of Baroda	6,731	6,547
Bank of India	7,768	7,619
Bank of Maharashtra	2,683	1,876
Canara Bank	8,609	7,754
Central Bank of India	8,510	7,459
Dena Bank	3,534	3,534
Indian Bank	4,005	3,295
Indian Overseas Bank	3,992	3,404
Oriental Bank of Commerce	803	744
Punjab & Sind Bank	2,073	1,970
Punjab National Bank	6,095	5,923
Syndicate Bank	7,166	6,409
UCO Bank	5,484	4,865
Union Bank of India	4,303	4,037
United Bank of India	3,007	2,599
Vijaya Bank	2,581	2,526
Total of 18 Nationalised Banks	80,644	73,666
Total of 26 PSBS	**1,26,733**	**1,01,764**

branches as delays in remittance of cash snow- balled to over five days with the banks too understaffed to clear transactions in time. In normal cases, the transfer of money takes place on the same day or the next day. The VRS in banks has definitely resulted in disproportionate downsizing of staff, regional imbalances in the staff, rise in the work load of the existing staff and frustration among the staff.

Thus the VRS, though was being trumpeted as a major achievement, the whole process seems to be driven less by a strategic assessment of long-term manpower requirements than by a compulsion to slash numbers in the immediate future for making the privatisation bid charming and successful.[13]

Prudential Reserves Mars Efficiency

The commercial banks have been stipulated to maintain liquidity reserves under CRR and SLR for prudential purposes. These reserves have steeped up to an unreasonably huge levels – though during the reforms period were brought down considerably – which are being utilised for wrong priorities mostly at the cost of priority sectors and the efficiency of the banking industry.

While the reserves meant for prudential purposes averaged below 8 percent in the developing countries and only 2-3 percent of the deposits in the developed countries, in India the reserve peaked to 61.5 percent in 1991, which is now rightly reduced to half of it. It is however discomforting to note that while these reserves are meant to ensure safety and liquidity of the banks, these were used as a means to finance huge deficits and other credit needs of the public sector at subsidised interest rates[14].

According to the latest Annual Report of the RBI, banks are investing heavily in Government securities although the demand for credit has picked up from industrial and other borrowers. One of the main reasons why banks continue to invest heavily in Government securities is the RBI stipulated norm of at least 9 percent capital adequacy ratio to be achieved by 2000 AD. In other words, banks are supposed to raise their capital base by 9 percent with every Rs.100 lending, whereas similar need does not arise in the case of investments in Government securities[15]. This practice of banks has led to hampering their profitability and thereby the capacity to serve the people in general.

Decline of Credit to Agriculture

The main concern of the Narasimham Committee was the decline in productivity and efficiency of the financial services industry, and it identifies the directed investments and credit programmes, as well as rapid branch expansion as the major responsible factors. A clearly defined objective for the financial sector in the report is competitive efficiency and it is with this in mind that distortions in allocation of resources are to be removed and profitability as well as portfolio quality of the banking system are to be restored. Within the framework of competitive efficiency, the report argues that the expansion of priority sector lending since its introduction in the post-nationalisation phase has had its effects upon drastic increases in borrower accounts with adverse consequences for bank's incomes through concessional interest rates and high administrative costs of such loans[16].

There have also been changes in the sectoral flow of credit, following the introduction of reforms. Table 2 captures the period-wise trend in the share and rate of growth of bank credit in the three broad economic sectors, viz., agriculture, industry and tertiary. During the 1970s, the agricultural and tertiary sectors witnessed higher rates of growth of bank credit than the industrial sector. However, during 1990s, the rate of growth of credit to both agricultural and tertiary sectors has considerably slowed down. There has also been a decline in the rate of growth of credit to the industrial sector during this period, but this is still higher at 5.8 percent than the total credit expansion at 4.9 percent.

Table 2: Sectoral Share and Rate of Growth of Bank Credit

Period	*Agriculture*		*Industry*		*Tertiary Sector*		*Total Bank Credit*
	Share in total Credit	*Average Annual Rate of Growth*	*Share in Total Credit*	*Average Annual Rate of Growth*	*Share in Total Credit*	*Average Annual Rate of Growth*	*Rate of Growth*
1972-79	9.1	15	45.2	5.8	43.9	18	11.7
1980-89	13.3	9.8	35.9	7.2	50.8	6.5	7.2
1990-99	12.4	0.5	46.7	5.7	40.9	1.8	3.4
1992-99	11.8	1.2	46.9	5.8	41.3	4.9	4.9*
1992-99	11.8	6.6	42.9	6.1	45.3	7.8	6.8

Note: The growth rate comes down to 1.5 percent for 1992-99, if we omit the abnormal rise of 28.5 percent in 1995.
Source: RBI, Statistical Tables Relating to Banks in India.

So far as the share of agriculture in the total bank credit is concerned, it was rising with fluctuations, until 1990, when it reached a high level of 15 percent. Thereafter, there has been a steady decline and the share reached a low of 10.6 percent in 1998. This has to be seen against the background that, under the priority sector lending, a share of 16 percent of the total net bank credit has been prescribed as mandatory lending to the agricultural sector. So far as the tertiary sector is concerned, its share in the total bank credit reached an average of 51 percent in the 1980s, but registered a declining trend in the 1990s, with the average for 1992-99 being 41.3 percent. By contrast, the share of the industrial sector in the total bank credit which declined from 45.2 percent in the 1970s, to 35.9 percent in the 1980s, has registered a sharp rise to 47 percent in the post-reform period. Thus, while the overall rate of growth of bank credit has slowed down in the post-reform period, the contraction has been felt mainly in the agriculture and tertiary sectors; the industrial sector has been relatively immune from the impact of the decline in the rate of credit expansion. The reason for an industrial sector getting a larger share of the bank credit in the post-reform period has to do with the bank's perception that the loans to the industrial sector are less risky than those to the agricultural and tertiary sectors.[17]

In the post-reform period, ceiling of short term credit to be considered under priority sector has been increased to Rs.1 lakh. Demand for crop loan by small and marginal farmers is definitely not of this order. There will, therefore, be a tendency to move away from small and marginal farmers with regard to crop loans as fewer accounts can service higher amount of loan.

In this category of direct advances to agriculture, new acquisition of jeeps, pick-up vans, mini buses, etc., have been included. These will again definitely not be acquired by small and marginal farmers. Secondly, these vehicles are not used for transporting agricultural produces to improve their marketability and hence production level. This is only going to help the affluent farmers in diversifying their activities to non-farm activities. Even the absentee land owners and non-serious farmers will be found eligible for credit for such purposes under agricultural loan. Less attention will be paid to the agricultural affairs. At the same time because of social value, they will not like to sell their lands. As a result agricultural production is going to suffer.[18]

Conclusion

The excess SLR investments offer a good opportunity to banks to widen the investor base. The banks should encourage average investors to invest in Government

Securities rather than add to the deposit base of the banks. They can use this technique to augment their fee base incomes. Banks can provide depository services in respect of the average investor's holding of government securities. They can also earn suitable commission on each sale and repurchase of Government securities by the investor, so that the average investor enjoys liquidity for his investment while at the same time earning a return that would be higher than what he currently earns on bank deposits. It is of particular advantage to both the depositors and the bank to convert the long term deposits into investments in government securities. Banks could also minimise their asset liability management problem through this mode.

After examining the existing evidence on the costs and benefits of priority sector lending in India, it has been argued here that credit policy in this regard needs to be re-appraised and geared towards more specific objectives. These objectives could be defined locally on the basis of a bank-industry exchange that could guide the banks as to which firms or industries are to be financed. Lending to agriculture in general and to the small and marginal farmers in particular needs to be enhanced beyond the prescribed targeted levels, since the definition of agriculture is unreasonably widened.

REFERENCES

1. Kurup., N.P., "Banking Sector Reforms and Transparency", *Economic and Political Weekly*, March, 23, 1996., p. 747.
2. Janki Ballesh, *IBA Bulletin,* Vol XXIII Nos. 4 & 5 April–May, 2001, p. 8.
3. Sushil Khanna., "Financial Reforms and Industrial Sector in India", *Economic and Political Weekly*, November 6, 1999. pp. 32-31.
4. Kurup, N.P., *op.cit* p. 745.
5. Deena Khatkhate; 'Timing and Sequencing of Financial Sector Reforms: Evidence and Rationale," *Economic and Political Weekly*, July 11, 1998, p. 1838.

6. Bhide. M.G., *et. al.*, "Banking Sector Reforms: A Critical Overview"; *Economic and Political Weekly*, February 2, 2002, p. 400.
7. Krishna Murthy, G., "Old Private Sector Banks: Emerging Challenges Strategies and Solutions", *IBA Bulletin*, March, 2001. p. 32.
8. Bhasin.T.M., 'E-Commerce in Indian Banking" *IBA Bulletin.*, April-May, 2001. p. 24.
9. Girija Upadhyaya, "Technology and Banking: Challenges Ahead", *IBA Bulletin,* Marcch, 2001, p. 78
10. Shwetajain and Gourishukla, "A Not-so-Golden Handshake' *Business-standard,* October 8, 2002.
11. Chopra, V.K., 'Emerging Challenges, Strategies and Solutions in Indian Public Sector Banks" *IBA, Bulletin*, March, 2001, p. 48.
12. Shweta Jain and Gouri Shukla; *Op. Cit.*
13 Ram Mohan, T.T., "Setting the Stage for Bank Privatisation" *Economic and Political Weekly*, Jan 27, 2001. p. 265.
14 Bhatta Charya, Pradir, C, and Siva Subrahmanyam, M.N., "Aspects of Banking Sector Reforms in India" *Economic and Political Weekly*, October, 27, 2001, p. 4152.
15. Patil.R.H., "Industrial Finance and Capital Market: Changing Scenario", *Economic and Political Weekly,* January, 27, 2001, p. 360.
16 Renu Kohli, "Directed Credit and Financial Reforms" *Economic and Political Weekly*, October, 18, 1997, p. 2669.
17. Bhatta Charya, Prabiv.C., and Siva Subrahmanyam, M.N., *Op. Cit.* p. 4155 & 4156.
18. Dasgupta. Rajaram., "Priority Sector Lending: Yesterday, Today and Tomorrow", *Economic and Political Weekly*, October 12, 2002, p. 4240.

13

One Decade of Economic Reforms and Indian External Sector*

*Mrs. A. Sailaja Devi***
*Prof. M. Sundara Rao***

Introduction

Keeping aside the initial compulsions, largely driven by international oil price crisis, to open up a window or two to the world trade system, the feeling that the Indian economy could no more continue with its import substitution strategy, cultivated during 50s and 60s, Indian economy started opening up its frontiers to the world outside during late 70s and early 80s. It was the first time that efforts were made to improve 'productivity', 'efficiency' and 'competitiveness'. India could no more keep aloof from the rest of the world, particularly if technological advances occurring elsewhere would have to be assimilated and adapted to India's own production requirements. Anticipating export growth potential of certain areas, a selective import liberalisation approach was put into

* Research Paper submitted in favour of presentation in the National Seminar on "A decade of Indian Economic Reforms-Prospect and Retrospect" conducted by Department of Rural Development, Nagarjuna University, Nagarjuna Nagar.

** Mrs. A. Sailaja Devi is U.G.C Project Fellow and Prof. M. Sundara Rao is Head, Department of Economics, Andhra University. Dr. B. R. Ambedkar P. G. Center, Etcherla-532 402, Srikakulam (Andhra Pradesh).

operation to gain international competitiveness. Import of technology, modern capital equipment and its ancillaries, specified categories of industrial raw materials, etc., all on a highly selective basis, was the summary of the trade liberalisation philosophy of the eighties. Naturally, its impact was limited. Nonetheless, it set the trail ablaze. Since 1986 or 1987, every now and then, the economy witnessed one or the other liberalising element till we entered the nineties.

Economic Reforms on External Sector

In July 1991, a new economic era commenced. Wide-ranging policy reforms, encompassing all major sectors of the economy (trade, industry, agriculture, foreign investment and foreign technology, financial sector, public sector, and so on) were put through, with a rare degree of political resoluteness. The new trade policy aimed at eliminating discretionary controls on international trade transactions, reducing the nominal as well as the effective protection available to domestic industry, and bringing domestic prices closer to world prices. Three dimensions of the new trade policy, namely a rapid dismantling of quantitative restrictions on imports and exports, a substantial reduction on taxes and subsidies on trade and suitable adjustments in exchange rate, need to be underlined. The process of a near total dismantling of quantitative restrictions on imports and exports signalled a dramatic departure from the past policy regimes. In the sphere of exports also, the negative list consisted of the same three principal categories. Reduction in import and customs duties was the other landmark of the new trade policy.

Recently, India herself has completed the last bit of the opening-up on April 1, 2001. Furthermore, this is hardly the stage at which we can scientifically delineate the effect of a particular agreement, or a specific aspect of the same, on the concerned sector, free of other inter-connections.

Hence, the best we can do is to make some conjectures on the basis of what has been going on in the recent past. Indeed, this is our only analytical choice, since the kind of economic regime that may emerge in the next few years would only be reaffirmation, and a gradual extension, of the globalisation and trade liberalisation polices set afloat during the first half, and comprehensively expanded during the second half of the 1990s when WTO came.

In recent years, there have been intense discussions in the academic as well as policy circles regarding the second generation economic reforms in our country. It must be recognised that while the first generation economic reforms in July 1991 was initiated as per the conditionality of the IMF loan that we took at that time to salvage India's credibility in the world financial market, the second generation economic reforms at the turn of the 21st century have been guided by our compulsions to conform to the norms set by the WTO in matters of trade policy, to which India committed herself at the conclusion of the Uruguay round of GATT negotiations. Many of the changes that are now contemplated in the functioning of the Indian economy are basically the offshoots of the standards and norms prescribed by the WTO.

Foreign investment was now invited in a wide range of areas; investment collaborations were negotiated by dozens; technology import was no more a forbidden word; the public sector had started shedding its unproductive weight while the private sector, mature enough as it was believed to have grown by then, had started entering into those difficult and strategic areas that were once beyond their investment capability; external trade had opened up in a significant manner and the flow of exports and imports was freed of numerous procedures; a wide range of quantitative restrictions were done away with; international market calculations and 'getting the prices right', both nationally and internationally, were now given out to be the infallible panacea for growth, employment and economic welfare. In brief, every sector of the Indian economy was attuning itself to the changing economic environment. The state itself was striving to define its role in the new economic order. India's going to the WTO in 1995, and accelerating further the process of trade liberalization, would seem to be natural and inevitable.

Trade policy reforms over the last decade have aimed at creating an environment for achieving rapid increase in exports, raising India's share in world exports and making exports an engine for achieving higher economic growth. The focus of these reforms have been on liberalisation openness, transparency and globalisation with a basic thrust on outward orientation focusing on export promotion activity, moving away from quantitative restrictions and improving competitiveness of Indian industry to meet global market requirements. Over the years, significant changes in the EXIM policy have helped to strengthen the export production base, remove procedural irritants, facilitate input availability, besides focusing on quality and technological upgradation and improving competitiveness. Steps have also been taken to promote exports through multilateral and bilateral initiatives, identification of thrust areas and focus regions.

During 2000-01 special economic zones (SEZ) were set up to encourage export production. Evolution of a scheme for granting assistance to states based on their export performance for development of export related infrastructure was initiated. On the front of capital account, Foreign Direct investment (FDI) up to 100 per cent were permitted in e-commerce, subject to specific conditions. The dividend balancing condition for FDI in twenty-two consumer goods industries were removed. Similarly, during 2001-02 Quantitative Restrictions (QRs) on BOP grounds were removed by dismantling restrictions on the remaining 715 items. Partial back loading of withdrawal of tax benefits were offered to exporters under Section 80-HHC of the Income Tax Act. Agri-Economic Zones were set up for promoting agricultural exports on the basis of specific products and geographical areas. Market Access Initiative (MAI) scheme introduced to boost exports. On the capital account front, FDI up to 49 per cent from all sources was permitted in the private banking sector. 100 per cent FDI was permitted for B to B e-commerce, courier services, oil refining, hotel and tourism sector, drugs and pharmaceuticals etc. Non-Banking Financial Companies (NBFCs) were permitted to hold foreign equity up to 100 per cent in holding companies.

The EXIM policy announced in March 2001 has completed the process of removal of QRs on BOP grounds by dismantling restrictions on the remaining 715 items. Out of these 715 items, 342 are textile products, 147 are agricultural products including alcoholic beverages and 226 are other manufactured products including automobiles. The policy has, however, put in place necessary mechanisms to provide a level playing field to domestic players vis-a-vis imports. Trade policy reforms over the last decade have aimed at creating an environment for achieving rapid increase in exports, raising India's share in world exports and making exports an engine for achieving higher economic growth. The focus of these reforms has been on liberalisation, openness, transparency and globalisation with a basic thrust on outward orientation moving away from quantitative restrictions and improving competitiveness of Indian industry to meet global market requirements.

Against this background the present study attempts to evaluate the emerging trends on the different dimensions of the external sector of the Indian economy. Necessary information on related data have been collected from different issues of economics survey published by Government of India, reports of CSO, RBI and other governmental reports.

Trends in Balance of Payment Indicators during the Reform Period

The selected indicators of external sector presented in Tables 1, 2 and 3 reveal that there have been significant improvements in the structure of the external sector during the reform period. The export cover of imports rose sharply. The ratio of exports and imports to GDP rose during the reform period. The current account deficit as percentage of GDP declined during pre-reform to a well manageable level during the reform period. The capital account of BOP has also undergone a major structural change in favour of non-debt creating foreign investment flows. Foreign exchange reserves were built to a very comfortable level of about 8 months of imports from a critical level of about two months of imports in June 1991. External debt and debt service indicators marked sustained improvements over 1990. External debt as a per cent of GDP, declined gradually. Also debt service payments on external debt as a per cent of current receipts declined gradually. The strength of the external sector has enabled India to withstand fairly well the Asian financial crisis contagion and the related adverse spillovers. The Balance of payment summary presented in Table 3 indicate that during the reform period the current account deficit was contained. After some setbacks in 1998-99 capital flows improved significantly in 1999-2000. The moderation in current account deficit and the sharp increase in net capital inflows resulted in a large accumulation of foreign exchange reserves. Invisible flows maintain an upward trend during reform period. Private remittances account for the bulk of private transfer receipts.

India's Balance of Payments (BOP) remained reasonably comfortable in 2000-01 and the external sector marked distinct improvements. The improvement in the current account was largely due to a more dynamic export performance, sustained buoyancy in invisible receipts reflecting sharp increases in software service exports and

Table 1: Balance of payments Indicators (1990-91 to 2000-01)

BOP Indicators	*1990-91*	*1994-95*	*1995-96*	*1996-97*	*1997-98*	*1998-99*	*1999-00*	*2000-01*
1. Exports	18477	26855	32311	34113	35680	34298	37542	44894
2. Imports	27915	35904	43670	48948	51187	47544	55383	59264
Of which:POL	6028	5928	7526	10036	8164	6399	12611	15650
3. Trade Balance	-9438	-9049	-11359	-14815	-15507	-13246	-17841	-14370
4. Invisible	-242	5680	5449	10196	10007	9208	13143	11791
5. Current Account Balance	-9680	-3369	-5910	-4619	-5500	-4038	-4698	-2579
6. External Assistance (net)	2210	1526	883	1109	907	820	901	427
7. Commercial borrowing (net) @	2248	1030	1275	2848	3999	4362	313	4011
8. IMF (net)	1214	-1143	-1715	-975	-618	-393	-260	-26
9. NR deposits (net)	1536	172	1103	3350	1125	960	1540	2317
10. Rupee debt service	-1193	-983	-952	-727	-767	-802	-711	-617
11. Foreign investment (net) of which	103	4807	4615	5963	5353	2312	5117	4588
(i) FDI (net)	97	1228	1954	2651	3525	2380	2093	1828
(ii) FIIs	0	1503	2009	1926	979	-390	2135	1847
(iii) Euro equities & others	6	2076	652	1386	849	322	889	913
12. Other flows (net) +	2284	2604	-2235	-1131	-606	608	3940	-2291
13. Capital Account total (net)	8402	8013	2974	10437	9393	7867	10840	8409
14. Reserve use (-increase)	1278	-4644	2936	-5818	-3893	-3829	-6142	-5830

Table 2: Selected indicators for the External Sector (1990–91 to 2001–02)

(In US $ million)

	1990-91	1995-95	1995-96	1996-97	1997-98	1998-99	1999-00	2000-01
1. Growth of Exports-BOP (%)	9.0	18.4	20.3	5.6	4.5	-3.9	9.5	19.6
2. Growth of imports-BOP (%)	14.4	34.3	21.6	12.1	4.6	-7.1	16.5	7.0
3. Exports /Imports-BOP (%)	66.2	74.8	74.0	69.7	69.7	72.1	67.8	75.8
4. Imports cover of FER (months)	2.5	8.4	6.0	6.5	6.9	8.2	8.2	8.6
5. External Assistance (net)/TC %	26.3	19.0	29.7	10.6	9.7	10.4	8.3	5.1
6. ECB (net)/TC (%)	26.8	12.9	42.9	27.3	42.6	55.4	2.9	47.7
7. NR deposit/TC (%)	18.3	2.1	37.1	32.1	12.0	12.2	14.2	27.6
8. Short term debt/FER (%)	146.5	16.9	23.2	25.5	17.2	13.2	10.3	8.2
9. Debtservice payments as % of	35.3	26.2	24.3	22.5	19.1	13.0	16.2	17.1
		As per cent of GDP						
10. Exports	5.8	8.3	9.1	8.9	8.7	8.3	8.4	9.8
11. Imports	8.8	11.1	12.3	12.7	12.5	11.5	12.4	13.0
12. Tradé balance	-3.0	-2.8	-3.2	-3.8	-3.8	-3.2	-4.0	-3.1
13. Invisible balance	-0.1	1.8	1.6	2.7	2.4	2.2	3.0	2.6
14. Current account balance	-3.1	-1.0	-1.7	-1.2	-1.4	-1.0	-1.1	-0.5
15. External debt	28.7	30.8	27.0	24.5	24.3	23.6	22.2	22.3
16. Debt service Payments	2.8	3.4	3.4	3.2	2.7	2.6	2.5	2.9

Table 3: Selected Indicators of External Sector in 1980s and 1990s

Item	*1980-81 to 1991-92 (Annual Average)*		*1992-93 to 1999-2000 (Annual Average)*
Annual Average Growth Rates		Per Cent Per Year	
1. Growth of Exports-BOP (%)	7.6		10.0
2. Growth of Imports-BOP (%)	8.5		13.4
Non-POL-DGC&S (%)	6.6		13.2
Key Ratios		Averages for the Period	
3. Exports/Imports-BOP (%)	62.3		74.0
4. Import cover of FER (No of month)	3.8		7.2
5. External Assistance (net) /Tc (%)	41.6		18.9
6. ECB (net)/Tc (%)	25.1		22.7
7. NR deposits /Tc (%)	23.2		23.2
8. Short term debt /FER (%)	137.5		23.8
9. Debt Service payment as % of current receipts	31.8		22.2
Select Items in balance of payments		Per Cent of GDP	
10. Exports	5.1		8.4
11. Imports	8.2		11.5
12. Trade Balance	-3.1		-3.1
13. Invisible Balance	1.2		1.9
14. Current Account Balance	-1.9		-1.2
15. External debt	31.4		27.9
16. Debt Service Payments	2.8		3.0

Source: Government of India: Economic Survey 2000-01.

private transfers and the subdued non–oil import demand. The deficit on the trade account, of BOP narrowed to 3.1 per cent of GDP in 2000-01. On the front of capital account the recovery in capital flows was broadly maintained during 2000-01. Net capital inflows (excluding IMF) in the BOP account amounted to US $9.02 billion in 2000-01. The reduction in the net capital inflows was mainly due to the bunching of repayments of commercial borrowings and significant net outflows. At the same time, capital inflows were bolstered by the mobilisation of US $5.51 billion under the India Millennium Deposits (IMD) Scheme in October-November 2000. Official BOP statistics, as compiled by the RBI for the first half of 2001-02 indicates that the current account deficit in 2001-02 expected to remain within 1 per cent of GDP. The widening of the current account deficit is mainly due to poor export performance. Merchandise exports (in US dollar terms) remained almost stagnant with export growth of 0.6 per cent for the nine months of 2001-2002.

Trends in Foreign Investment Flows during Reform Period

The economic reforms are expected to increase the extent of foreign financial inflows into our country, which are in the form of Foreign Domestic Investment (FDI) in joint ventures/subsidiaries of MNCs; commercial borrowings from foreign investments/bank loans and grants from world monetary institutions or deposits from non-residents and foreign equity contributions etc. However, these foreign financial inflows would be beneficial only if these are non-debt generating, which would help to build up long lasting capital. The trends relating to the foreign financial inflows presented in Table 4 reveal that Indian global opening produced immediate promising results. Number of foreign technical and financial collaborations and FDI proposals started inundating the Indian economic environment. Also overall economic and industrial growth rate and saving and investment rates indicated a positive trend.

Table 4: Foreign Investment Flows by Different Categories

(US $ millions)

	1990-91	1991-92	1992-93	1993-94	1994-95	1995-96	1996-97	1997-98	1998-99	1999-00	2000-01
A. Direct investment	97	129	315	586	1314	2144	2821	3557	2462	2155	2339
a. RBI automatic route	-	-	42	89	171	169	135	202	179	171	454
b. SIA/FIPB route	-	66	222	280	701	1249	1922	2754	1821	1410	1456
c. NRIs (40% & 100%)	-	63	51	217	442	715	639	241	62	84	67
d. Acquistion of shares	-	-	-	-	-	11	125	360	400	490	362
B. Portfolio investment	6	4	244	3567	3824	2748	3312	1828	-61	3026	2760
a. FIIs	-	-	1	1665	1503	2009	1926	979	-390	2135	1847
b. GDRs/ADRs	-	-	240	1520	2082	683	1366	645	270	768	831
c. Offshore funds & others	6	4	3	382	239	56	20	204	59	123	82
Total (A+B)	**103**	**133**	**559**	**4153**	**5138**	**4892**	**6133**	**5385**	**2401**	**5181**	**5099**

Source: Government of India: Economic Survey 2001-02.

After a sharp setback in 1998-99, foreign investment inflows made a smart recovery in 1999-2000 and the position was broadly maintained in 2000-01. During the first eight months of 2001-02, total foreign investment inflows have risen by about 47 per cent. The source and direction of FDI remained unchanged during the 1990's. FDI is seen as a means to supplement domestic investment for achieving a high level of economic growth and development. Towards this end, the FDI policy has been constantly reviewed, and necessary steps have been taken to make India a favourable destination for FDI. Fresh inflows for portfolio investment by foreign institutional investors (FIIs) during 2000-01 were US $1.85 billion, slightly lower than the inflows of US $2.14 billion in the previous year. The policy in regard to portfolio investments by FIIs is reviewed constantly and major initiatives are taken, when necessary. In the Budget for 2001-02, it was proposed to raise the limit for portfolio investment by FIIs from the normal level of 24 per cent of the paid up capital of the company to 49 per cent. The outstanding balances under non-resident deposit schemes continued their increasing trend. Outstanding balances under all the non-resident deposit schemes amounted to US $24.65 billion at the end of November 2001.

Trends in Foreign Exchange Reserves during Reform Period

The sharp reduction in current account deficit and the funds raised under the IMD Scheme resulted in large accumulation of official foreign exchange reserves for the fifth year in succession during 2000-01 (Table 5). On BOP basis, the reserves increased by a substantial US $5.83 billion. During 2001-02 the foreign currency assets of the RBI have increased by about US $7.01 billion from US $39.55 billion at the end of March 2001 to US $46.56 billion at the end of January, 2002. Total foreign exchange reserves (including gold and SDRs) at the end of January, 2002 amounted to US $49.48 billion, providing cover for about 10 months of estimated imports in 2001-02.

Table 5: Foreign Exchange Reserves

Year	Reserves					
	Gold		SDRs		Foreign Currency Assets Rs. Crore	Total Rs. Crores (3+5+6)
	Tonnes	Rs. Crores	Millions	Rs. Crores		
1980-81	267	226	491	497	4822	5544
1981-82	267	226	425	444	3355	4024
1982-83	267	226	270	291	4265	4782
1983-84	267	226	216	248	5498	5972
1984-85	291	246	147	181	6817	7243
1985-86	325	274	115	161	7384	7820
1986-87	325	274	139	232	7645	8151
1987-88	325	274	70	125	7287	7687
1988-89	325	274	80	161	6605	7040
1989-90	333	281	82	184	5787	6251
1990-91	333	6828	76	200	4388	11416
1991-92	351	9039	66	233	14578	23850
1992-93	354	10549	13	55	20141	30745
1993-94	367	12794	77	339	47287	60420
1994-95	396	13752	5	23	66006	79780
1995-96	398	15659	56	280	58446	74385
1996-97	398	14557	1	7	80368	94932
1997-98	396	13394	1	4	102507	115905
1998-99	357	12559	6	34	125412	138005
1999-00	358	12973	3	16	152924	165913
2000-01	358	12711	2	11	184482	197204

Trends in Currency Depreciation during Reform Period

Economic reforms in the front of external sector are much considerable on the exchange rate regimes. The reforms on the exchange rate front have sharply depreciated the Indian rupee since 1997. The main reason responsible for this has been erratic behavior of foreign institutional investors who were permitted to trade on Indian stock exchanges since 1991 devaluation of currency in 1992 etc. Table 6 reveals that in terms of dollar, Indian rupee value has sharply depreciated. The recent trends on the front of Indian exchange rate indicates that the exchange rate of rupee against the dollar came under downward pressure.

The exchange rate of the rupee against the US dollar continued to be broadly market determined. The foreign exchange markets experienced considerable uncertainty with the rupee depreciating by 6.7 per cent between end of April and end of October 2000 from Rs. 43.655 per US dollar to Rs. 46.775. Since November 2000, the situation had shown large improvement and the forex markets were relatively stable. The world economy experienced one of the worst shocks in the aftermath of September 11, 2001 events in the United States. Foreign exchange markets in India also became volatile, with the rupee showing a depreciation of 1.3 per cent vis-a-vis the US dollar during the 10-day period of September 10-20, 20001. The situation necessitated a quick response to provide appropriate liquidity and overall comforts to the markets. The RBI announced some measures during the period September 15-25, 2001. These measures had the desired effect of moderating possible panic reactions and reducing volatility in financial markets, particularly in money, foreign exchange and government securities markets. As at the end of January, 2002, the exchange rate of the rupee was Rs.48.58 per US $.

The exchange rate management policy continues its focus on smoothing excessive volatility in the exchange rate with no fixed rate target, while allowing the underlying demand and supply conditions to determine the exchange rate movements over a period in an orderly way. Towards this end, the RBI monitors closely the developments in the financial markets at home and abroad and carefully coordinates its market operations with suitable monetary,

Table 6: Exchange Value of Rupee Vis-à-vis Dollar

Year	*Rs.Per $*
1990-91	17.94
1991-92	24.47
1992-93	30.47
1993-94	31.37
1994-95	31.40
1995-96	33.45
1996-97	35.50
1997-98	39.50
1998-99	42.07
1999-00	43.33
2000-01	45.68
2001-02	
April	46.78
May	46.92
June	47.00
July	47.13
August	47.12
September	47.64
October	48.02
November	47.99
December	47.91

Source: Government of India, Economic Survey, 2001-02, Ministry of Finance, New Delhi.

regulatory and other measures, as considered necessary from time to time. The exchange rate of the rupee remained broadly stable (Table 7), appreciating only marginally, in real effective terms during 2000-01, depreciating in nominal terms by about 5.1 per cent against the US dollar but strengthening against the other major currencies. The appreciation of the rupee in real effective exchange terms has, however, picked up during 2001-02 affecting the competitiveness of our exports.

Table 7: Trends in Nominal and Real Effective Exchange Rate of Rupee.

Year/Month	*Nominal Effective Exchange Rate (NEER)*		*Real Effective Exchange Rate (REER)*	
	5-Country Index	*10-Coutry Index*	*5-Country Index*	*10-Coutry Index*
1985	368.39	380.51	179.19	188.07
1986	313.27	316.51	165.84	169.68
1987	280.86	279.22	157.67	158.86
1988	251.78	251.15	149.85	151.35
1989	224.84	225.23	137.02	138.73
1990	200.74	196.93	129.15	128.08
1991	153.73	151.79	110.59	110.16
1991-92	143.92	142.4	105.88	105.57
1992-93	118.75	117.37	96.06	95.52
1993-94	110.21	111.36	95.51	96.80
1994-95	106.31	106.80	101.17	101.72
1995-96	97.57	97.35	97.99	97.75
1996-97	95.68	95.37	101.12	100.78
1997-98	95.05	96.52	105.19	106.40
1998-99	84.09	85.33	101.06	101.89
1999-2000	81.40	83.95	99.68	102.08
2000-01	80.35	84.45	99.04	103.04
2000-01 Apr	81.79	85.67	99.89	103.65
2001-02(P) Apr	80.69	84.76	101.33	105.13

Source: Government of India: Economic Survey 2001-02.

Trends in External Debt during Reform Period

During the reform period trends in the external debt front of the Indian economy are presented in Table 8. During the reform period the external debt to GDP ratio has been declining continuously the rates improved from 23.6 per cent at the end of March 1999 to 20.7 per cent at the end September 2000. The external debt-GDP ratio has

Table 8: India's External Debt Outstanding

(US $ billion)

Categories	*End - March*							*End*
	1991	*1992*	*1995*	*1998*	*1999*	*2000*	*2001R*	*-Sept. 01*
1. Long-term debt	75.3	78.2	94.7	88.5	92.6	94.4	96.1	97.58
2. Short-term debt	8.5	7.1	4.3	5.0	4.3	3.9	3.5	2.80
Total debt	**83.3**	**85.3**	**99.0**	**93.5**	**96.9**	**98.3**	**99.6**	**100.38**
External debt-key indicators (ratio as per cent)								
Total external debt to GDP	28.7	38.7	30.8	24.3	23.6	22.2	22.3	21.0
Short term to total debt	10.2	8.3	4.3	5.4	4.4	4.0	3.5	2.8
Short term debt to foreign currency assets	382.1	125.6	20.5	19.4	14.5	11.2	8.8	6.7

Source: Government of India: Economic Survey 2001-02.

been declining continuously over the years. The ratio improved from 38.7 per cent at end-March 1992 to 22.3 per cent at end-March 2001 and further to 21 per cent at the end of September 2001. The share of short-term debt to total debt declined from 10.2 per cent at the end of March 1991 to 2.8 per cent at the end of September 2001. The debt service ratio declined from a peak level of 35.3 per cent of current receipts in 1990-91 to 16.3 per cent in 2000-01. The improvement has been the result of concerted and continued efforts of prudent external debt management strategy undertaken by the Government. It is particularly noteworthy that for the first time, the World Bank has classified India as a less-indebted country.

Conclusion

On the external front, reforms have enhanced India's competitiveness in labour and skill intensive industries, reduced the dependence of competitive industries on inefficient domestic suppliers and infrastructure and enhanced domestic competitive conditions, exports have been growing at 20 percent in dollar terms. What is more significant is that the share of manufactured goods in the exports basket has risen while that of primary products has fallen. Various BOP indicators bring out continued improvement in the external sector. The achievements in the external sector appear to be more credible. This is perhaps because the measures taken have been coherent and were so far reaching. The best way to ensure continued stability and viability of the BOP is by increased foreign exchange earnings from the export of goods and services to a sufficient level to pay for the imports and all other external payments on the current account. This requires control of inflation to maintain appropriate real effective exchange rate vis a vis other competing nations.

The above-mentioned trends on the front of major dimensions of the external sector indicate that the external sector reform has not bestowed its much favourable influence on the Indian economy. The full benefits of external sector reforms are yet to be achieved. It may be due to slow pace of India's opening up. Trade growth and FDI inflows to India have yet to come in a big way. Also reforms are yet to influence the exchange rate regimes and external debt front on more favourable lines. However, India's external sector has emerged with considerable inner strength to meet the challenges of foreign as well as domestic shocks, following the economic reforms in the 1990s. The Indian economy is now more open than ever before. As the economy opens up further, it will derive efficiency gain but will not remain insulated from adverse effects of external shocks, through trade and financial linkages. India can cushion against the adverse effects of such shocks by further strengthening the country's economic fundamentals.

REFERENCES

1. Government of India, Economic Survey 2001-02, Ministry of Finance, New Delhi.
2. Nayyar. D, "Globalization The past in our Present", Indian Economic Journal. Vol. 43 No. 3. (Jan.-March 1996) pp. 1-17.
3. Qureshi. L., "Globalization, New opportunities, Through Challenges", Financial Development, (March1996).
4. Sen., "Economic Reforms, Employment and Poverty, Trends and options", Economic and Political Weekly, Vol. XXXI (1996).
5. Tata Services, Statistical Year Book of India, 2000.
6. Pankaj Cheman Lal and Murali Patibanda, "India's exports since the Reforms", EPW, Vol. XXXI, No. 20 May 16-2,1998.

14

Economic Liberalisation: Prosperity or More Poverty?

*Prof. S. Janakarajan**

We need to keep in mind three important issues:

1. Economic reform, WTO and GATS are closely interrelated.
2. The basic philosophy and the hidden agenda and economic reform is deregulation:

   This means nothing but privatisation of all sectors including services.
3. Do we have the enabling environment to adopt such a policy in India?
4. Let us take some specific cases, where reform process has already been started:

Reforms in Power and Water Sectors

It is necessary to study a decade of economic reform in India in an historical context. After the October Revolution, slowly and steadily, the entire world was divided into two blocks, controlled by the US and the former Soviet Union. The political, economic and trade policies of the countries representing these blocks were

* Professor, Madras Institute of Development Studies, Chennai.

determined by their respective bosses. Under such circumstances, GATT existed but mostly to regulate trade among the developed countries. However, after the collapse of the Soviet Union, there was an urge to coordinate all economic and trade activities of the world countries under a single umbrella. GATT was insufficient to achieve such an objective. That is when the whole idea of economic reform and WTO were mooted.

To regulate trade in goods, the WTO was created and to regulate trade in services, GATS was formed. It is however, interesting that it was basically G7 (currently G 8) nations, which were instrumental in the formation of all rules and regulations and conditionality pertaining to international trade. The IMF and World Bank were instruments through which conditionality were enforced. Nevertheless, when these rules and regulations and conditionality were framed, there was not an iota of concern whether developing and poor countries have the capacity to absorb them. The Western World have the required capacity; but most of the Asian, West African and Latin American countries are already struggling to cope up with many international pressures and debt burden. The conditionality of WTO and GATS are going to tighten further the grip and for them, the trap is widened.

The arguments that were advanced in favour of the reform process were,

- Any country which does not want to initiate the reform process and which does not want to sign the WTO and the GATS will be isolated from the rest of the world community.
- Being a signatory, a country's competitiveness will go up, there will be an export boom, more foreign exchange earnings, more foreign investments leading to faster economic growth and above all more employment opportunities.

- It will increase the quality of life of a common man and will contribute to decrease in poverty.

  Let us take the case of India. It is more than a decade since the economic liberalisation process was initiated. Let us look at our own performance with some key indicators (Chandrashekar, C.P.2000).

- There is an overall increase in GDP – from 5.5 percent witnessed in the 1980s to 6 percent achieved during 1990s. However, while looking through various sectors, the picture one gets is a dismal performance.
- Agricultural production has slowed down: During the 12-year period preceding 1991, there was a secular rate of growth of 2.4 percent of foodgrain production, which was above the population growth rate. It is however declined to 1.2 percent during the period 1990-91 to 1997-98 which is less than the rate of growth of population.
- Paradoxically, despite declining growth rate of foodgrain production, the bufferstock has swollen to 64 million tones. What is the mystery? It is entirely due to increase in the PDS prices, which has considerably reduced the off-take from the central pool, resulting in bursting of godowns. One of the conditionally imposed on us was to lift all subsidies, in particular agriculture and PDS. As a result, the central issue price for foodgrains (to be distributed through PDS) has gone up considerably. For instance, for the above poverty line group, the issue price of wheat has gone up from Rs.450 to Rs.682 per quintal between February and April 1999. Similar increases have been made in the issue price of rice also. Indeed, there is very little difference between the price offered in the PDS shops and the open market.

- The economy is flooded with a variety of luxury and consumer goods which has indeed let down our domestic industries very badly (e.g., soft drinks, consumer durable industries); prosperity induced due to such trading and industrial activities are short-lived and will mostly cater to the needs of urban upper middle class population.
- Otherwise, the overall industrial performance was dismal. The average annual growth rate of 8.4 in industrial production witnessed during the period 1985 – 1991 has come drastically to 5.7 percent during the period 1991-1998.
- Estimates of poverty in India, which stood at 55.3 percent in 1972-73 came down to 34.1 percent in 1989-90. The subsequent NSS rounds up to 1997 indicate that the poverty level averaged at 38 percent, during the 1990s, which is above the 1989-90 level (Chandrashekar.C. 2000). The increase in poverty is largely due to lack of purchasing power among agricultural workers and other weaker sections which is due to steady increase in PDS prices of foodgrains and declining employment opportunities.

Do we have the enabling the environment and the capacity to absorb the shock generated by the economic liberalisation process?

Even after 55 years of Independence, the Indian economy is confronting several chronic problems, which hinder developmental process:

- Lack of purchasing power and persisting poverty.
- Raising unemployment.
- Mass illiteracy, in particular among women, SCs and STs.

- Lack of access to basic infrastructure such as safe drinking water and sanitation, housing, roads, electricity, communication and transport.
- Lack of good and affordable health care system
- Maladies such as dowry deaths, female infanticide, and sex selection at birth.
- Above all, corrupt governance and competitive populist measures, which not only stagnate the economy but also result in huge wastages and leakages of public resources.

General Agreement on Trade in Services (GATS)

GATS is one of the sub-agreements that was adopted as a part of Uruguay Round of Multilateral Trade Negotiations (1986-1994). GATS is a legally enforceable agreement aimed at deregulating and privatising international trade in services such as in health, education, transport, insurance, banking, telecommunication, water supply and sanitation. While WTO regulates trade in commodities (in favour of the developed world), the GATS is attempting to regulate 'trading in services'. Unlike WTO, which has generated a good deal of debate in the sub-continent and in other parts of the world as well, GATS is still not debated enough. In fact, opposition to GATS from the developing world was almost negligible in the Doha ministerial conference held in November 2001. As a result, Paragraph-15, which encompass the section on GATS, was one of the least controversial issues at Doha (Equations, Campaign against the GATS, 2002). As a matter of fact, GATS will have far reaching repercussion on a number of sectors in the economy. For instance, due to the economic liberalisation process, agricultural sector is already stressed heavily due to multiplicity of factors such as removal of subsidy on fertilisers, no remunerative price for agricultural output, environmental degradation and pollution of water bodies, transportation of water from rural to urban areas, removal of subsidy on surface water, removal of subsidy on well digging and electricity for pumping groundwater, huge reduction of public sector investment on agriculture and other allied activities and so forth. On top all these, GATS will impose additional costs on all agriculture related services, which is categorised as 'services incidental to agriculture, hunting and forestry'. These services, which will be privatised soon, include marketing, soil testing, agricultural extension and so on. Apart from agricultural services, whole range of services is included under GATS. Some of the key services which, could drastically affect poor are, legal (no more free legal aid), medical (no free government hospitals), veterinary, education at all levels starting from primary school, adult education, transport of all kinds, PDS and so on. In addition, services such as electricity generation and distribution, drinking and irrigation water, insurance, tele-communications and banking will affect very badly the poor population.

Three key sectors, which need to be mentioned in this context, are public distribution system (PDS), public transport system and education. If PDS is privatised and if the subsidy element is lifted on foodgrains, it would have drastic impact on marginalised and low-income groups who depend on these sources for subsistence. Similarly, if public transport is privatised, the private operators will terminate all non-profitable transport routes. It would have serious impact on poorer sections of the population, in particular rural areas, whose mobility for marketing, education and for other links with urban areas depend entirely upon public transport system. Most important of all is the 'knowledge industry' (education). Education will be treated purely as a commercial and tradable commodity. The role of education for nation building, as a store-house of knowledge, as a vehicle to transmit culture, as a medium to popularise science and technology and above all us a vehicle for change will be completely disregarded.

In the next few paragraphs let me briefly discuss the impact of liberalisation process on land, water and electricity sector as case studies.

Privatising Common Land to Corporate Sector

It is quite disheartening to note that in the Tamil Nadu State, even public land is going to be given away to multinationals and other companies in the corporate sector under what is called 'wasteland development programme'. A series of measures have already been issued to this effect. For instance, G.O.No.189, dated 2-07-2002 says, the policy is that the government shall act as a facilitator bringing corporate houses and small land holders to bring maximum extent of fallow and wastelands under cultivation. In reality, no plot of land can be called a wasteland. Poromboke land (government land is classified as Poromboke land in Tamil Nadu) could be classified as (a) occupied Poromboke with B memo and (b) unoccupied Poromboke. The latter category of land includes road, canal, burial ground, lakes and tanks and foreshore area, thrashing floor and so on. Some of these plots of lands are used as grazing lands for cattle. And, very often, people in rural areas cut across these parcels of lands to reach their destinations. If these parcels of public land are given away to corporate houses it will have serious impact on lifestyle and livelihood of farming community. Above all, the common land (what is regarded as 'wasteland'), if given away to corporate houses, will reinforce feudal/new-zamindary system through backdoor. Since the objective of the wasteland development programme is of develop export-oriented horticultural cultivation, the corporate houses will have no hesitation to sink deep bore-wells (without any limitation) in several parts of land and could extract groundwater round the clock. This will result in groundwater depletion which will affect very badly farming community why would not be in a position to compete with corporate houses in deepening wells. The direct consequence is the loss of wells and land to farmers who will be compelled to sell their lands to corporate houses. Thus, corporate houses who lease-in land under this programme, would own not just land but also aquifers. And precisely for this reason corporate houses will soon become local zamindars. Almost all opposition parties in the state have criticised this programme. And, there have been widespread protests to this programme from the farming community. A public interest litigation case has already been filed against this programme in the Madras High Court.

Privatisation of Water

Privatisation of water assumes greater significance due to rapid urban expansion and accelerated industrial progress. This has resulted in competing demand for water across sectors such as agriculture, fishing, industry, and domestic uses and to preserve ecology and environment. Privatisation of water is talked about in India in several major cities after the globalisation process has been initiated. Notable among them are Delhi, Bangalore and Chennai. The contract to be awarded is of the order of Rs.400 crore for five years to distribute water on an experimental basis in two areas in Bangalore. Two French companies (with 44 professionals already camping in Bangalore) are trying to initiate the project. The monthly fee of 44 French professionals works out to Rs.2.4 crore, whereas the monthly salary bill of 2900 employees of Bangalore Water Supply and Sewerage Board works out to only Rs.4.34 crore. These two companies are operating in 120 countries and their combined turnover is $64 billion (The Hindu, 2-8-2002). Similar efforts are being made in Delhi to bring water from Tehri Dam to which the global water giant called Suez-Degremont has been approached. This company operates in 130 countries. This company has already set up a treatment plant with 636 million liters/ day capacity in Delhi at a cost of Rs.180 crore. All other metropolitan cities are also contemplating to privatise water supply and sewerage system. However, the case of Tiruppur Municipality is quite an interesting one.

Tiruppur is a town around 400 kms west of Chennai city and located a distance of about 40 kms from Coimbatore town. Tiruppur town has already entered into the global map due to large concentration of knitwear and dyeing and bleaching industries. The knitwear products exported from Tiruppur account for 20 percent of total garment exports from India. It contributes to about Rs.5000 crore by way foreign exchange annually.

The population of this town according to 1991 census is 2,35,000. This town however starves due to inadequate water for both industries as well as for domestic use. Agriculture is also badly affected and stressed due to lack of water. This region does not have any perennial water supply from surface sources. The ground water is depleted with water dropping up to 1200 feet in many parts of the district.

A company called New Tiruppur Area Development Corporation (NTADCL), has been initiated to supply water to the industries of Tiruppur town and to the domestic users. This is a project in which many agents are participating: They are, Tamil Nadu Government, Tiruppur Exporters' Association (TEA), Tiruppur Municipality. Infrastructure Leasing and Financial Services, Ltd (IS & FS), the Tamil Nadu Corporation for Industrial Infrastructure Development, Ltd. (TACID), New Tiruppur Area Development Corporation (NTADCL) and Indo-US Financial Institutions Reform and Expansion (FIRE) Project. This project aims to supply 185 million liters of water per day (from Bhavani river) to cater to the needs of about 1000 dyeing and bleaching units located in this areas as well as to supply water to 1.6 people located in the Tiruppur municipality and the adjacent Panchayats. The detailed project components are the following:

- treated piped water supply of 60 million liters per day (MLD) to Tiruppur municipality and 21 adjoining towns and village Panchayats.
- treated water supply of 100 MLD to over 400 dyeing and bleaching industries within the Tiruppur Planning Area.
- sewerage system for Tiruppur
- onsite sanitation facilities for 88 designated slum areas within Tiruppur municipality

NTADCL will be responsible for transmission, treatment of water supply, distribution of water outside municipal limits where most of the industry is located, treatment of the collected sewage and maintenance of the sewage treatment plants.

Resource Mobilisation for the Project

Basically, TEA, TACID and IL & FS together are responsible to design and execute the project. Therefore, a public limited company called New Tiruppur Area Development Corporation (NTADCL) was formed in 1995 to see through the project. The NTADCL will contract out the construction and maintenance of the systems to a Build, Operate and Transfer (BOT) consortium, which is the Mahindra Consortium (Mahindra & Mahindra, United International, North West Water, and Bechtel). USAIAD has provided long term (30 years) loan guarantees for US$ 25 million with IF & FS to help finance this project (The NTADCL, web page). Total estimated cost of the project is Rs.12 billion of which equity share of Rs.3.9 billion will be contributed by the union government, IL & FS, the Tamil Nadu Corporation for Industrial Infrastructure Development, the Tiruppur Exporters Association and the Mahindra-led consortium – the EPC contractor-cum- BOOT operator. The project has a debt component of Rs.6.98 billion and a subordinate debt of Rs.750 million.

The State CM has already laid the foundation stone on June 20, 2002. The project is supposed to be in full operation within six years. It boasted, this is the first public-private partnership project to access commercial funds for the water sector in India. The Tiruppur experiment is going to be the benchmark for private initiatives in the sector and it will build a strong case for private financing of water projects in India in the future.

Treatment of effluent generated by the industries is not taken care of by the company. One of the important processes in the making of knitwear products is dyeing and bleaching. This particular process not only consumes enormous quantity of water, but almost the same quantity of water is discharged as effluent. The major part of effluent is discharged as effluent. The major part of effluent is discharged into the **Noyyal River** and to a significant extent in other small streams such as Nallar and Jamunai rivers. The available evidence confirm that the effluent discharged by these units are quite hazardous causing serious health problems. This is evident from the type and the extent of chemicals used in the bleaching and dyeing process. In the process of dyeing and bleaching, the chemicals used for a 100 kilograms of clothes are, wetting oil (100%) 500 grams, caustic soda 4 kgs, hypern 750 grams, sodium peroxide 4 kgs, hydrochloric acid 8 kgs, soda ash 15 kgs, acetic acid 3 kgs, common salt 10 kgs and petroleum oil 2 kgs. This particular process is heavily water consuming and requires 40,000litres. On an average, a dyeing unit can process 20 tonne of clothes per month or about 700 kgs per day, consuming about 8 million liters of water per month or 28,000 liters of water per day (Palanichamy, N.V and Palanisami, K, 1994). The estimated water requirement of the bleaching and dyeing units in Tiruppur is about 94 million liters per day (mld) of which about 60 percent is met by groundwater as transported by the tanker-trucks from the rural neighbourhood. This was in 1994. The requirement of water today has crossed 120 million liters per day. What is really disturbing is the fact that a comparable quantity of water is let out as effluent in the Noyyal river and other streams, which has already caused permanent damage to the river, top soil and the most important of all, the groundwater. Even before 30 years, the local textile operators have confirmed that groundwater is contaminated around the areas where dyeing and bleaching units discharge their effluent. In the absence of any perennial source of surface water, the villages around Tiruppur entirely depend upon groundwater for agriculture. As groundwater is contaminated, agriculture as the key occupation seems to have been abandoned in many villages (Stanley Report, Vol. II).

The government Order (G.O.No.213, I) dated 30-03-1989 prohibits establishment of any polluting industry at a distance of 1 km adjacent to the rivers. This G.O. has been subsequently amended with the effect that 1 km norm has been extended to 3 km. Noyyal is one of the notified rivers in the GO. The Tiruppur dyers' Association wanted exemption from this GO, since according to their claim, the Noyyal River is dry and whatever water that flows in the river is not used for irrigation. On the other hand, the government of Tamil Nadu has constructed a dam across this river (called Orathapalayam dam) in the year 1992, about 10 km below the Tiruppur town, with a view to providing irrigation for 8000 hectares. This dam's catchment area is 2245 sq. km, which includes most of the area in which the dyeing and bleaching units are located. The construction of this dam has turned out to be a mockery and has resulted in the wastage of public resources. As it so happens, water that is stored in the dam is much more than the actual flow in the river. This is simply because a large quantity of water (about 120 mld/day) consumed by the Tiruppur dyeing and bleaching units is conveniently let into the Noyyal river (in the form of untreated trade effluent), contributing thereby to the 'additional storage level' of the dam. Thus, the dam effectively performs the role of a storage reservoir for the contaminated water, contributing quite significantly to the pollution of environment, in particular, groundwater. Unless 20,000 cusecs of water is released into the river Cauvery (a major river into which Noyyal joins in the downstream), the release of water from the Orathapalayam dam would be extremely harmful to the crops, soil, animals and groundwater. However, in February 1997 when there was no appreciable flow in the river Cauvery, the water from the Orathapalayam dam was released with a view to minimising the damage to the villages around the dam. Since the dam was opened without any prior public notice, it resulted in a great havoc to crops, animals, soil and groundwater. This polluted water of the Noyyal river joined Cauvery 32 km down the Orathapalayam dam. It is reported that hundred animals after drinking this water reported to have collapsed. A few petitions were filed in the High Court protesting against the decision of the Government in releasing the polluted water and claimed compensation for the damages. The Tamil Nadu Government realised the danger and had decided to release 20,000 cusecs of water from the Mettur dam even though it was a scarcity period, basically to absolve the polluted water in the Cauvery.

Further, in all the villages all along the river course from the Tiruppur town to the dam at Orathapalayam, a distance of about of 10 km, and villages along a distance of about 20 km of the river's downstream below the dam, groundwater and agriculture have been seriously affected. Blomqvist's (1996) field visits confirm that the groundwater in both sides of the Noyyal river has become brackish and considerably harder in the last 10-15 years. It is reported that the water quality remains bad even at 300 feet depth, rendering it unfit even for irrigation.

If the new water company in Tiruppur brings additional water (185 million liters per day) the pollution threat is going to escalate further. The existing CETPs (a total of 8) in this area hardly function, but satisfy the Supreme Court order. Further, these CETPs are not designed to treat the TDS which is the biggest pollutant. Since the RO system is very expensive, no industry owner is willing to treat the effluent. Therefore, the new company will pose additional problems by bringing more water to the town.

The other problem related to water company is the fixing of the price for water for the domestic users. The rates are not decided so far but it goes without saving that the rates for water is going to adversely affect the common man in the region.

Privatisation efforts in the power sector

Power is one of the most vulnerable sectors in India. The State Electricity Boards (SEBs), in almost all States perform very badly and dance according to the whims and fancies of the respective State Governments. The heavy transmission and distribution losses, theft, huge dues to be collected from industrial houses and all other un-metered consumption account for massive losses every year. In other words, inefficiency coupled with corrupt governance result in irredeemable losses to the SEBs. But of late, the Government of India, on the pretext of redeeming the SEBs, buckled under the pressure exerted by the World Bank and passed an Act called Regulatory Commissions Act (1998), which enables each state to set up a commission (SERC-State Electricity Regulatory Commission). In a State like Tamil Nadu, SERC is trying its best to lift free electricity, provided to the agricultural pumpsets since 1991.

The introduction of new agricultural bio-chemical technology and the neglect of traditional surface irrigation have contributed for a rapid growth of well irrigation in the State as well as in other parts of the country. As a consequence, wells were deepened in a competitive manner in order to get access to assured, timely and better quality of irrigation. In some sense, free electricity has also contributed to the indiscriminate and unregulated pumping. We also encounter a situation in which about two-thirds of the wells are owned by farmers who have a less than or equal to five acres. And one-third of wells are owned by small and marginal farmers who have less than 2.5 acres of land. This is a paradoxical situation in which there seems to be equity in access to ground water. But it reinforces a new class among farmers: Those who have struck good aquifers quite early on the day, large land owners who are better endowed with resources and potential water sellers have all prospered; But a large number have been deprived: for those of small and marginal farmers, who are the late exploiters of groundwater, there is a high probability of getting displaced in the process of competitive deepening. In a fast depleting groundwater regime, every bit of investment falls disproportionately on the small and marginal farmers. This is because, while large farmers have an incentive of irrigating a larger extent of land, small and tiny holders have the constraint of area that they can irrigate. Similarly, while large operators of land can sustain the event of an unsuccessful investment in well digging and deepening or persisting drought conditions (as occurred in the 1980s), for a small farmer it would be an unsustainable blow. Further, the very high incidence of joint well ownership (Sharing a well) complicates the matter. In all the river basins studied by the author, 40 percent to 50 percent of the wells are jointly owned. The problem gets further compounded because the incidence of joint well ownership is seemingly quite high in the small and marginal categories. For these farmers, re-introduction of electricity tariff would be a severe blow. They may even take recourse to closing down or be compelled to sell away their wells. In these farmers go out of orbit, it would result in unemployment, loss of production and so on.

15

An Inquiry Into the Poverty Decline in Rural India During 90s

*K. Hanumantha Rao**

Strong apprehensions have been expressed that the New Economic Reforms would adversely affect the well-being of the poor. Contrary to these, the poverty estimates based on large samples of National Sample Survey Organisation (NSSO), during the first decade of reforms in India have been exhibiting declining poverty trends. Several scholars have therefore, examined this paradoxical situation even while focusing on the scope for poverty reduction when the country itself is ill-equipped to opt for structural changes. {Gupta SP (1999), Gaurav Datt (1999), Sundaram (2001), Deaton and Dreze (2002)}. The present paper makes another attempt to seek some plausible explanation for poverty decline in rural India by shifting evidences in the agriculture sector and rural labour markets. Section-I portrays the poverty scenario that emerges from the NSSO data on consumption expenditure in rural areas. The groups which were adversely affected in the development process are identified. The performance of agriculture during 90s is reviewed in the next section since the rural poverty is

* Associate Professor, National Institute of Rural Development, Rajendranagar, Hyderabad–500 030.

highly correlated with nature and extent of agricultural growth. Since most of the poor participate in labour markets to take out their livelihoods, the changes in rural labour markets are depicted in the subsequent section with a view to linking them with the trends in poverty indicators. To obtain the insights into the development process which might have resulted in poverty decline during 90s, the partial elasticities of poverty vis-à-vis several key parameters were worked out. The last section presents the conclusions of this study.

Trends in Poverty Indices

The estimates of rural poverty in India during the new economic reforms era indicate a declining trend if one considers the NSSO's large sample data i.e. 43rd round (1987-88), 50th round (1993-94) and 55th round (1999-2000). The poverty decline was higher i.e. 4.56 percent per annum during late 90's compared to early 90s i.e. during 1987-88 to 1993-94 of less than one percent (Table 1). Even poverty estimates adjusted for changes in questionnaire design during 1999-00 and corrections for poverty lines confirm the declining trends in poverty in both rural and urban sectors1 (Deaton and Dreze, 2002); the extent of fall, however, varied.

The poverty estimates based on thin sample data reveal that during the early phase of reforms, poverty levels were fluctuating and were stable at 38 percent in the later period. In fact, the controversies about poverty trends in 90s revolve around the reconciliation of the estimates of poverty based on 'thin' and 'large' samples besides paucity of supporting evidence to justify such trends. It is to be noted that subjects of inquiry for these thin sample rounds are not 'consumption expenditure'. Thus, poverty analysis in this paper has been done mainly taking the large sample survey data.

Table 1: Levels of Poverty and Poverty Gap Index-Rural India

S. No.	*Year/Period*	*Poverty Ratio*	*Poverty Gap Index (PGI)*
1.	1983-94	45.7	12.32
2.	1987-88	39.2 (-2.4)	9.11 (-6.5)
3.	1988-89*	39.2	9.5
4.	1989-90*	34.3	7.8
5.	1990-91*	36.4	8.64
6.	1991-92*	37.4	8.29
7.	1992-93*	43.5	10.88
8.	1993-94	37.3 (-0.77)	8.45 (-1.21)
9.	1994-95*	38.8	8.63
10.	1995-96*	38.3	8.34
11.	1997*	38.5	9.03
12.	1999-00	27.1 (-4.56)	5.2 (-6.41)

Note: Figures in parentheses are growth rates over the previous period (with large sample size i.e. years without asterisk marks).

Source: Planning Commission, GOI.
Datta & Sharma (2002) for the Years with * marks.

Data on poverty gap index which measures the aggregate shortfall in consumption expenditure as a percentage of the poverty line also confirms the declining trends in poverty indicators. Thus, poverty decline in rural India was also accompanied by the reduction in inequalities in consumption expenditure among the poor in 90s.

Since rural poverty is heavily concentrated in socially disadvantaged groups like Scheduled Castes (SCs) and Scheduled Tribes (STs) and in agriculture dependent population i.e. Agriculture Labour (AL) and Self-Employed in Agriculture (SEAG), data on rural poverty across social groups and important occupational groups are presented in Tables 2 and 3. During early 90s, the rates of decline in poverty among SCs and STs were higher than those for

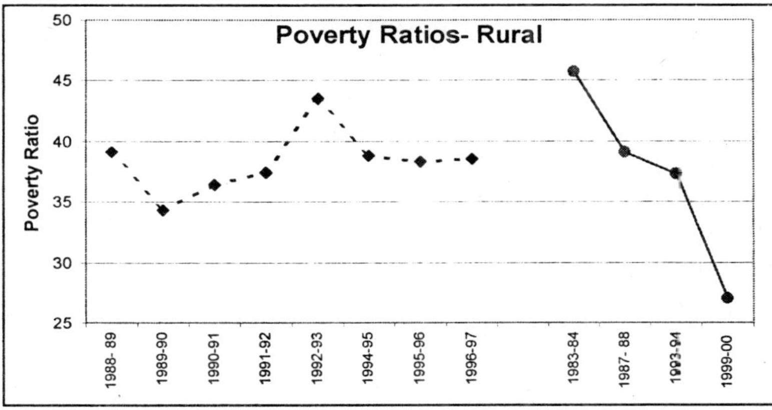

other groups. The poverty levels were further reduced at an accelerated pace for 'All classes' and 'SCs' in the subsequent period. In regard to STs, there was deceleration in the fall of poverty suggesting that the growth opportunities have been relatively reduced to them. The agriculture dependent population also gained more from the development process during late 90s. In other words in the initial phase, non SC & ST classes and agriculture labour did not benefit much compared to the rest. Since most of the SC adults are engaged in the agriculture and allied activities, the source of poverty reduction among SCs could be agriculture development mainly.

Table 2: Social and Economic Group-Wise Poverty in Rural India

	Poverty Levels (%)		
	1987 - 88	*1993 - 94*	*1999 - 2000*
All Classes	39.1	37.3 (-0.77)	27.1 (-4.56)
SC	55.2	48.3 (-2.08)	40.0 (-2.86)
ST	59.9	52.0 (-2.2)	48.2 (-1.22)
Agriculture Labour	61.8	56.8 (-1.35)	41.4 (-4.52)
SE in Andhra Pradesh	37.3	29.0 (-3.71)	20.4 (-4.94)

Note: Figures in parantheses are annual growth rates over the previous period.

The acceleration in poverty decline in Period-II for non- SC and ST classes indicate that these classes gained from the development of agriculture and non-agriculture activities. So, the poverty trends suggest that during period-I, the poverty decline was attributable mainly to agriculture growth and in the subsequent period, the growth in farm as well as non-farm sectors contributed to fall in poverty levels.

Table 3: Number of Poverty Persons-Rural India

	No. of poor persons (Millions)		
	1987 - 88	*1993 - 94*	*1999 - 2000*
All Classes	232	244 (0.86)	193 (-3.48)
SC	57.3[24.7]	68.9 (3.37) [28.2]	58.4 (-2.54) [30.3]
ST	34[14.7]	35.1 (0.54) [14.4]	35.0 (-0.05) [18.1]
Agriculture Labour	98.3[42.4]	106 (1.31) [43.4]	85.6 (-3.21) [44.3]
SE in agriculture	72.7[31.3]	69.4 (-0.76) [28.4]	52.0 (-4.18) [26.9]

Note: Figures in ( ) parantheses are percentage change per annum over the previous period
Figures in [ ] brackets are shares in total poverty
SE: Self-employed

From Table 3, it is evident that absolute number of poor increased in Period-I by less than 0.9 percent per annum. Similar is the case with respect to poor among SCs, STs and agriculture labour; exception being SE in Agriculture. The data also confirm the view that share of socially disadvantaged was almost 40 percent in poverty and those of agriculture-dependent population was about 75 percent in early 90s. The shares of SCs and agriculture labour in poverty had gone up during period-I, though moderately. These percentages were higher than their shares in rural population confirming the vulnerability of these sections.

Period-II was characterised by reduction in the number of poor in all categories; the extent, however, varied across the categories. The SCs and STs account for almost 50 percent of the total poor (it was 39 percent in 1987-88 and 43 percent in 1993-94). The share of agriculture labour was almost stable at 42-44 percent; on the contrary, share of 'SE in Agriculture' fell from 31 percent in 1987-88 to 27 percent by 1999-00. The variations in the shares of different socio-economic groups could be due to several factors which include varying rates of growth of population of the specific categories and differential effects of economic growth during 90s.

Agricultural Growth and Rural Poverty

Given the dependency of rural people on agriculture for their livelihoods, an inverse relation between agricultural growth and rural poverty is expected though such relationship seems to have weakened in several states. During this decade the share of agriculture to total GDP has slipped from 28.7 to 23 percent while the dependency on agriculture for employment has not reduced much.

Table 4 contains data on the performance of the agriculture sector. The GDP from agriculture grew moderately in period-I and later remarkably. The labour productivity in agriculture registered a low but negative growth in Period-I and it expanded at over 2 percent per annum in late 90s. The fall in labour force participation rates more so, of female workers during 1999-00 could be attributable partly to the rise in the growth rate of labour productivity. Thus, agriculture sector might have contributed substantially for poverty reduction in Period-II in rural India. Since many studies have shown high (negative) correlation between foodgrain output and poverty, the observed rise in production of foodgrains in 90s might have benefited the low-income classes. Thus, rise in the supply of foodgrains has helped the bottom deciles in terms of employment and also increased availability of grains for consumption at affordable prices.

Table 4: Foodgrains output, GDP from Agriculture and Labour Productivity

	1987-88	*1993-94*	*1999-00*
A. GDP from Agriculture TE (at 1993-94 prices) (R. Crore)	210965	221834(0.86)	66292(3.34)
B. Labour productivity * in agriculture (Rs.)	1145	1090(-0.80)	1227(2.09)
C. Foodgrains output TE ending with (MT)	144.1	177.4 (3.86)	201.6(2.27)

* GDP from Agriculture (at 1993-94 prices) divided by the estimated number of workers engaged in agriculture.
TE: Triennium; MT: Million Tonnes.
Source: CSO., 'National Accounts Statistics', GOI., Economic Survey; 1999-2000, Shariff and Gumber (1999).

Rural economy is getting diversified but the farm sector still occupies an important position. The contribution of farm sector on poverty is traced indirectly by examining the rates of growth of crop output and crop productivity during these two periods. It is clear from Table 5 that crop output and its productivity measured at 1990-93 prices have been rising steadily. The contribution of area to output expansion was about 0.3 percent per annum during 1980/83 to 1992/95 and in the later period-it was even negative. Thus, the improved performance of farm sector might have had favourable effects on the dependent population.

Table 5: Growth of Agricultural Crop Output and Productivity (at 1990-93 prices)

	1980-83	*1992-95*	*1998-2000**
Agricultural Crop Output (Rs in billions)	843.47	1260.4(4.1)	1782 (7.53)
Agricultural Crop Productivity (Rs per hectare)	5090	7388(3.76)	10498 (7.65)

Source: For the period 1980 - 83 and 1992 - 95, the values are taken from Bhalla and Singh (2000)
* Using the approach of Bhalla and Singh, values are estimated for the period 1998-2000

Changes in Labour Market

There have been marked improvements in the rural labour markets during the last few decades (Hanumantha Rao, K; 2000). For instance, literacy levels of rural males and females have gone up from 44.9 and 21.9 percent in 1983 to 58.8 and 38.5 percent respectively by 1999-00. The Quality of Labour Index (QLI) (15 years and above age) 2 - indicates an overall improvement in the capabilities of the workforce (see Table 6). The Index Occupational Distribution (ODI)3 of workers point out that workforce has been getting diversified initially but the process was reversed in late 90s perhaps due to limited number of opportunities in the non-agriculture sector (for both males and females). The rural labour markets have been characterised by increased casualisation which will enhance vulnerability or reduce livelihood security. The Index of Employment Opportunities (EOI)4 reveal that during late 90s, the rural labour markets have not been providing ample opportunities. e.g. the percentage of households with no employed persons has gone up to 4.7 in 1999-00 from 3.1 in 1993-94. Similarly, the percentage of households with one male and one female employees has gone down to 22.8 in 1999-00 from 29 in 1993-94.

Table 6: Changes in Rural Labour Markets-Key Indices

	1987-88		*1993-94*		*1999-2000*	
	M	*F*	*M*	*F*	*M*	*F*
ODI	56.1	68.9	56.3	74.9	52.3	71.6
QLI	14.6	7.04	21.0	6.58	24.2	8.58
IOC	31.4	35.5	33.8	38.7	36.2	39.6
EOI	68.8		73.0		71.0	

ODI: Occupational Diversification Index;
QLI: Quality of Labour Index (based on literacy and education levels);
IOC: Incidence of casualisation (or percentage of casual workers)
EOI: Employment Opportunities Index (for households)

The qualitative changes in rural labour market, ceteris paribus, are likely to influence the poverty scenario, more so among those households with wage income as the principal source of income.

Though labour force participation rates have not either improved or fallen during 1999-005, the absolute number of labourers registered arise and male labourers grew at a higher rate than the female group (following the usual status approach) (see Table 7). The number of workers/employed persons - both males and females, grew steadily in the two periods. The unemployed persons declined during period-I more so in the case of female workers and the second portrays provides a disturbing picture of rise in the number of unemployed persons. The rate of growth of female unemployed was high indicating that the later part of 90s was unfavourable to females (Hanumantha Rao and Rajya Lakshmi, 2002).

Table 7: Estimated Labour Force, Employed and Unemployed Persons-Rural India

Figures in Millions

Sl. No.	*Particulars*	*1987-88*		*1993-94*		*1999-2000*	
		M	*F*	*M*	*F*	*M*	*F*
B.	Labour Force *	155.3	88.7	168.8 (1.45)	93.8 (0.96)	189.3 (2.02)	101.5 (1.37)
C.	Employed *	152.5	86.7	166.4 (1.52)	93.1 (1.23)	186.1 (1.97)	100.5 (1.32)
D.	Un-Employed *	2.8	2.0	2.4 (-2.48)	0.7 (-10.8)	3.2 (5.83)	1.0 (8.33)

Note: Figures in parantheses are growth rates over the previous period.

* Usual status approach considering principal and subsidiary statuses.

Since current Daily Status (CDS) approach is superior to the Usual Status (US) and Current Weekly Status (CWS) approaches, the employment and unemployment days for males and females were worked out using CDS approach (see Table 8). The number of employment days for males per week has gone up from 992 millions in 1987-88 to 1061 millions in 1993-94 and then to 1172 millions by 1999-00. The employment grew at a moderate pace but the unemployment has also gone up at an alarming level, exception being the decline in unemployment for females during 1993-94 over 1987-88. Once adjusted for the size, the average number of days of employment per annum was steadily declining for male workers; while it was fluctuating in the case of female workers. The difference between male and female workers in employment was reduced from 105 days to 42 days during early 90s confirming that this period was favourable to women workers. Period-II was unfavourable to both male and female workers. So, decline in employment days per worker and reduction in poverty cannot to be corroborated unless the wages in real terms might have risen significantly. Table 9 contains data on wage earnings of casual agriculture laboureres expressed at 1987-88 prices. It can be gleaned from the Table that the wage earnings registered a marginal rise in the Period-I but late 90s witnessed a phenomenal rise in the wage earnings. Juxtaposing the two i.e. employment and wages, one can infer that the loss in employment was over

Table 8: Growth of Employment and Unemployment (CDS)*

(Million person days)

	1987-88		*1993-94*		*1999-2000*	
	M	*F*	*M*	*F*	*M*	*F*
Employment(days per week)	992.2	388.8	1061.36 (1.16)	435.64 (2.01)	1172.33 (1.74)	481.13 (1.74)
Unemployment(days per week)	47.5	28.17	63.44 (5.59)	25.62 (-1.51)	90.37 (7.21)	36.27 (6.93)
Employment per worker (days/year)	338	233	333 (-0.25)	291 (4.15)	309 (-1.20)	238 (-3.04)

* Using the Current Daily Status approach

compensated by the rise in wages. The qualitative changes in labour market and hike in real wages could provide plausible explanation to poverty decline, to a certain extent.

Table 9: Wage earnings of casual labourers in Agriculture and other activities (at 1987-88 prices)*

(Rs/day)

	1987-88		*1993-94*		*1999-2000*	
	M	*F*	*M*	*F*	*M*	*F*
a. Agriculture						
i. Public works	12.62	9.31	14.03 (1.8)	10.4 (1.9)	29.7 (18.6)	19.9 (15.2)
ii. Other works	10.73	9.17	12.10 (2.1)	8.50 (-1.2)	25.6 (18.6)	16.5 (15.7)
b. All activities	12.30	7.60	12.97 (0.9)	8.61 (2.2)	25.6 (16.2)	16.5 (15.3)

Source: NSSO.
Note: Figures in parantheses are growth rates over the previous period.

Before analysing the impact of the changes in rural poverty due to several factors relating to agriculture sector and labour market, the trends in per capita monthly consumption expenditure are examined (see Table 10). The

Table 10: Estimated Per Capita Consumption Expenditure

(Rs/month)

	1987-88	*1993-94*	*1999-2000*
All Classes	157.66	281.4 (13.08)	486.1 (12.12)
SC	139.02	238.9 (11.98)	391.00 (10.61)
ST	130.48	234.4 (13.27)	365.74 (9.34)
Share of B-30 in Consumer Expenditure	15.6	18.2 (2.78)	18.8 (0.55)

Note: Figures in parantheses are growth rates over the previous period.

consumption levels grew faster in period-I compared to period-II for all groups and for SCs and STs. The deceleration was noticed more for STs. The improvements in the share of bottom - 30 percent of rural population in the consumption expenditure augurs well with reduction in poverty ratios. During the initial period, the inequality reduced sharply than in the latter period.

The partial elasticities of rural poverty were computed by calculating the ratio of growth in poverty to growth in the (selected) parameter during the reference period. It is evident from Table 11, that the impact of agriculture related parameters on poverty was more during period-II. Similarly, the labour market related parameters have also made higher dent on rural poverty in late 90s.

Table 11: Partial Elasticities of Rural Poverty

	Parameter	*Period-I*	*Period-II*
1	GDP from Agriculture	-0.89	-1.36
2	Crop output/Crop Productivity	-0.19	-0.61
3	Foodgrains output	-0.89	-2.01
4	Per capita consumption expenditure	-0.05	-0.38
5	Inequality in consumption expenditure distribution - share of Bottom - 30% population	-0.32	-8.60
6	Labour productivity	0.96	-2.18
7	Employment of male workers (CDS approach)	-3.08	-3.8
8	Wage rate of male casual workers	-0.85	-0.28

Period-I: 1987-88 to 1993-94
Period-II: 1993-94 to 1999-00

Conclusions

- NSSO data on consumer expenditure based on thick samples and corrections applied (by others) for changes in recall period and also price indices, which reflect more aptly the inflationary trends confirm the view that poverty in rural India had declined in the first phase of the new economic reforms i.e., the decade of 90s.

- Poverty gap indices reveal that inequalities among poor have also shrinked during this period.
- Effects of economic growth were uneven and rates of poverty reduction differed across socio-economic (occupational) groups. In the initial period i.e. during 1987-88 to 1993-94, poverty decline was more conspicuous among the socially disadvantaged. However, the late 90s did not benefit the STs much. The 'agriculture labour' could not reap much from development initially unlike the self-employed in Agriculture. The poverty decline in Period-I was mostly ascribable to the growth in agriculture and to the entire rural economic prosperity in the latter period.
- Due to varying rates of population growth and the differential effects of development, the share of SCs and STs in poverty had gone up in the reforms era from less than 40 percent to about 50 percent.
- The rates of growth of GDP, labour productivity and those of crop output and its productivity indicate that the effect of agriculture development on rural poverty could be more during the second period.
- The labour market changes are more favourable during period I than in period-II. The growth rates of employment and unemployment were higher in second period and the net effect might be beneficial to low-income classes in the light of the observed poverty decline. Female workers were (relatively) at a disadvantage during late 90s.
- On the whole, the employment per annum for male workers was steadily reducing while that of females was fluctuating. The rising unemployment levels for both males and females warn that the initial era of the new economic reforms was unfavourable to rural workers. However, the impressive gains

in real wage earnings might have compensated the loss in the employment opportunities. The real causes of steep rise in wages of the casual workers need further scrutiny besides the observed improvements in labour and land productivities.

- The partial poverty elasticities together confirm that several factors were at play for the observed poverty decline during 90s and the changes in rural labour market and agriculture performance could provide needed explanation partly if not totally.

END NOTES

1. The poverty estimates for rural India adjusted for questionnaire design and revised poverty lines are given below (see Deaton and Dreze).

	1987-88	*1993-94*	*1999-00*
a Adjusted for changes in questionnaire Design	39.4	37.1	30.0
b Revising the poverty line	39.4	33.0	26.3

2. Quality of Labour Index (QLI) is constructed by taking weighted average the workforce with different literacy and educational levels. Scores of 0,1,2,3,4 and 5 were assigned for illiterate, literate and up to primary, middle, secondary, higher secondary and others, respectively.

$$\text{QLI} = \sum_{i:0}^{5} (\text{PiWi}) \times 100$$

Where **Pi** proportion of workforce in i th category of education level, **Wi** the score for i th category.

3. Occupational Diversification Index (ODI) is calculated as follow

$$\text{ODI} = \left\{ \sum_{i:1}^{n} (a_i)^2 \right\} \times 100 \qquad \text{n: g}$$

Where ai is proportion of workers in i th industry
I: 1, ... n is 9-fold industrial classification
Higher the value of ODI, greater is the concentration of workforce in a few industries; a lower value indicates diversification of occupational distribution.

4. Index of Employment Opportunities (EOI) is obtained by

$$EOI = \sum_{j:0}^{4} \left(x_j s_j\right)$$

Where xj proportion of households in I th category and sj is the corresponding score. Households are categorised into: households with no employed person, with one female employee, with one male employee, with one male and one female employed and others.

REFERENCES

1. Abusaleh Shariff and Anil Gumber (1999) "Employment and Wages in India: Pre and post Reform Scenario", Indian Journal of Labour Economics Vol. 42 (2).
2. Bhalla GS and G. Singh (2000)., "Indian Agriculture: Four Decades of Development" Sage publications, New Delhi.
3. Datt Gaurav (1999a)., "Has Poverty Declined since Economic Reforms?", Economic and Political Weekly, December 11-17.
4. Datta KL and Savita Sharma (2002)., "Facets of Indian Poverty" concept Publishing Co. New Delhi.
5. Deaton A and Jean Dreze (2002)., "Poverty and Inequality in India: A Re-examination" Economic and Political Weekly September 7.
6. Gupta, SP (1999): "Tricle Down Theory Revisited: The Role of Employment and Poverty", V B Singh Memorial Lecture, 41st Annual Conference of the Indian Society of Labour Economics, November 18-20, Mumbai.
7. Hanumantha Rao K and K. Rajya Laskhmi (2002)., "Structure of Employment and Casualisation in Rural India during Pre and Post Reforms Regime", Journal of Rural Development Vol. 21 (1).
8. Hanumantha Rao. K. (2000), "Changes in the Structure of Employment in Rural Areas" NIRD, Hyderabad. National Sample Survey Organisation, Reports Nos. 461, 457, 458.
9. Sundaram, K (2001a): "Employment—Unemployment situation in the Nineties: Some Results from NSS 55th Round Survey", Economic and Political Weekly, March, 17.
10. Sundaram, K (2001 b): "Employment and Poverty in 1990s: Further Results from NSS 55th Round Employment-Unemployment Survey, 1999-2000", Economic and Political Weekly August 11."

16

Impact of Economic Reforms on Growth and Poverty

*S. Subrahmanyam**

India's development strategy after attaining Independence can be divided into three distinct phases. During the first phase, which extend for three decades, the country followed economic policies, which gave the government primary role. This period witnessed a low growth rate of 3-4 percent per annum. The second phase, the decade of eighties, is a period of partial liberalisation. During this phase the country attained a high growth rate of more than 5 percent in its real Gross Domestic Product (GDP). This high performance is mixed with fiscal and foreign exchange crises or internal and external crises. The balance of payments crisis became so serious that the reserves plummeted to less than ten days of imports. This is due to the trade liberalisation policies adopted during the decade. Imports grew at a high rate with no commensurate growth of exports. The internal crisis is due to increase in fiscal deficit from 7 percent of the GDP at the beginning of the decade to 9.4 percent by the end of the decade. As a result of this, public debt as a ratio of GDP increased from 30 to 60 percent. The credit rating by the international agencies has gone down to a low level forcing the country to approach the International Monetary Fund (IMF) for a loan of $1.8 billion in 1991. India had to

* Professor in Centre for Economic and Social Studies, Hyderabad.

agree for introducing wide ranging reforms in order to get the loan from the IMF. The World Bank/IMF strategy for development is to reduce the role of the government to the minimum and removal of trade restrictions. Hence this strategy is designated as liberalisation, privatisation and globalisation model. With establishment of the World Trade Organisation (WTO) in 1995, globalisation has become compulsory for the country. A study based on the data from 20 developing countries shows that economic performance does not differ greatly between fully-fledged market economies and partially liberalised ones. Further, there is little difference in manufacturing and agricultural growth between full and partial liberalisers, yet the overall growth is more rapid for the former because of the high growth of the service sector (White Howard and Jennifer Leavy, 2000). This paper examines the performance of the Indian economy in terms of growth, regional inequalities and poverty in India during the decade of partial reforms and full-fledged reforms.

Review of Economic Reforms

The control of the public sector is removed from 15 out 18 industries that were hitherto under control. Only defence equipment, atomic energy generation and railway transport were retained in the list of industries reserved for the public sector. Reservation of industries for small-scale sector is reduced (54 items are removed from the reserved list in 2001 and 2002). Licensing by the Central Government is almost abolished except in the case of hazardous and environmentally sensitive industries. In the pre-reform period investment by large industrial houses needed a separate clearance under the Monopolies and Restrictive Trade Practices Act. Now the condition is removed and the act is going to be replaced by a new competition law. In trade policy import licensing was abolished for capital and intermediate goods industries in 1993. There was a switch to flexible exchange rate regime.

Quantitative restrictions on imports of manufactured consumer goods and agricultural products were removed on April 1, 2001 partly because of a ruling by a WTO dispute settlement panel on a complaint brought by the United States. Liberalising foreign direct investment is another important aspect of economic reforms. A large number of industries are now allowed to have 100 percent foreign ownership. Further, except in banking, insurance, telecommunications and airlines, all other industries are allowed to have majority ownership by foreign companies. Industries eligible for automatic approval with foreign equity levels of 100 percent, 74 percent and 51 percent are specified so that potential investors within these limits need not wait for approval and it is enough if they just register with the Reserve Bank of India. The Foreign Investment Promotion Board will consider the applications when investment of a higher share of equity is involved. The reform process neglected agricultural sector partly because it comes under the state subject. The policies introduced for promoting foodgrain production are still followed. Huge subsidies are provided on power, water and fertiliser and on the other, investment in agriculture declined. However, there is improvement in investment in agriculture in the 1990s.

The size of the external reserves crossed $60 billion. Significantly foreign exchange reserves have been accumulating when the external environment is not very conducive for developing countries. However, accumulation of reserves is due to lower oil imports reflecting recession in the industrial sector. On the other hand, the problem of fiscal deficit could not be tackled. Though it could be reduced in the initial years, it has again gone back to the pre-reform level after mid-1990s. The blame is thrown on the public savings, which were found to be negative after mid-1990s. This may be due to the disinvestments of profit making units and keeping the loss making units. There is no increase in the investment ratio in the nineties, indicating that the scope for increasing the growth rate does not exist. Tax revenues of the Center declined from 9.7 percent in 1990-91 to 8.8 percent in 2000-01. This is due to poor performance of indirect taxes, Customs duties were reduced deliberately as a part of trade reforms.

Between 1991 and 2001, FDI approvals in these states came to Rs.1588.6 billion which comes to Rs.2014 per capita. However, Maharashtra attracted the highest amount of Rs.5780 in per capita terms. Karnataka, Gujarat and Tamil Nadu also attracted a high amount of FDI (more than Rs.4000 per capita). These four states attracted two-thirds of the FDI during the 1990s.

Growth Performance of Indian Economy

India's growth performance improved marginally during the 1990s as compared to the 1980s (5.24 to 5.53 percent). This acceleration is not only marginal, but also unsustainable. It is unsustainable because the commodity producing sectors namely, agriculture as well as manufacturing, experienced deceleration in growth. For instance, GDP from agriculture decelerated from 3.1 percent during the 1980s to 2.8 percent during the nineties. This is after taking into account the shift to value addition activities even in agriculture. The growth rate of manufacturing sector decelerated from 7.1 percent in the eighties to 6.2 percent in the nineties. The registered part of the manufacturing was hit more severely than the unregistered part. While the latter maintained its earlier growth rate, the former experienced fall in the growth rate from 8 percent during eighties to 6.4 percent during the nineties. The unsustainable nature of the growth of nineties also arises because of the deceleration in the growth of electricity, gas and water supply. The former experienced decline in growth from 8.9 percent in the 80s to 5.7 percent in the 90s. This slow growth will affect the commodity producing sectors adversely.

It is significant to examine whether the acceleration in the service sector growth and deceleration in the growth of commodity producing sectors occurred in the initial period of reforms (before 1985) or later period of reforms (after 1985). The early part of the 90s, in fact, experienced acceleration in agricultural growth. On the other hand, the acceleration in the growth of service sector occurred only during the later part of the 90s. In fact, the early part of the 90s witnessed deceleration in growth. This high growth in the service sector is partly due to the rise in the salary structure of the government employees as a result of the implementation of the recommendations of the Fifth Pay Commission and partly due to IT boom.

The issue of poverty has become important in the nineties because of the policy debate on the effects of economic reforms introduced in 1991. The data on poverty are available from two large sample surveys conducted during 1993-94 and 1999-2000 (50th and 55th rounds of NSSO) and four small sample surveys conducted during the intervening years. The controversy about the trends in poverty during the nineties is mainly due to the change in methodology of data collection since 1994-95. In all the four small sample surveys, this new reference period is adopted for one half of the sample and old reference period for the remaining half. The results based on week reference period showed significantly higher level of consumption and hence lower incidence of poverty between 1993-94 and 1998-99. The incidence fluctuated between 36 and 43 percent as compared to 37 percent in 1993-94 in rural areas 32 and 35 percent in urban as compared to 33 percent in 1993-94. But in 55th round relating to 1999-2000 both reference periods are included in the same questionnaire and with this change the gap in per capita expenditure between the two estimates almost vanished and there was steep increase in the estimates based week reference period. The estimate of poverty for 1999-2000 is found to be 26.1 as against 36 percent 1993-94. A lot of energy is being spent in adjusting the estimates of consumption and poverty for design changes. For instance, Deaton and Dreze (2002) adjust for design changes and show that the incidence rises slightly from 26.8 to 30 percent in rural areas and 24.1 to 24.7 percent in urban areas after adjustment. They conclude that the decline in the incidence of poverty in the nineties is real. However, these results have to be taken with a pinch of salt and no definite conclusions can be drawn till the results of the next NSS round are available. The evidence from growth of real wages and growth of food grain prices relative to the growth of overall price index do not support the hypothesis of poverty reduction in the nineties. The growth rate of wholesale price index as well as that of foodgrain prices are higher in the 1990s as compared to the 1980s. Further, while foodgrain price index grew at a lower rate than wholesale price index in the 1980s, the opposite had happened in the 1990s.

Regional Inequality

One of the most debated issues with reference to economic reforms is the issue of regional inequalities. Among the 17 states considered for the analysis, three states occupy top position with per capita SDP exceeding Rs.19000 per annum, another three states have per capita income of Rs.16000-17000, five states have income level of Rs.13000-15000, four states have Rs8000-11000 and two states occupy the bottom-most position with per capita income less than Rs.6000. Thus the gap between the top and bottom states is more than three times. There is no change in the ranks of the top four states either in the 80s or in the 90s. Similarly, there is not much change in the ranks of bottom four states except those caused by deterioration in the ranks of Jammu & Kashmir and Assam. All changes in ranks took place in the middle level.

Tamil Nadu and Andhra Pradesh are significant beneficiaries in the 80s with their ranks improving from nine to five in the case of the former and twelve to nine in the case of the latter. West Bengal showed significant deterioration during the 80s. Kerala improved its position significantly during the 90s. Except in the case of the top two states whose growth rate is found to be less than 4.7 percent, there appears to be systematic positive association between per capita income and growth rate of per capita income. During the 90s, Gujarat, Maharashtra, Karnataka, Tamil Nadu and Kerala attained growth rates of more than 6 percent per annum. These are the states where FDI is concentrated.

Whether incomes are converging or diverging is examined by finding the coefficient of variation in per capita NSDP across states for the three periods and also by estimating the growth regression. These results show that regional inequalities are increasing since 1981, but the divergence is more glaring during the 90s.

On the basis of the above analysis, it may be concluded that full-scale liberalisation has not helped the country either in poverty reduction or in reducing regional inequalities, though overall growth could be maintained. The sector-wise growth trends indicate that this growth is not sustainable.

17

New Economic Policy In India: The Caste Dimension

*Prof. K.S. Chalam**
*Dr. D. Francis***

Introduction

The social order in the Indian society reckons with the varnashrama dharma in which the four varnas shall always perform their assigned duties so as to keep the equilibrium. The first three varnas are called as the *dvijas*, the twice born and the fourth varna is put in position to serve the *dvijas*. Therefore, they are called the shudras. There are several layers among the shudras and they are manipulated and ordered to work as per the requirements of the *dvijas*. The panchamas, the fifth category has always been outside the order as an experimental group. Keeping this social structure in view, several attempts have been made to develop the socio-economic conditions of the people. Interestingly, those who have migrated to other faiths over centuries have not behaved very differently and therefore, fit into the varnadharma. There seems to be an agenda hidden or public according to which the social and economic processes take place in India. Unless one understands this, it is very difficult to analyse any developments in the

* Professor of Economics and Director, UGC-Academic Staff College, Andhra University, Visakhapatnam.

** Research Associate, UGC-Academic Staff College, Andhra University, Visakhapatnam.

country, be it contemporary or historical. An attempt is made in this paper to analyse the new economic policy from this perspective.

Caste as property

Caste in the Indian subcontinent is considered as an important social category. But, caste is hardly analysed by social scientists as an economic category. Though its manifestation is social, its essence is found to be purely economic. In fact, the first social anthropologist H.W. Wiser who examined caste and introduced the concept of "Jajmani" for the first time in the 1930 had analysed the transactions among different castes in a village and found them as purely economic. The real transactions between Brahmins and Kshatriyas and between the '*dvijas*' and other servile castes and among the servile castes and untouchable castes were found to be purely economic in nature. He even estimated the values of products and services transacted between castes in Kalimpur village. It was clearly established that the Brahmin gives only intangible service and takes the highest value of goods and services from others. At the lowest level, the untouchable provides the maximum value in terms of goods and services and in return receives the lowest value. If these values are translated as returns from each caste's property, the concept of caste as an economic category will be clear. Marx has mentioned that social relations are always embedded in economic relations. These relations are nothing but property relations. In this context, caste needs to be understood as property in India. However, considering the hindu caste as property has certain limitations. The character of property as a thing to exchange with others or sell it to outsiders is very much limited here. Therefore, caste is to be considered here as communal possession and not as private property. Wiser has mentioned in his study that caste was a corrupted form of ancient system of the custom of communal ownership directed by the Panchayat.

In other words, caste is a hindu category of property where the brahmin possesses the highest value and the lowest value is assigned to untouchable. Viewed from this angle, caste system as described by Kelkar and adopted by Ambedkar is not just division of labourers. In the division of labourers, the individual labourer is considered as a unit of analysis. But the Indian caste system is a division of groups of people, each being assigned with a particular duty and economic value. That is why, the members of a family in a caste produce finished goods and not parts of a good. This is generally understood as division of labour in economics. The castes being economic entities, accumulate these values over a period of time. But, the hindu super structure which has been protecting this economic caste base, did not allow the non-*dvija* castes to accumulate and capitalise their value. The *dvija* castes of Brahmin, Kshatriya and Vaisya are given the right and opportunities to education, assets, weapons etc., which naturally accumulate (may be primitive accumulation) capital over a period of time and improve their value of human capital. But it is denied to the Sudras and untouchables. As a result, the social manifestation of unequal exchange between castes is now synthesised as property relations.

Caste being a property of a group of people can be utilised for the advantage of the members of the group. This has also been used for the exploitation of others and also empowering of one's own group. These concepts have been used here to understand the economic power of the dominant *dvija* castes particularly Brahmin caste in India today.

In a modern democratic society, the struggle among different political groups is aimed ultimately to distribute resources. Those who are the winners in the race will have control over the resources and provide opportunities for their supporters to have access to these. In the Indian situation, the Brahmins have remained arbiters and enjoyed the patronage of both the winners and also the runners. Kautilya, the Brahmin Intellectual had laid a strong foundation for a brahminical political economy as distinguished from western political economic theory much before western economic theory emerged. The basic principle on which Kautilya laid his political economic theory is that every person is dishonest as against the western idea that man is rational. He mentioned in his **Arthasastra** how the state should get revenue and how it should spend the money. In the hierarchy of the state, the ministers who are in general were drawn from among the Brahmins, came first, and then the purohit enjoyed the highest status. He had even gone to the extent of saying that the king can cheat gullible people in getting revenue for the exchequer. Kautilyan principles have been followed by almost all the kings in the country till the emergence of urban economy. The vaishyas have cooperated with the King in carrying out the internal and external trade. Thus, the *dvijas* had the opportunity to run the State.

The Dvija Project

Dvijas as the twice born are basic pillars of the Indian society. There is absolute understanding and cooperation among the three groups to maintain equilibrium. It is found sometimes, that one category among the three is benefited, and it is their unwritten denotation that the other will not grudge. In times of crisis they get united and share the pillage. This is abundantly clear in the economic reforms of post-independent period. There seems to be at least one adjustment and reform in a period of one decade starting with the First Five Year Plan. Each adjustment made the *dvija* groups to modernise and adjust to the changing times. They get distributed among different groups and platforms and argue and speak differently ultimately to benefit the *dvijas*. For instance, the abolition of privy purses made the Kshatriyas to turn out as capitalists, the public sector modernised the Brahmins, the license raj benefited the Vaishyas and so on. This is the *dvija* project which has been in operation for quite sometime. There are however, certain aberrations here and there when some upper sudras tried to climb the ladder in the guise of a *dvija*. In such cases, they are either thrown out of the system or absorbed depending upon the circumstances and the strength of the beholder. The economic reforms or the so called New Economic Policy need to be analysed from this perspective to draw meaningful conclusions.

Several developments have taken place in the Indian economy and polity during the last 50 years. But, the basic structure of the society remained the same with few opportunities provided first to the upper sudras and later to some OBCs. Some of the dalits and OBCs who have been coopted into the system have slowly formed into a bahujan group as a political category. The emergence of regional parties and groups is an indicator of the upsurge of this category, particularly the OBCs.

Planning was introduced in the country in the1950s and investments to the extent of several thousands of crores during the plan periods were basically managed and enjoyed by the brahmin and *dvija* bureaucrats. Public property was slowly converted into private property through black money, scandals, bribes and other economic crimes. By the end of 1980, most of the upper castes acquired properties worth crores of rupees in the form of urban property, real estate, shares in private companies and they were also in a position to develop an independent economy. Several studies in the area of social economy of Tamil Nadu revealed that the reservation policy of the DMK Government reduced job opportunities to Brahmins. This made enterprising Brahmins like T.V.S.Iyengar and Sundaram Finance, to develop private enterprises with public money from the centre. Any casual observation of all our metropolis and urban areas reveal that posh localities and government developed estates are occupied by the upper castes. All the banks in the country are either managed or owned by them. Further, public higher education helped them to become most lucrative NRIs. Most of the NRIs today are from *dvija* groups only. The Mandal Commission report has provided data on the numerical strength of the Brahmins in the Indian Bureaucracy.

Meanwhile, the license raj helped them to develop independent industry at the cost of the public sector. Some scheduled caste and tribes have started entering into public sector employment through reservations to challenge the hegemony of *dvijas*. In the south, OBCs have also joined the ranks of secular job seekers in the modern public sector. The Brahmins who have swelled their private exchequer with public money thought that it would not be beneficial any more if they continued in the public sector They envisaged that it becomes risky if the public sector continues further as the dalits are emerging as a formidable force. The results of R & D of the public institutions have been slowly passed into private individuals or corporate bodies. The Official Secrets Act is being used by the bureaucrats to syphon off money and other resources for private gains. This made the public sector dry and inefficient. The jolt given by the *dvija*s to the public sector tycoons like Krishna Murthy, Steno Harshad Mehta, Ketan Parekh, RBI, SEBI personnel and others show the nexus between them and their control over the economy. Already the saffron entrepreneurs have collected thousands of crores of rupees from the gullible OBCs and sudras. They have captured power by using the 'Bhasmasura' technique on the sudras. Meanwhile, the bahujan concept also started gaining momentum. Therefore, they thought that it would be beneficial for them to survive both economically and politically if the economy is made private and linked it to the international market. The brahmin experts in the World Bank and the brahmin bureaucracy in Delhi conspired and mortgaged the economy when the bahujans were emerging as a force to manage the economy and enjoy the benefits of it. They thought that it is difficult to fight the bahujans if the struggle to control the economy is an internal issue and conspired to make it an international issue. The alleged international manoeuvring for an Aryan hegemony by combining Germany, Russia and India is only a move to curb the emerging bahujan power and to get international support to crush the indigenous bahujan majority. The New Economic Policy and the WTO must be seen in this context. This is the *dvija* project in operation in an era of liberalisation.

What is New Economic Policy

Liberty, the concept on which the whole edifice of new economic policy is built now was first enunciated by J.S.Mill to enhance individual choice and for the organisation of production. Mill never advocated liberty for the sake of exploitation and profit making. The economic reforms of the Government of India in 1991 based on the principle of liberty, however consisted of broadly two kinds of policies. One, the stabilisation policy which was implemented in response to a payments crisis in 1991 as India was running a current account deficit of around $10 billion and the reserves were down to two weeks of imports. Second, the structural reforms which were initiated in the early 1980s but slowed down later and again vigorously pursued as a package of economic reforms in 1991. The stabilisation policy, which was purely on account of trade deficit and earlier policies of the Government was embarked upon as an inevitable strategy to come out of the crisis. In fact, the economy as a whole was not that bad and it was growing at 5.5 percent just before the economic reforms (1980-90) as compared to 3.6 percent of the previous period (1965-80). But, the economy slipped into a crisis in the later part of 1990 due to several factors that were not purely economic in nature. The liberal licensing policy of allowing foreign automobile manufacturers to start production of two wheelers and four wheelers that consume oil, forced the country to import more oil straining the foreign reserves. It has been argued that India had entered the decade of nineties with large internal and external imbalances which made the economy highly vulnerable for any kind of shocks. It is further elaborated that the Gulf crisis has added a serious blow to the system and its foreign reserves dropped dramatically and the international credit ratings placed India at a very low position particularly between August 1990 and July 1991. This situation has forced the government to adopt an adjustment strategy by borrowing heavily from the international agencies. It has devalued its rupee three times during a period of two months and instilled confidence in foreign funding agencies and borrowed heavily from the World Bank and IMF. Along with these changes, the country has also agreed to follow the economic prescriptions dictated by these agencies. Though the government may say that it is pursuing a structural reform, it is in fact providing opportunities to control the economy through market. Therefore, the following prescriptions are implemented:

1. In the realm of trade policy the new policy replaces import licensing

2. In the area of industrial policy, the system of licensing that regulated the entry and the expansion of firms has been largely eliminated. The industrial policy of 1956 and 1980 which envisaged 'commanding heights' for public sector is given up.

3. In the area of public sector, the exclusive reservation of certain key industries have been curtailed and foreign investment in these areas has been openly invited.

4. Some of the public sector units are open for private initiative by slowly converting the equity and allowing private enterprises and business houses to hold the equity of the public sector including defence.

5. Reduction of fiscal deficit is envisaged by way of reducing aggregate expenditure in areas like the so called unproductive items which generally create scope for new jobs.

6. Encouraging the economy to link itself with global markets to improve competitiveness and efficiency.

The above policy prescriptions have really helped the *dvija* project to intensify its operations. The VRS as an exit policy targeted the dalits and OBCs to drive them off the public sector. The fifth pay commission abolished around 5 lakh jobs mostly belonging to the backlog vacancies.

Macro Economic Indicators

Despite the adverse effects of the policy, the government has vigorously implemented it as there was no constructive opposition from political groups. It appears that there is almost an agreement among all the *dvijas* spread in all political parties on this. Therefore NEP continues. As seen from Table 1, the macro economic indicators show the results of the economic reforms. It is found that the economy is growing at an average rate of around 7 percent after 1992-93. It has slowed down after the NDA regime. The increase is found to be more in manufacturing and in services sectors. The inflation rate is now brought down to the single digit level from that of 12 percent in 1990-91. The fiscal deficit is also brought down to around 5 percent of GDP from that of 8.3 percent in 1990-91. The savings and investment ratios as a percent of GDP have however, remained less than the pre-reform period. The current account deficit is remained at 0.5

Table 1: Macro Economic Indicators

	1990-91	1991-92	1992-93	1993-94	1994-95	1995-96	2001-2002
1. GDP(annual percentage change)	5.2	0.5	5.3	6.0	7.2	7.1	5.4
Agriculture & Allied Sectors	4.2	-1.8	6.1	3.6	4.6	-0.1	5.7
Manufacturing	7.0	-1.2	4.2	8.5	10.2	13.6	3.3
Services	4.3	4.1	5.5	7.3	7.5	8.8	6.5
2. Inflation(percentage per annum)	12.1	13.6	7.0	10.8	10.4	4.4	7.0
3. Broad Money M3(annual percentage increase)	15.1	18.5	11.2	18.2	14.9	13.2	11.2
4. Reserve Money (annual percentage increase)	19.7	12.9	10.4	15.6	5.7	19.6	5.6
5. Gross Domestic Investment (percentage to GDP)	27.7	23.4	24.0	23.6	26.0	27.4	24.0*
6. Gross Domestic Savings (percentage to GDP)	24.3	22.8	22.1	23.1	24.9	25.6	23.4*
7. Gross Domestic Capital Formation (percentage to GDP)	27.7	23.4	24.0	23.6	26.0	27.4	26.3
8. Current Account Deficit (percentage to GDP)	-3.2	-0.4	-1.8	-0.5	-0.9	-1.7	-0.5*
9. Fiscal Deficit (percentage to GDP)	8.3	5.9	5.7	7.4	6.1	5.8	5.5*
10. India's External Debt (percentage to GDP)	30.4	41.0	39.8	35.9	32.7	28.7	22.3*

Source: Economic Survey of India, Govt. of India, Various Issues.

* Relates to 2000-2001.

percent of GDP, though it is found to be less than what it was in 1990-91 (3.2 percent). All these modest achievements of the economic reforms can be attributed to the sacrifices made in terms of the reduction in the domestic capital formation and the external debt remaining around the pre-reforms level of around 22 percent of GDP. The fiscal deficit is covered by disinvestment of some of the profit making public sector units and in reducing public expenditure on social sectors like education, health and welfare programmes. The impact of these changes need to be examined in detail with reference to the socially disadvantaged groups who are more vulnerable than any other marginalised sections in the world. Out of the super 100 firms reported in Business India, none appears to be owned by a dalit. However, out of the super losers in 1999 compared to their position in 1991, one firm reported to be from an OBC in liquor trade.

Manifestation of *Dvija* Project in Stock Market

The opening of the economy to global opportunities is a spout for the *dvijas* to publicly acknowledge and declare their accumulations. In fact, the so called technology transfer or foreign technology agreements and FDI approvals without any exception benefited the *dvijas* with a few spill overs to upper sudras from regional groups. During the last one decade, around 20,000 technical and investment approvals with a projected investment of Rs.2.70 lakh crore are reported in the economic survey of 2001-2002. These collaborations and technological transfers have taken place through informal sources. A *dvija* NRI with the tacit approval of the foreign collaborators nominates his kith and kin as a promoter in India. The promoter with the help of brokers and fraudulent operators enter the stock market and manipulate the capital market to their advantage. For instance, if the Infosys hold about 29 percent and Wipro 84 percent of their shares respectively, then the market capitalisation naturally benefits them. Speaking on such manipulators Mr. A.K. Gupta, Deputy Director, CBI said:

> The gullible public and the inefficient banking system provide ample opportunities for the financial institutions to play and squander the public funds. The overheated stock market and the laxity of the financial institutions and the watchdogs like SEBI are the other major contributory factors. The modus operandi is fairly simple. The investors are lured to part with their savings by promises of unrealistic returns. The banks and financial institutions are made to part with their funds either by misrepresentation or through forgery or by simply corrupting the bank officials. The funds are placed at the disposal of scamsters who use these in the stock market operations. As the bubble bursts, which is inevitable, everyone becomes a loser. Investigation, arrest and prosecution deters them for sometime but in due course new scamsters and new scams emerge (Alternative Economic Survey, 2001-2002, p.124).

The so called boom in software technology and the clamour for body shopping, it is said, resulted in the current crisis in IT. It is reported that during the boom period, shares of even loss making companies commanded with premium. Another major scandal of the initial period was that the promoters, especially MNCs, issued preferential shares at prices far lower than the then prevailing market prices. All the operators in the stock market belong to the *dvija* castes and manage the moneys of first generation non-*dvija* investors. In the US, the stock market operators are professional managers but in India caste, family and primordial relations enter the market. The data in Table 2 indicate the shares of different categories of shareholders in market capitalisation. It is found that out of Rs.636045 crore total market capitalisation as on April 2002, Rs.611794 crore or 96 percent are held by 2574 companies. Studies undertaken by ISID have revealed that 61.73

percent of the market is held by top 10 companies. The total turnover of the stock market in a year is estimated to

Table 2: Share of different categories of shareholders in market capitalisation

Category	*Market capitalisation (Rs. Crores)*	*Share in market capitalisation of non-government companies (%)*
A. Total market capitalisation (MCAP)#	6,36,045	—
B. Of which, MCAP of 2,574 companies for which shareholding data are available	6,11,794	—
C. MCAP of 67 public enterprises (within B)	1,71,634	—
D. MCAP of 2,507 Non-Government Companies (B) – (C)	4,40,160	—
Composition of (D)		
1. Indian and Foreign Promoters including persons acting in concert with them	2,10,597	47.85
2. Institutional Investors	1,08,281	24.60
a. Foreign Institutional Investors (FIIs)	53,741	12.21
b. Banks and Financial Institutions	30,506	6.93
c. Mincluding persons acting in concert with themutual Funds	23,044	5.46
3. General Public: Indian	79,086	6.93
4. Private Corporate Bodies	17,582	3.99
5. Non-Resident Indians and Overseas Corporate Bodies (OCBs) controlled by them	6,997	1.59
6. Others (including GDRs)	17,617	4.00

MCAP is available for 2055 companies;
Source: Alternative Economic Survey, 2001-2002.

be Rs.28,80,990 crore in the year 2000-2001 which is higher than that of the GNP during the year. This indicates the economic capacity of the stock market and thus the *dvija* project.

A new generation of journalists, academics, economic consultants, chartered accountants, etc., have emerged during the post-liberalisation period. The single point agenda of these people is to eulogize the benefits of liberalisation and the efficiency of the market. Majority of these consultants are involved in government policy making and there is circumstantial evidence to prove the nexus between the consultants and the policy prescriptions they recommend. About two years ago, the government of the *dvijas* has created a separate ministry of disinvestment to take control of the public sector units, where the poor and the dalits have invested their future through the government. No one knows how the ownership of the PSEs are transferred and to whom? Even the profit making organisations are transferred to private individuals or companies. Invariably all the new owners are either the *dvijas* or MNCs with *dvija* control. A new brand of multi-caste corporations (MCCs) have emerged with the *dvija* agenda. Some academics like Bardhan, Corbridge and Harris have recognised the fact that caste interests have played a role in the new economic policy in the backdrop of mandal and bahujan upsurge. But, no serious evaluation and discussion on the issues raised by the academics has taken place either in the mainstream academic discourse or in the press.

According to the new economic policy, market is given the supreme position in the allocation of resources to various sectors and groups. It is generally claimed that those sectors and groups, which are found to be efficient and competitive would alone survive and those which are weak would perish in the market. When this market strategy is translated into practice, it would be clear that those sections and sectors, which have been given importance in the policy formulation and implementation will get strengthened. They alone would stand in the competitive world now. And those sections/sectors which are given help or subsidy for sustenance would not be in a position to compete in the market. It means that the reservation groups will have to face a greater challenge than others.

The impact of the new economic policy appears to be adverse and serious in the case of dalits. The common property resources such as water bodies, forest, and seacoast, which were freely used by these communities have been appropriated by powerful lobbies after liberalisation. There are some studies that have proved that after liberalisation, the living conditions of groups like fishermen, service castes and dalits, have deteriorated. It is time that a serious attempt is be made to study the impact of the policy on specific groups in a society like India where social inequalities are further accentuated by economic inequalities.

REFERENCES

1. Anne O. Krueger, *Economic Policy Reforms and the Indian Economy,* Oxford, 2002.
2. Bardhan Pranab, *The Political Economy of Development in India,* Oxford, 1998.
3. Chalam K.S., *Economic Reforms and Missing Safety Nets,* Vikas, Adhyana Kendra, Bombay, 2000.
4. Corbridge S and John Hariss, *Reinventing India, Liberalisation, Hindu Nationalism and Popular Democracy,* Cambridge, 2000.
5. Jean Dreze and Amartya Sen, *India: Development and Participation,* Oxford, 2002.
6. Jenkins Rob, *Democratic Politics and Economic Reforms in India,* Cambridge, 2000.
7. Kohli Atul, "Politics of Economic Liberalisation in India", *World Development,* Vol. 17, No. 3, 1989.

8. Panini, M.N., "The social logic of liberalisation", *Sociological Bulletin,* Vol. 44, 1999.

9. Patnaik Prabhat, "Notes on the political economy of structural adjustment", *Social Scientists,* Vol.22, 1994.

10. Srinivasan, T.N, *Eight Lectures on India's Economic Reforms,* Oxford, 2000.

11. Varshney, A, "Mass politics or elite politics: Indian Economic Reform in comparative perspective, in Jeffrey Sachs and Others (Ed.), *India in the era of Economic Reforms,* Oxford, 1999.

18

The Post-Reform Thoughts on Trade Union Movements

*Prof. P.A. Vasudevan**

Trade Union (T.U) movement has a long history of struggle for a better living of workers and for the right of the workers to control the system of production. The movement wa a real search for economic democracy. For long labour has been in an adversarial role against capital, mostly because of the oppressive attitude of the capital owing class. They made profit the central aim of production and wage was treated as a unnecessary evil and an unnecessary flab in the cost of production.

Struggle for liberation and right living countinues in every system. The nature and challenges of these struggles are different. That is the case with T.U.Movement is these days of globalisation and corporate production system. The movement should realize the present realities, which require a shift grom the past and conservative role. Some of the arguments in this context require careful study since T.U. are going through an identity crisis. New models of industrial organsation and management have necessitated this is forge a future course of action.

The movement requires an operative strategy in the back drop of the neo-liberal policies in the third world

* "AKSHARAM". Vidyuth Nagar, Palghat-678001 Kerala.

countries, especially in India, the labour movement should consolidate well as long as import substitution industrialisation (I.S.I.) strategy existed in countries like India and Brazil. The domestic market was predictable. Then came the shift from labour-long industries like textile, leather to 'capital-long' ones like engineering and capital goods that led to new patterns of work orientation, employment creation, international linkages etc. This considerably weakened the collective bargaining position of T.U.

The neo-liberal preferences gave a turn-about towards export-oriented industries (E.O.I.). The signal aim was to slim the per unit cost of production, which led to search for cheap labour via child labour, feminisation, casualisation, and flex labour. State, which had a pro-labour attitude, took to pro-employer attitude, which led to serious problems to the T.U.Movement. The T.U.Movement in India, South Asia and Latin America was pushed to the defensive position. This was inevitable, when the economies of the developing countries started turning out – ward looking. The first casuality, when an economy takes itself to transnational functioning is the cohesiveness of the T.U.movement. The movement should seek alternative operative methods, forgetting its conservative model.

The new form of industrialsation is part of globalisation, which aims at higher competitiveness and profit. Given the changes taking place in the national and international markets, the new organisational forms try to weaken the position of T.U. with respect to employment conditions and power relations. The challenges before T.U. in the context with effectively safeguard its interest in the changing scenario of macro political economic circumstances.

The various organisational forms that came into existence in the process of graduating towards globalisation, have been aiming at reducing the economic and political importance of workers in decision-making. This was done by changing the industrial relation pattern and thus the trade union involvement.

Under proprietary capitalism, the problem was building up competitiveness and in the absence of innovative technology, the only option was squeezing of labour cost. Managerial capitalism, which was an American variat, aimed at capturing world market, with lower unit cost and hence higher competitiveness. Here the strategy was to incorporate T.U. in a drive to lower cost of production through a package deal. It included higher wages to appease workers by the stripping away their role, antagonistic bargaining process and claim for better working conditions.

The collective capitalism model, which is a Japanese variat, aims at still higher profit, through further lowering of labour cost. This system projects superior enterprise network with other institutions, flexibilities through sub-contracting and major organisational re-structuring, characterized by continuous innovation. This was an organisational trap, when workers become permanent partners of the capitalist production system, negating their adversarial role. Stretched beyond the limit this will definitely weaken the T.U.Movement.

We should know that organisational forms and perennial innovations are used cryptically by the elite corporate production system, to ensure the submissive role of workers, which is strategically forced upon them. Management as a part of the strategy now compete with T.U.'s for the loyalty of workers even at the cost of providing them with extra facilities. This is to weaken the cohesiveness of relationship among workers to move towards a common cause. These are some of the in-roads cut by the capital-owners into the domain of working class solidarity. Since this is a reality now, we should not just wish them away.

Global finance capital, is trying every possible strategy, to eliminate to the maximum labour content in the production process and introducing technology to supplant human effort. The new technology is more labour saving rather than energy and input saving. This is an ideological distortion on the part of the capital owners in the new era, that labour is the one segment that keeps the cost of production high and reduces competitiveness in the international market. So technological R & D are oriented towards labour saving techniques. The excessive reliance on the other inputs has resulted in energy and resource constraints, whereas labour, the only organic input in production was rendered surplus and redundant.

The market-friendly production system today, is not creating technology for mass but aims at expansion of market. Market is created through advertisements for commodities that are hi-tech in nature, which enjoy cost advantage. The markets thus exclude a large chunk of the consumers and the elite corporate production system caters only to the rich and medium consumers, which maintain or increase their level of profit. Naturally they can axe away a big segment of the labour force, which do not find alternate employment in a highly technical production system. Such a highly sophisticated production system mostly negates the role of T.U. Also this system has a flexible production pattern, suiting to the requirements of the elite society, in which the labour tenure is not secure.

The absence of awareness among workers about the new economic and technological changes and sweeping shift in ideological field needs concern. We have myriads of sectoral unions, which require a thorough orientation towards the macro changes taking place in the background of globalisation. This prime function is on T.U. movement, which lacks the professionalism required for it. There is need for union schools, for retraining the workers, to suit their new demand for workers, but the altered production system should flush out a part of workers who cannot gainfully fit into the new system.

For long, state was the protector of the labour interests. Globalisation has resulted in a diminutive state. When everything is hinged on the cost effectiveness and when state is not able to provide welfare measures at a cost effective rate, workers are directly face to face with employers. Also in pursuit of rapid industrialisation the state has amended labour laws, favouring employers. Not only that the workers have lost the insulation of the state, but also that they have to confront an anti-labour government.

The bulging informal and unoranised sector has weakened the decisive role of T.U.s in policy making. Most of the Naion's States are now under the global market policies dictated by TNCs. The National political and economic policies are subservient to global policies. The public and the organized sector where the unions are strong have suffered serious threat of being eliminated. The huge informal and tertiary sectors stand beyond the control of T.Us, a vital issue the T.Us should address itself most urgently.

We must be more aware of our problem than the prospects, to keep the movement relevant and coherent in the present changing scenario. Some of the gloabalisation trends in the present post reform India that are relevant to the movement can be summarized.

1. There is a sharp reduction in the permanent workforce, as there is considerable casualisation of workforce in ancillary units, which serve the main industrial units.
2. Aggressive attitude by the employees aided by the pro-employer legislations, have caused job insecurity in the minds of workers, who often are hesitant to disclose their loyalty to unions. Eg:In 1980's, except in 1986 more days man were lost

due to lock-out, than due to strike. In 1991, in the dawn of reforms, lockout, loss of work was almost double that of strike-loss.

3. There is a fast disintegration of organized sector, in India, which is adverse to the T.U.solidarity. The organized sector employees nearly 8.5 percent of the workforce only and even among them only 4.5 percent people are in the unions. This fall in number of organized workforce, compels the state to turn pro-employer.

4. In the modern production system dominated by sophisticated technology, traditional labour, with strong unionisation is found redundant and firms, instead of giving retraining to old workers, go in for, new recruits, who lack the spirit of unionisation.

Globalisation establishes an agenda in which state is decimated and organized workforce is emasculated. It has a variety of strategies for this purpose. The T.U. activities and academicians should have a close grasp of these realities and should form a new operating strategy. Ultimately, all efforts should be to strengthen this movement, which is the hub of economic democracy. Some vital points in this direction are as follows:

1. We must realize that there is still a good terrain of struggle for the T.U. The national governments are as aggressive as the M.N.Cs and the struggle should be from all angles, against the national governments, that pledge in the rights to foreign agencies. In the process the T.Us should see that they are not weakened by political fragmentation.

2. T.Us should be more beyond sheer economism and should be part of a right social process.

3. We must go beyond national government to establish solidarity with global workers unions.

4. The conservative functioning is out of tune with the new order and the T.Us should have more pro-active role, addressing itself to issues related to influencing labour market, creation of employment and income distribution.

5. Strong regional unions to influence regional industriailisation technological development and migratory patterns.

When things around us are changing, it is wise to evolve a new formula for gainful survival and right living. It requires a solid professional approach like networking with experts and globally concerned groups.

19

Food Security and Working of PDS in Andhra Pradesh

G. Sridevi *

Introduction

Food security means access to enough food by all people at all times. The food insecurity can be either transitory or chronic in nature. Transitory food insecurity arises due to fluctuations in food production. While the chronic food insecurity arises due to the inability of the household to acquire food on account of green revolution and buffer-stock operation, the country has been able to reduce transitory food insecurity but it has failed to make a dent on chronic food insecurity.

Increased food production is considered to be necessary, though not a sufficient condition for improving food security to the poorest segments of the population till the 1970s. However, it is now recognised that the ultimate aim of food security is not only provision of food grains for the entire population on a stable basis throughout the year but also to provide economic access to food. In the absence of such preconditions, even with improvement in food supply the market mechanism may not always and automatically

---

* PhD Fellow, Institute for Social and Economic Change, Bangalore.
Thanks are due to Professor. R.S. Deshpande, ISEC, Bangalore, for his valuable comments.

transfer food to the poor. Hence in order to improve food security for the poor, the government relies on a set of policy instruments such as food rationing, price subsidies, and employment programme. Public distribution is given an important role in protecting the vulnerable sections against price rise and for stabilisation of prices in Indian food policy over a period.

Since 1991 Indian economy has been exposed to economic liberalisation and globalisation in line with structural adjustment and stabilisation policies initiated by IMF and World Bank. Structural adjustment policy advocated privatization, import liberalisation, and export-led growth while stabilisation policy emphasises reduction in fiscal deficit through withdrawal of subsidies given to industry, trade, agriculture and food subsidies. Reducing food subsidies is seen as an important way of reducing public expenditure. In India since 1991 the government has been looking at ways of reducing the food subsidy, by increasing the food prices and the policy has attempted to cut back coverage and consumption by means of targeting.

What are the implications of structural adjustment for food security? It is suggested that structural adjustment in the economy affects the availability of food at the national level and food security at the household level (FAO, 1989). There are four types of perceived effects on food security:

(i) With a shift in strategy towards a more export-oriented economy, patterns of production in the agricultural sector are likely to change and food production for the domestic economy to be affected.

(ii) Devaluation and other macro economic changes affect the absolute and relative price of food commodities as well as food price inflation.

(iii) Changes in the pattern of public expenditure

that affects food subsidies and expenditure on agriculture through changes in input subsidies and capital formation.

(iv) Economy-wide changes in poverty; inequality and unemployment are all likely to affect real incomes and household food security.

In this context it is relevant to consider the role of PDS in providing food security to the poor. In this paper an attempt is made to study the role of PDS in providing food security at the state level.

PDS in Andhra Pradesh

Several earlier studies have dealt with different aspects of the subsidised rice scheme in Andhra Pradesh; Venugopal (1992) examined the impact of the welfare scheme on the reduction of hunger. Sastry, et al (1990) attempted to estimate leakages in the PDS. Krishna Rao (1993) made a critical evaluation of the scheme. The impact of alternative intervention policies has been analysed by Radhakrishna and Indrakant in1988 and by Indrakant in1996.

Andhra Pradesh is one of the states pursuing a vigorous public distribution policy. Since the early 1980 onwards PDS coverage has been almost universal, although the scale of rations, commodities supplied and ration prices have varied across different sections of the populations. In Andhra Pradesh Rs.2 per kilo of rice scheme was started in 1982-83. Under this scheme, families having income less than Rs.6000 per annum are provided rice at a subsidised rate (Rs.2 per kg). The scheme provides 5 kgs per month per person subject to a ceiling of 25 kgs per month per family. Ever since the TDP was propelled in to power largely on the basis of its electoral promise of cheap rice, rice subsidies, PDS policy has become an important issue in the election battles.

Under this rice scheme based on 1981 census, 8.29 million households were identified. Serious problems arose when the results of the enumeration emerged in April, 1983. Against the maximum projection of about 8 million households that were expected to be the beneficiaries of the rice scheme, the number that actually emerged was 10.85 million, which is almost the number of the total households in the state (11.35 million in 1983). A drive had therefore, to be launched to eliminate the ineligible households and in subsequent months, nearly 1.2 million green cards meant for the identified poor households for the issue of subsidised rice were either cancelled or converted into yellow cards, meant for the non-poor households.

Prior to 1983, the PDS in Andhra Pradesh was handicapped by two factors (i) The low quantities of rice released for use in the PDS and (ii) The non-utilisation in full, even those quantities by the state. In keeping with its poll promises, the new Government (TDP) in 1983 tried to rectify this situation. The new Government's objective was to make rice available at Rs.2 per kg. to all the poor, both in urban and rural areas. It therefore, became necessary to identify poor households using a verifiable economic criterion that could be uniformly applied all over the state. The Government, as a working rule, regarded the households having an annual income of less than Rs.6000 per annum as poor and issued green cards to them. Other households were issued yellow cards. A household with a green card was entitled to 5 kgs of rice per person per month subject to a ceiling of 25 kgs, at Rs.2 per kg. Besides rice, they were entitled to sugar and kerosene. A household with a yellow card, in the initial years, was permitted to purchase rice from fair price shops but at a higher price of Rs.3.50 per kg. Later on, this facility was withdrawn.

In rural areas, households having less than 1.5 acres of wetland under assured water resources or 2.5 acres of wetland under other irrigation sources or 3 acres of dryland under commercial crops and 5 acres of land under other crops were issued green cards. The Congress Government in 1991 modified the subsidised rice scheme. The ceiling on rice for white cardholder was initially reduced to 16 kgs but later on it was increased to 20 kgs. On account of the increase in issue price of rice by the FCI, the State Government increased the ration price of rice to Rs.3,50. Further, the green cards were replaced with white cards and yellow cards by pink cards. In 1994, the Telugu Desam Government restored the ceiling on rice to white cardholders to 25 kgs. Further, the price was raised to Rs.5.25 per kg and the ceiling was reduced to 20 kgs per card.

At present there are 113.60 lakh white cards and 53.97 lakhs pink cards. The Government of Andhra Pradesh has introduced coupons system for all eligible white cardholders and coupons have been issued to 1.05 lakh. There are 39,648 fair price shops in the state, out of them 6,974 are in urban areas and 32,674 are in rural areas. The following statement indicates the number of white cards and quantity of rice distributed from time to time by the State Government.

No of white cards distributed increased during 1990s but the number of people below poverty line remained to be more during this period (Table 1) which indicates that still many of the poor households are not included in the targeting of the PDS. The subsidised rice scheme is covering nearly 70 percent of the population while only about 30 percent of the population is estimated to be poor. Thus, many non-poor households enjoy the benefit of the scheme also. Venugopal (1992) has estimated the number of bogus cards in the state using 1981 census data. In 1986, the number of ration cards in circulation (139 lakhs) exceeded the estimated number of households (121 lakhs) by about 15 percent (18 lakhs). At the micro-level studies reveal, a large number of poor households do not have ration cards.

Table 1: No of Ration Cards in the State

Year	*Number of white cards (in lakhs)*	*Quantity of rice distributed (in lakhs Mts.)*
1983-84	96.47	18.14
1984-85	101.03	17.76
1985-86	104.33	20.34
1986-87	95.14	22.36
1987-88	96.25	21.98
1988-89	99.22	17.86
1989-90	99.22	21.40
1990-91	99.22	21.17
1991-92	107.16	22.42
1992.93	106.46	18.84
1993-94	100.71	22.50
1994-95	99.26	22.55
1995-96	99.26	25.20
1996-97	112.66	23.60
1997-98	112.66	21.60
1998-99	113.25	23.00
1999-2000	113.60	19.92
2000-2001	113.60	17.39

Source: Commissioner of Civil Supplies, Government of Andhra Pradesh, HYD.

Poverty in A.P. (Lakhs)

Year	1973-74	1977-78	1983	1987-88	1993-94	1999-2000
Rural (A.P)	178.21	149.13	114.34	96.38	79.49	58.13
Urban (A.P)	47.48	48.41	50.24	64.05	74.47	60.88
Combined	225.69	197.54	164.58	160.43	153.97	119.01

Source: Economic survey, Government of A.P. (2001-2002).

Figure—1

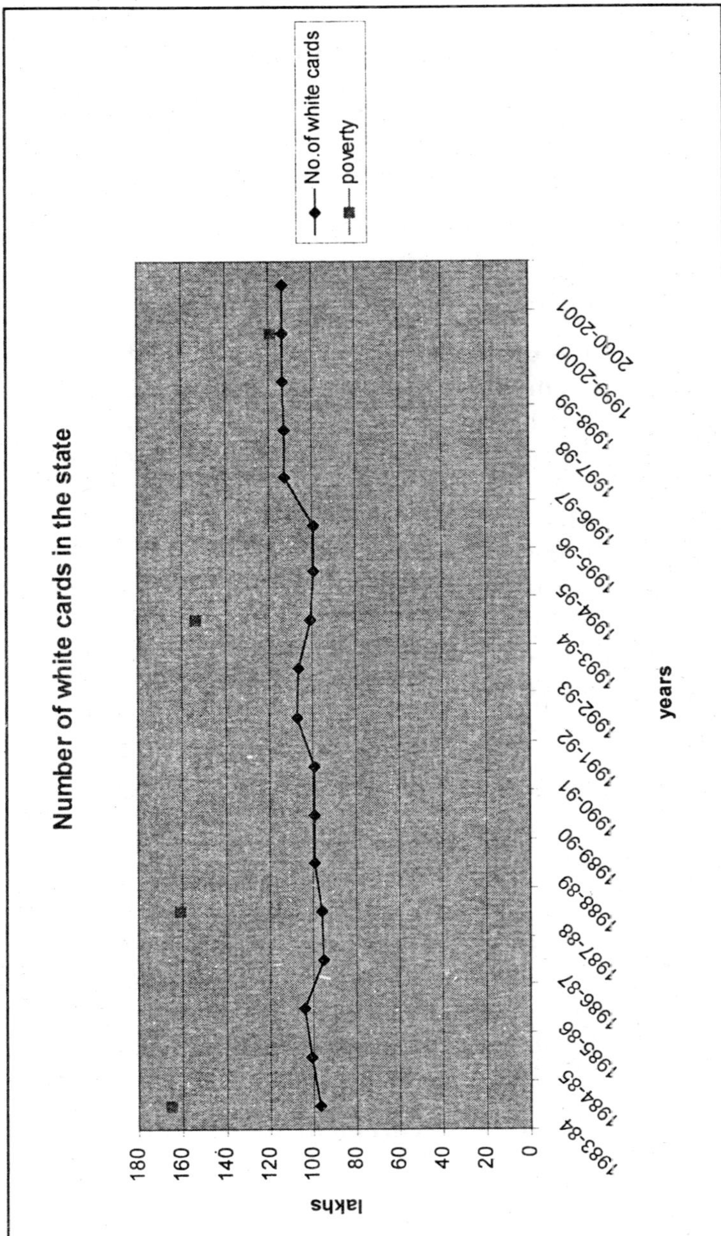
Number of white cards in the state
No.of white cards
poverty
lakhs
180
160
140
120
100
80
60
40
20
0
1983-84
1984-85
1985-86
1986-87
1987-88
1988-89
1989-90
1990-91
1991-92
1992-93
1993-94
1994-95
1995-96
1996-97
1997-98
1998-99
1999-2000
2000-2001
years

Trends in Procurement and Distribution

The Government of Andhra Pradesh introduced a compulsory levy on producers fort the first time in 1965/66 and entrusted the FCI with the responsibility of undertaking procurement directly from producers. The scheme was abandoned after a trail of barely four months. The main reason for the failure of this scheme was that there was no advance preparation for its implementation.

In 1968/69, the Government of Andhra Pradesh imposed a compulsory levy on all traditional Sheller and Huller-cum Sheller mills as well as modern rice mills operating in the private and co-operative sectors. All the 'Huller mills' and some of the non-trading Huller-cum-Sheller mills were excluded from the purview of the compulsory levy. The exact proportion of the levy varied from time to time, depending on the public procurement target and crop situation in a particular year. The procurement policy in 1985/86 was that the millers were required to give one unit to the FCI as a levy and half unit to the Andhra Pradesh Civil Supplies Corporation Ltd (APSCSC), at a negotiated price. Only then they were permitted to sell half a unit of levy-free rice within the state and one unit anywhere in the country (Radhakrishna and Indrakant, 1988).

Trends in procurement, procurement-output ratio are tabulated in Table 2 It can be seen that the procurement has risen from 0.70 million tonnes in 1980-81 to a large amount of 3.17 million tonnes in 1999-2000. Procurement as a percent of production after 93-94, but distribution as a percent of procurement declined during this period.

The extent of procurement in the early 1980s was substantially higher than that of all India. There was a phenomenal jump in the quantity procured in 1982-83 on account of the introduction of a new welfare scheme. The volume of rice procurement depends on level of rice output

Table 2: Trends in Procurement and Distribution of Rice in Andhra Pradesh

Year	*Procurement (in mts)*	*Production (in mts)*	*Procurement as % of production*	*Distribution (in mts)*	*Distribution as % of procurement*	*Percapita quantity (in Kgs)*
1980-81	0.70	7.01	9.98	–	–	–
1981-82	1.10	7.87	13.97	–	–	–
1982-83	2.00	7.67	26.07	1.37	68.5	24.98
1983-84	2.42	8.79	27.53	1.83	75.62	32.59
1984-85	2.74	6.91	39.65	1.89	68.98	32.91
1985-86	2.48	7.61	32.58	2.15	86.69	36.61
1986-87	2.03	6.59	34.90	2.21	96.08	36.82
1987-88	2.41	7.08	34.04	1.87	77.59	30.49
1988-89	2.78	10.62	26.18	2.00	71.94	31.94
1989-90	3.59	9.96	36.04	2.12	59.05	33.17
1990-91	3.32	9.65	34.04	2.42	72.89	37.11
1991-92	2.26	9.25	24.43	1.78	78.76	26.76
1992-93	3.30	8.79	37.54	1.99	60.30	29.34
1993-94	3.30	9.56	34.51	2.25	68.18	32.50
1994-95	3.35	9.27	37.75	2.26	64.57	32.00
1995-96	3.67	9.01	40.70	2.52	68.66	31.18
1996-97	4.50	10.68	42.13	2.36	52.44	28.74
1997-98	3.85	8.51	45.24	2.28	59.22	28.24
1998-99	5.07	10.66	47.56	2.28	49.97	26.92
1999-00	3.17	10.6	29.9	2.28	71.92	26.20
2000-01	6.9	12.4	55.6	1.7	24.63	–

Source: Civil Supplies Department, Government of Andhra Pradesh.

Figure—2

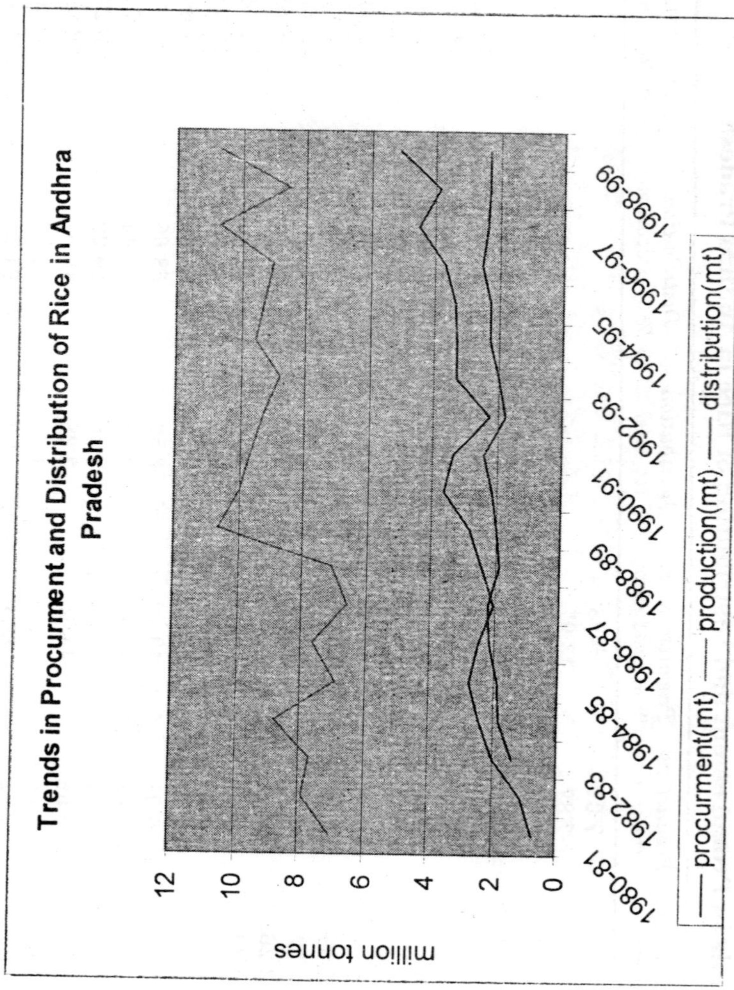
Trends in Procurment and Distribution of Rice in Andhra Pradesh
million tonnes
12
10
8
6
4
2
0
1980-81
1982-83
1984-85
1986-87
1988-89
1990-91
1992-93
1994-95
1996-97
1998-99
procurment(mt) production(mt) distribution(mt)

and the level of procurement price in relation to the open market price, which will benefit mostly large farmers and millers. The two-rupee kilo rice scheme might have influenced the procurement in 1982-86. The quantity distributed through the PDS generally varied in the range of 2 to 2.5 million tonnes. The quantity procured is increasing with the increase in production but the quantity distributed is declining (2000-2001), this may be due to increase in prices and the quality of the rice distributed through PDS. The annual per capita quantity distributed through the PDS varied in the range of 25 kgs to 37 kgs. During the last five years, the quantity distributed through PDS has not changed much, while the population of the state has been steadily increasing and therefore, the per capita quantity distributed has been declined.

Subsidy on Rice Scheme

The Government of Andhra Pradesh introduced the subsidised rice scheme in early 80s to improve the consumption levels of the weaker sections of the society. The subsidised rice scheme involves the provision of subsidy by both the State and the Central Government. The central subsidy per tonne increased from Rs.534 in 1982-83 to Rs.4748 in 1998-99 (refer Table 3). This increase was partly due to regular enhancement in procurement price and partly due to rise in administrative cost of FCI.

The mounting buffer-stock is responsible for increase in the storage cost. During the same period, the state subsidy per tonne increased from Rs.29 to Rs.2512. It may be noted that in 1983-84, the state subsidy per tonne jumped by about Rs.500 i.e. from a low level of Rs.29 to Rs.523. This jump is on account of introduction of the subsidised rice scheme. In spite of hike in central issue price, the Government of Andhra Pradesh kept the retail issue price at Rs.2 per kg. In 1991, it was raised to Rs.3.50 per kg, but in January 1995 it was again reduced to Rs.2 per kg. As a

Table 3: Central and State Subsidy on Rice Scheme in Andhra Pradesh (Rs/tonne)

Sl.No	Year	Central subsidy	State subsidy	Total subsidy
1	1980-81	340	–	340
2	1981-82	429	–	429
3	1982-83	534	29	563
4	1983-84	667	524	1191
5	1984-85	749	725	1474
6	1985-86	773	613	1386
7	1986-87	804	818	1622
8	1987-88	809	994	1803
9	1988-89	817	809	1626
10	1989-90	1242	1390	2632
11	1990-91	1280	1512	2792
12	1991-92	805	1973	2778
13	1992-93	869	1206	2075
14	1993-94	967	1504	2471
15	1994-95	1379	2882	4261
16	1995-96	1495	4133	5628
17	1996-97	2371	3106	5477
18	1997-98	3296	2608	5904
19	1998-99	4748	2512	7260

Source: Economic survey, Ministry of Finance, Govt. of India.

result, in 1995-96 subsidy per tonne registered a peak level of Rs.4133. It declined during the later years as retail issue price was raised Rs.3.50 per kg in August 1996. Now it is raised to Rs.5.25 per kg. Olsen (1989) examined the cost involved in the subsidised rice scheme. She points out that in 1987-88 the subsidy on rice scheme was more than the entire state expenditure on public health. From 1996 onwards state's subsidy was reducing when compared with central subsidy on rice. But the question is whether this subsidy is reaching the poor or not?

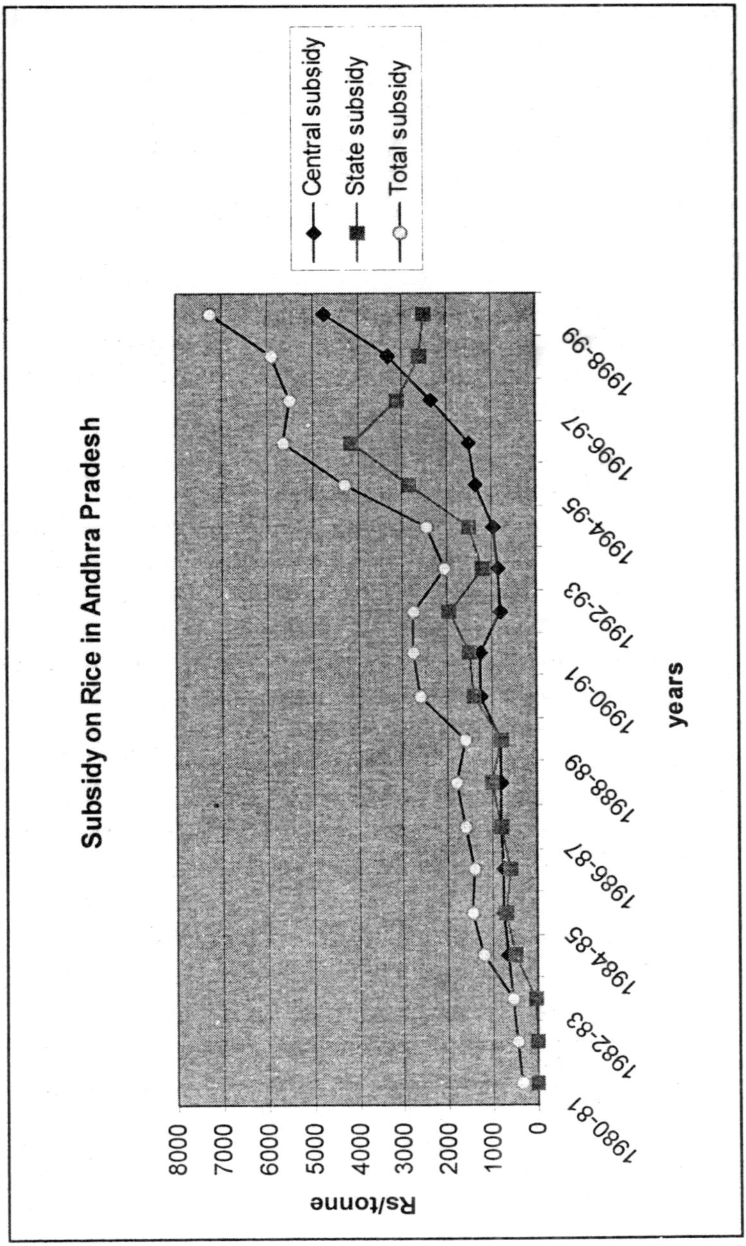
Subsidy on Rice in Andhra Pradesh
Central subsidy
State subsidy
Total subsidy
Rs/tonne
8000
7000
6000
5000
4000
3000
2000
1000
0
1980-81
1982-83
1984-85
1986-87
1988-89
1990-91
1992-93
1994-95
1996-97
1998-99
years

In 1993-94, the cost of providing one rupee of subsidy was Rs1.71 for entire population. Some portion of PDS supplies is leaked into the market, the larger the diversions, greater will the costs of using food subsidies to transfer income to target groups. When we compare the average per capita PDS off-take to the average per capita consumption of PDS rice (from NSS consumption survey) in order to quantify the extent of leakages it shows that nearly15 percent of rice supplies in A.P do not reach PDS consumers. This must be an important reason explaining why income transfers are costly. The other reason why the cost-effectiveness ratio is greater than one might be that the government is inefficient, relative to private trade, in delivering foodgrains through the PDS.

Errors of targeting arise when attempts are made to distribute the benefits of a welfare scheme to a specific target group. Targeting errors will arise in the system due to factors such as imperfect information and measurement. There can be two kinds of targeting errors. Errors of wrong inclusion refer to the inclusion of non-eligible persons or households in a programme, these were termed as F1 mistake. Errors of wrong exclusion refer to the exclusion of genuinely poor or deserving households from a programme. These were termed as F2 mistake (Cornia and Stewart, 1993). A higher proportion of the upper deciles in rural A.P use the PDS. The magnitude of F1 error in urban A.P (4.29) and that of in rural (22.35) indicates that an average per capita consumption of PDS grain by the upper deciles is significantly higher in rural A.P. The magnitude of F2 error in urban A.P (36.4) and that of in rural (20.42) indicates

Table 4: Targeting Errors in A.P

	Rural	*Urban*	*Combined*
F1	22.35	4.29	14.35
F2	20.42	36.4	22.29

Source: Bhaskar Dutta, Bharat Ramaswami (2001).

utilisation of the PDS, both in terms of the fraction buying PDS grain as well in terms of the quantities bought, amongst the bottom deciles it is significantly higher in the rural sector compared to the urban sector in A.P.

Utilisation of PDS

National Sample Survey Organisation (NSSO) in its 42nd round i.e., 1986-87, collected information on utilisation of PDS. The result of the survey reveals that in case of rice and sugar, nearly 60 percent of the rural households depend partially or wholly on PDS. In urban area, half of the households purchase rice and kerosene from fair price shops. If the total population were considered, then the per capita quantity of rice distributed through PDS would be only 2.5 kg. This reduction is mainly because only white cardholders are entitled for rice. About a quarter of the households in rural area could not buy rice because either they had no entitlement or no ration card (refer *Table 5*).

Table 5: Percentage of persons having no entitlement/ no ration card

Item	*Rural*	*Urban*
Rice	24.14	44.83
Sugar	17.53	53.82
Kerosene	41.60	53.42

Source: NSSO (1986-87).

Extent of Food Security

Rice is the most popular cereal item distributed through the PDS in Andhra Pradesh. Therefore, the extent of food security provided by the PDS in Andhra Pradesh can be measured by (i) The percentage of PDS rice purchases in total rice purchases, and (ii) The percentage of PDS rice purchases in total consumption. The analysis reveals that in rural Andhra Pradesh, nearly 32 percent of rice purchases are made from FPS and it forms over 22 percent of total rice consumption. The percent of the PDS rice purchase has declined to 21.5 in rural and 12.60 percent in urban A.P. over the ten years (refer Table 6).

Table 6: Extent of food security provided by PDS in Andhra Pradesh

Sl.No	*Region*	*% PDS rice purchases in total rice purchases*		*% PDS rice purchases in total rice consumption*		*% PDS rice purchases in total rice cereal consumption*	
		1988	*1999*	*1988*	*1994*	*1988*	*1994*
1	Rural	32.54	21.5	23.07	23.3	18.19	19.3
2	Urban	21.47	12.60	20.00	14.10	17.53	12.76

Source: 1. NSSO (1989) 2. NSSO (1994).

Similarly, in urban areas, PDS purchases account for nearly 22 percent in total purchases, and forms 20 percent in total rice consumption. Percent of PDS rice purchases declined to 14 percent in 1994 whereas in rural it remains more or less the same, hence the extent of food security provided by PDS appears to be better in rural areas, but many of the beneficiaries are non-poor. Urban poor are prone to be more food insecure when compared to the rural poor.

Regional Disparities in Access to PDS

In Andhra Pradesh, white cardholders are entitled to highly subsidised rice. The distribution of white cards across the region is in favour of better-off regions. Over 47 percent of white cards are in circulation in coastal Andhra, which accounts for less than 39 percent of poor people in the state. The share of coastal Andhra in white cards is higher than their share in population. On the other hand, in Rayalaseema less than 18 percent of white cards are in circulation in spite of the fact, that 22 percent of the poor people in the state reside in Rayalaseema. Similarly, Telangana accounts for nearly 40 percent of poor people but has only 35 percent of white cards in the state. The better-off districts have managed to get a larger share in white cards. For instance, West Godavari with less than 2 percent of poor people is having over 6 percent of white cards. Similarly, East Godavari possesses over 7 percent of white cards, while it accounts for less than 3 percent of poor population. In contrast, the backward districts could not get their due share. Mahaboobnagar and Anantapur each accounts for 9 percent in poor population, their share in white cards is only about 4 percent. The share of each district in white cards more or less matches with its share in population and not with its share in poor population (Sudhakar Reddy, 1991). This pattern of distribution of white cards is unlikely to reduce the existing regional imbalances.

In the unirrigated area, the economic conditions of some of the households even having more than 5 acres of land, is not sound. Due to the impositions of ceiling on landholding, some of the poor households are also excluded from the scheme. While fixing the ceiling on land for the distribution of white cards in the state, the variation in land productivity across the districts and regions must be given due importance. This indicates that a large number of households above the poverty line are enjoying the benefits under the scheme.

Concluding Observations

A household is said to be food secure when it has the necessary purchasing power to buy foodgrains and access to the required amount of foodgrains. The causes of food insecurity are poverty (transient or chronic) and inadequate foodgrain production. Even in the absence of these two causes, there can exist food insecurity due to market imperfections. PDS is perceived to be the main safety-net to protect the poor from potential short-run, price-induced adverse effects in Andhra Pradesh. It influences the consumption of foodgrains and nutritional status through the income effect by increasing the purchasing power of beneficiary households since they can buy larger amount of food at the same cost, and through the substitution effect by reducing the price of food relative to the prices of other goods.

From the analysis we found that the present scheme has certain shortcomings:

(i) A large number of poor households do not have ration cards while many non-poor households have white cards.

(ii) About a quarter of the households in rural area could not buy rice because either they had no entitlement or no ration card.

(iii) The PDS price paid by higher income groups is not substantially higher than the price paid by the poorer groups.

(iv) The cost of delivering a rupee of subsidy is more than Rs1.50 in the state.

(v) The percent of PDS rice purchases in total rice purchases are declining over the years, this may due to increase in prices and targeting to some sections of the population.

(vi) The present PDS favours better-off districts and developed villages and hence is unlikely to reduce the reasonal imbalances.

An adequate quantity of grain needs to be distributed to make a sizeable contribution to household food security. Major improvements are needed in the administration of PDS to ensure a non-corrupt and efficient delivery system. Decentralisation can improve the working of the delivery system.

REFERENCES

1. Bhaskar Dutta and Bharat Ramaswami, (2001), "Targeting and Efficiency in the Public Distribution System: Case of Andhra Pradesh and Maharashtra", *Economic and Political Weekly,* No: 18, May 5th-11th
2. Cornia G.A. and Framces Stewart, (1993), "Two Errors of Targeting", *Journal of International Development,* Vol 5, No.5.
3. Indrakant. S, (1996), Food Security and Public Distribution System in Andhra Pradesh—A Case Study, CESS, Hyderabad.
4. NSSO, (1988), "Consumer Expenditure Pattern", Report No.355/2.
5. NSSO, (1989), Utilisation of Public Distribution System, Report No.362.
6. NSSO, (1994), Report on Household Consumer Expenditure, 50th round.
7. Ossen, Wendy. K., (1989), Eat Now Pay Later "Impact of Rice subsidy scheme", *Economic and Political Weekly* Vol.24, No.28, pp. 1597-1611.
8. Radhakrishna. R., K.Subba Rao, S. Indrakanth and C. Ravi (1997): India's Public Distribution System—A National and International Perspectives, World Bank discussion paper No.380.
9. Radhakrishna. R, S. Indrakanth, "Effects of Rice Market Intervention Policies in India: The Case of Andhra Pradesh", CESS, Hyderabad.
10. Reddy Sudhakar. S (1991): Poverty and Agriculture Growth In Rural Inter District Analysis—Center for Economic and Social Studies, Hyderabad.
11. Subba Rao. K, (1987), Interventions to Fill Nutrition Gaps at the Household Level: a Review of India's Experience, Institute of Economic Growth, New Delhi.
12. Venugopal. K.R., (1992), The Public Distribution System in India—Deliverance from Hunger.
13. Food and Agricultural Organization (FAO), 1989, 'Effects of Stabilisation and Structural Adjustment Programmes on Food Security', Economic and Social Development Paper 89, Rome.
14. Swaminathan. M, (2000), Weakening Welfare in the Public Distribution of Food in India, Left Word Books.

15. Krishna Rao. I.Y.R, (1993), 'Andhra Pradesh: an Experiment in Food Security', *Economic and Political Weekly,* 24.

16. Sastry, K.V.S., K. Hanumantha Rao and M. Narsing Rao, (1990), 'Welfare Implications of Rice Subsidy Scheme', Paper Presented at the AP Economic Association, CESS, Hyderabad.

20

Reform for Making Indian Agriculture Strong, Sustainable and Globally Competitive (Valedictory Address)

*Dr. K.C. Hiremath**

Friends,

Let me, at the outset, thank the organisers of this National Seminar for inviting me to address this august body of the intellectual cream of the country at the concluding session of this Seminar. I am fully aware of my inadequacies for this high honour. There are many among this audience who are far more qualified to do this job. However, having been pushed forward, let me try my best.

The topic that I have chosen for this valedictory address is *"Reforms for Making Indian Agriculture Strong, Sustainable and Globally Competitive"* which forms a sub-set of the main theme of this National Seminar on *"A Decade of Economic Reforms–Retrospect and Prospect"*. My purpose here is not to inflict on you a pretentious and pedantic address but to present briefly an introspection of the Economic Reforms of the first phase, analyse quickly the agricultural situation, and also to raise some very vital

* Professor of Agril.Economics (Retd.), University of Agricultural Sciences, Dharwad-3, Karnataka State.

issues for your consideration to carve out a policy framework for the second phase of reforms for our agriculture.

The First Phase Economic Reforms

The 1990s have been a decade of radical economic reforms in terms of liberalisation, privatisation and globalisation (LPG), including entry into the World Trade Organisation (WTO) which in itself constitutes a milestone and a great economic reform in world trade. Good or bad, a new chapter has been opened in our economic policies and development strategies. The basic tenets of our economic reforms (LPG) have come to be regarded as "structural adjustments". The introduction of these economic reforms has been hailed as "historic" and the beginning of a silent revolution in India. Of course, on all counts it has been a piece of innovation and a crucible of change. Although these economic reforms have not worked wonders, a good beginning has been made. The initial period has not been altogether disappointing as in other countries of the world particularly the South-East Asian countries. Given the severe economic, social and political constraints in our country, namely, social inequality, the caste system, patriarchy, feudal setting, illiteracy, poverty, multi-party polity etc. within which the new economic reforms had to function.

You may be aware that these economic reforms of the last decade were triggered by the balance of payment crisis of 1991. It was but natural to institute reforms in the foreign trade sector in the first place. The reforms in the foreign trade were followed by domestic reforms, doing away with a large number of centralised controls, regulations as well as different forms of restrictive trade practices. In other words, it virtually amounted to dismantling of the "Permit-License-Quota Raj". These were followed by reforms in the financial sector. There were also some over-lapping, even mutually conflicting measures in different sectors of the economy. The reforms are, thus, marked by a sequential approach rather than a comprehensive approach, encompassing all sectors of the economy in one sweep. Secondly, the reform process has been slow and halting, and the execution of the reforms itself has been much slower and even casual. Furthermore, several decisions have been of an adhoc nature. Besides, some compromises in competitive policy, labour policy, pricing policy, taxation policy and disinvestment and privatisation policies have been adopted due to political compulsions.

The real issues that matter here are:

1. Whether due to these economic reforms the rate of growth of the economy has been accelerated, and
2. Whether the plight of the vulnerable sections of the society has become less serious.

These questions are yet to be answered convincingly and with clear empirical evidence. We have, therefore, to identify the real constraints and hurdles in agriculture, industry and service sectors of the economy in order to overcome them, and to remedy the deficiencies and defects so that the Indian economy can attain a high growth trajectory. Appropriate policy framework has to be developed, exercising extra care that it would not produce any injurious side-effects or adverse fall-outs. Formulation of the second phase of economic reforms, embracing all sectors of the economy is admittedly, a much more difficult task than before. Further, in the second phase the issues of equity, sustainability, regional and sectoral allocation and institutional and infrastructural changes will become prominent and over-riding considerations. Hard decisions on several ticklish and sensitive policies are unavoidable. Reforms are also imperative to remove bottlenecks in the energy-transport-water infrastructures and in the development and diffusion of new technologies.

The Economic Development Models

The first N-M (Nehru-Mahalanobis) Model that loomed large in the pre-Economic Reforms period generated what is popularly termed as the "Hindu" rate of economic growth. This model was marked by a faith in the central control on the allocation of resources, greater emphasis on the public sector and more stress on the "heavy industries". It was mostly inward-looking with the key role being assigned to the bureaucracy in the implementation of development strategies. These ingredients were deftly re-adjusted in the second N-M (Narasimha Rao – Manmohan Singh) Model. In fact, the second N-M model broke a new path in economic policies and development strategies. This was followed by the WTO regime.

The Agricultural Scenario

It is in the above perspective that we are to review the agricultural scenario of our country and identify the roadblocks created by the agricultural policy measures from 1950-51 to-date, and think of the imperatives for the next phase of reforms in order to make our agriculture strong, sustainable, globally competitive and domestically lucrative. Unfortunately, Indian agriculture has not yet received the attention it should. The policy changes in agriculture in the first phase of reforms were much slower. Greater reliance had been placed on the agricultural price policy measures, while non-price policy measures such as development of technologies and creation of infrastructure were, in fact, much more important than the market-oriented measures. The Government had been more particular about food security rather than about livelihood security. In the new economic policy reforms, the agricultural sector remained unprotected, while many developed countries of the world continued to protect their agriculture. There was, in fact, no major policy reform for the agricultural sector in the Economic Reforms of 1990s. It was assumed that the market-determined exchange rate and reduction of protection for industry would benefit the agricultural sector, and with the removal of quantitative restrictions on agricultural exports, Indian farmers will have access to the world markets.

The Critical Areas in Indian Agriculture

Unless we address ourselves to the following issues and bottlenecks, things would be much more difficult.

1. Conflicting domestic policies relating to production, pricing, procurement and distribution of agricultural commodities,
2. Ineffective and inefficient agricultural subsidies,
3. Lack of infrastructure facilities in the rural areas,
4. Low agricultural productivity,
5. Recent deceleration in the productivity growth of all major agricultural commodities in the 1990s,
6. Poor value-addition to agricultural products,
7. Adhoc agricultural export policies,
8. High dependence on rain-fed agriculture,
9. High incidence of rural poverty,
10. Low proportion of acreage under modern agricultural practices,
11. Over-exploitation of groundwater resources,
12. Degradation and degeneration of land resources,
13. High regional disparity in the agricultural development,
14. Preponderance of small and marginal landholdings,
15. Low benefit cost ratio of agricultural enterprises,
16. Decay of self-help institutions at grass-root levels etc.

The inclusion of agriculture within the purview of WTO and our joining the WTO have thrown up challenges, while opening new vistas of opportunities for growth and diversification of agriculture and its exports. Indian agriculture must grow annually at more than 4 percent to meet the growing domestic demand and also to take advantage of the expanding external market. Long-term growth of the agricultural sector as a whole is essential to achieve food as well as livelihood security at the household level, generate more employment opportunities and to bring about equity in the distribution of income and wealth, all resulting in rapid reduction in poverty levels, simultaneously leading to self-reliance and sustainability at the national level.

The Innate Strength and Competitiveness of Indian Agriculture

Fortunately, India is endowed with rich and diverse agro-climatic resources where crops can be grown throughout the year. There is still enormous untapped potential in Indian agriculture and its bio-diversity. We have to find out now, what really prevents us from unleashing a series of revolutions in succession in our agriculture? We should strive hard to locate the major issues and problems hindering growth of this vital sector of the Indian economy on which all other sectors of the economy are dependent and to develop a policy framework that has the potential

1. to boost a higher growth,
2. to raise farmers' income
3. to alleviate poverty at a much faster rate; and
4. to ensure both food and livelihood security.

As Indian agriculture is to be gradually integrated with the global economy, the question that stares us into the face is—How will Indian agriculture fare in the new context? Which sub-sectors in Indian agriculture will ride the wave of liberalisation and globalisation and which ones would be threatened? This is a critical issue, since the trade liberalisation and globalisation processes would have significant repercussions not just on agricultural trade balance but also hold deeper implications on the overall welfare of producers and consumers and all other sections of the economy dependent on agriculture.

Indian agriculture is, by and large, competitive and capable. Fruits, vegetables, flowers and cotton are the potential exports since they are even now export competitive. This holds true for rice and wheat also to a certain extent. Most of our pulses and coarse cereals can help avoid imports, though are not export competitive at present. The traditional exports-tea, coffee, spices and tobacco-are likely to continue to be export-competitive, though the competing exporting countries are occasionally eating into India's share. The only major commodity group which is not competitive even as import substitute is the oilseeds and edible oils group. But they possess the innate strength and potentiality to become export competitive, provided proper measures are taken up in an integrated manner and on war-footing.

The Measures for Making Indian Agriculture Strong, Sustainable and Globally Competitive:

The agricultural policies in vogue are rooted in an era of shortages as a result of which there are some serious conflicts in the domestic policies relating to production, pricing, procurement and distribution. The present agricultural marketing system still continues to be highly restrictive. Therefore, reforming the domestic policies relating to these spheres is very important for exploiting the gains from the policy of liberalisation and globalisation and making our agriculture competitive.

Despite significant changes in the productivity growth of Indian agriculture after the Green Revolution, our agricultural productivity is still very low compared to the world standards. What is more appalling is that there has been a deceleration in the productivity growth of all the major crops in the 1990s. This has been largely due to the slow-down in the technological development, distortions in the incentive structure and declining investment in agriculture. Therefore, there is an urgent need to re-assess, re-prioritise and re-vamp the current expenditure and investment patterns in agriculture in order to release resources for investment in those activities that would enhance the productivity growth of the agricultural sector as a whole.

There is gross inadequacy in the pre- and post-harvest infrastructure facilities in the rural areas which have been leading not only to inefficiencies but also to colossal wastages. The low value-addition and poor quality standards further make our agricultural products un-competitive in the international market. To a greater extent, this is due to obsolete methods of processing, packaging, storage and transport of agricultural commodities which need to be modernised on top priority.

To overcome these constraints, we have to find out innovative ways and means of generating more resources for investments in rural roads, electricity generation, rural godowns, agro-processing centres, irrigation facilities, land reclamation, land development etc. We should also create a congenial environment for attracting more private sector investment and involvement in storage, transport, post-harvest management and processing. Further, agriculture being a state subject, needs large scale participation of State Governments in reforming agriculture. The centre should, therefore, motivate and encourage States to initiate reforms in the agricultural sector by setting specific targets and linking disbursements with the achievement of targets.

Domestic support and export subsidies maintained deliberately at high levels in the rich and developed countries make export of our agricultural products un-competitive not only in the international markets but also in our domestic markets where the developed countries are dumping their agricultural produce and products. The serious tariff and non-tariff barriers imposed by the developed countries have added to the problems of promoting our agricultural exports. To overcome these obstacles, India will have to take a pro-active and aggressive stance in all the rounds of the WTO negotiations to champion the cause of the developing countries of the world.

The Next Phase of Land Reforms

There have been some lacunae and loopholes in the land legislations and consequential evasion of some provisions of these legislations, especially in Land Ceiling Acts of different States. Moreover, the implementation of land reforms has been tardy. However, several important desirable changes have taken place. The notable ones among them are:

1. Prevention of enlargement of landholdings beyond the ceiling limit,
2. Reduction in the phenomenon of absentee-landlordism,
3. Greater convergence of land-ownership and land-management, and
4. Emergence of a more or less uniform land-tenure system (Ryotwari) throughout the country

Whatever may be the equity implications, the land reforms have failed to contribute to the overall growth in agricultural productivity. A large number of agricultural holdings remained deficient in production or at best self-sufficient. In any case, they have not been able to transform our agriculture into a surplus generating and high-value agriculture and much less into precision-agriculture. In view of low-value agriculture on a large number of landholdings, it has now become necessary that more capital is to be injected in farming in order to raise productivity. The ceiling on landholdings has been a major stumbling block for high capital investment in agriculture. Encouragement of the contract farming system in high-value crops is, therefore, the need of the hour. Relaxation of ceiling on landholdings at this stage may not be appropriate since it is likely to swell the army of landless workforce in agriculture. This step may have to be deferred until the needed resilience is built into our rural economy. There is, however, a clear and convincing case for liberalising tenancy provision. It would be quite appropriate to allow the land-lease market to function now. Relaxation of the Tenancy Laws would produce a positive impact on both the leasers and the lessees. We should, however. introduce two safeguards that the investment in land made by the tenant is appropriately compensated, and that the land owner will not lose his/her ownership right. Such a move will import the necessary assurance and flexibility in the land-market. And at the same time, un-freezing of land-lease market should be guaranteed.

The Reforming of the Agricultural Price Policy Structure and Agricultural Subsidies Policy

The objectives of the present four-tier Agricultural Price Policy, comprising the Minimum Support Prices, the Procurement Prices, the Bufferstock Operation and the Public Distribution System (PDS), have been often conflicting and counter-productive. This price policy structure worked well to close the gap between demand and supply of foodgrains from the domestic production in a closed economy, and acted as a cushion against the price-induced risk. Since, the situation has totally changed now, several distortions, and discrepancies, have cropped up in the existing system. There is, therefore, a need to take a serious look at the scope, instruments and institutions of the Agricultural Price Policy Structure. The *"high-cost and high-subsidy"* regime has been eating into the vitals of our agricultural economy by diverting the resources from the more productive uses such as investment in agricultural research and development (R&D) and agricultural extension services, and creating better rural infrastructure facilities. Further, the present Agricultural Price Policy Structure has proved to be a weak instrument of income transfers.

The present Input Subsidies System has been fast losing its significance and relevance and is becoming an unbearable fiscal burden. This has come to be branded as *"cheap-input and cheap-output"* policy. The Public Distribution System has also failed to serve its basic objective and philosophy.

It is, therefore, necessary to introduce a new agricultural price policy. Greater- reliance needs to be placed on crop insurance and forward markets. Similarly, rationalisation of the agricultural subsidies policy is also essential (i) by putting a ceiling on subsidies in the budget and (ii) by announcing a phased programme of progressively withdrawing subsidies. The amount thus saved from agricultural subsidies should be earmarked as addition to the funds for strengthening the rural infrastructure, agricultural R&D facilities and agricultural extension services. Further, the Food Corporation of India (FCI) should be the buyer of last resort and not first resort, the FCI should open its procurement centres all over the country where they do not exist, and it should dispose of excess stock procured or procure additionally by open tender immediately after harvest in order to stay close to bufferstock norms. The PDS should be made primarily the responsibility of States and Panchayati Raj Institutions and the PDS should confine itself to the public welfare and relief programmes only.

The Agricultural Trade Policy Reforms

India can exploit the international market to its advantage by making best use of its natural endowment resources. Emphasis should be laid on export of commercial crops where India has comparative advantage and competitive edge. The policy of canalisation of exports through public organisations, fixation of arbitrary minimum base prices for exports and the *"stop-go"* policy based on adhoc considerations will have to be replaced by a well-thought comprehensive agricultural trade policy and long-term strategies for agricultural exports in tandem with domestic economic policies. The agricultural price policy structure must be dove-tailed with the agricultural trade policy. Co-ordination between various policy instruments and institutions becomes necessary with emphasis on agricultural export promotion, on one hand and commitment to self-reliance in food grains and food as well as livelihood security, on the other hand.

Since agriculture is a vast, diverse and complicated subject, I have chosen and focused only on some selected areas of concern that need to be addressed effectively among others to keep myself within both the space and time limits allowed to me. A thorough re-vamping of the agricultural policies in all sectors of the agricultural economy of India in tune with the macro economic policy reforms of the country, however, is an imperative need in the next round of economic reforms in order to make Indian agriculture vibrant, and competitive, ensuring sustainable growth and prosperity of the agricultural sector as a whole. More importantly, there should be a strong and solid partnership between the farmers, Centre and States, between agriculture and industry, between the internal and external agricultural trade and between the macro-economic policies at the national level and those at the State and sectoral levels.